Irish Immigrants

IN

New York City,

1945–1995

Irish Immigrants

IN ❧

New York City,

1945–1995

LINDA DOWLING ALMEIDA

Indiana University Press

BLOOMINGTON AND INDIANAPOLIS

This book is a publication of
Indiana University Press
601 North Morton Street
Bloomington, IN 47404-3797 USA

www.indiana.edu/~iupress

Telephone orders   800-842-6796
Fax orders   812-855-7931
Orders by e-mail   iuporder@indiana.edu

The paper used in this publication meets the minimum requirements of American National Standard for Information Sciences—Permanence of Paper for Printed Library Materials, ANSI Z39.48-1984.

MANUFACTURED IN THE UNITED STATES OF AMERICA

Library of Congress Cataloging-in-Publication Data

Almeida, Linda Dowling.
    Irish immigrants in New York City, 1945–1995 / by Linda Dowling Almeida.
        p.   cm.
    Includes bibliographical references (p.   ) and index.
    ISBN 0-253-33843-3 (alk. paper)
        1. Irish Americans—New York (State)—New York—History—20th century. 2. Immigrants—New York (State)—New York—History—20th century. 3. New York (N.Y.)—Emigration and immigration—History—20th century. 4. Ireland—Emigration and immigration—History—20th century.   I. Title.

F128.9.I6 A46 2001
974.7′10049162—dc21

                                                                00-044974

1 2 3 4 5   06 05 04 03 02 01

In memory of Nana, whose stories sparked my interest in the immigrant experience

To Ed, Cionna, Devin, and Eamon, whose love and support kept me going

Contents

Acknowledgments

The foundations for this book were laid more than ten years ago when I published my first article about the New Irish. Along the way I have been encouraged, prodded, and inspired by dozens of people and stories. I'd like to acknowledge every one but I'm afraid of omitting as many as I include. So I'd just like to thank anyone who has ever listened to, contributed toward, or commented on any aspect of this work. I could not have finished it alone and am constantly overwhelmed and humbled by the generosity of those I've encountered in the course of this endeavor.

Having said that, I do want to single out certain individuals for special praise. My family deserves the biggest thanks. My husband and children suffered through my distraction, late hours, and Irish anecdotes with good humor and kind words (most of the time). But I think they were relieved when it was finally finished. I love them all.

As for scholarly assistance I must recognize all my colleagues at New York University. Dave Reimers worked with me for years, making suggestions and reading drafts. Marion Casey was always ready with a reference, a contact, and, most importantly, her friendship. Hasia Diner read the draft and encouraged me to go forward. Thanks to everyone at Ireland House, in particular Bob Scally and Joe Lee, who read drafts, offered suggestions, and lent moral support. My association with Ireland House also introduced me to my editor, Ralph Carlson, whom I can thank for placing my manuscript with Indiana University Press and for his solid advice and patience.

My appreciation extends as well to all the Irish advocacy agencies, church groups, and government programs for their goodwill and graciousness in the face of my endless questions and requests for information. This includes everyone at Project Irish Outreach, the Irish Immigration Reform Movement, the Emerald Isle Immigration Center, the Irish Consulate, and the Aisling Center, among many others. Special thanks as well to Kevin Morrissey and the Irish Institute.

To all those who participated in my surveys, sat for interviews, or sent me clippings, memoirs, and anecdotes, thank you. Your contributions made it possible to go forward and enriched a history that needed to be recorded.

To my parents, sisters and brother, and my in-laws, thank you for your interest and cheerleading over the years.

Finally I'd like to recognize two women who inspired me and nudged me toward the study of Irish American history. My immigrant grandmother piqued my interest in our family's past and the study of the Irish in America with her stories about leaving the old country and making a life in America. She never thought that what she did was "historical" or special and never quite got why I was so eager to hear about her past. I cherish the time we spent sharing that past together. This book is for her.

I was lucky to know another woman whose work and family life I've admired since my years as an undergraduate. Adele Dalsimer was an inspiration and role model for me and hundreds of other students she reached as teacher and director of the Irish studies program at Boston College. She died in 2000 and will be missed by many.

So thank you all. The work has been rewarding and the process an education all its own. While the following has been touched by many hands, in the end I take final responsibility for its content and tone.

Irish Immigrants

IN

New York City,

1945–1995

Introduction

At the beginning of the twenty-first century it is estimated that one in three New York City residents is an immigrant. No other American city has a population composed of so many different nationalities—more than a hundred at last count.[1]

Of these "foreign-born" a relatively small percentage come from Ireland, but the Irish presence in the city (and in the country) in the last half of the twentieth century was ubiquitous. In the 1990 census forty-four million Americans identified themselves as having Irish or Scotch-Irish ancestry. Of these over half a million lived in New York City. From a president who has taken a personal role in the Northern Ireland peace process (and who claims Irish ancestry himself); to Frank McCourt and Alice McDermott, whose books have topped the best-seller lists and captured the Pulitzer Prize and the National Book Award; to films such as *My Left Foot, The Crying Game* and *The Brothers McMullen;* to musicians such as Sinead O'Connor and the bands U2 and Black 47; to the phenomenally successful *Riverdance,* the Irish presence is everywhere.

Ironically, while thousands of books and articles have been written about the Irish in America, relatively little information is available on post–World War II immigrants. Hence this book. I identify two distinct waves of Catholic Irish immigrants: one in the 1950s and one in the 1980s. These were the largest postwar groups to come out of Ireland, and they were the first to leave an independent Ireland.

This book grew out of surveys conducted among the 1980s group—the self-proclaimed New Irish. These surveys revealed a tense distance between the eighties migrants and the established Irish American and immigrant community, and with a little probing it became obvious that the breach was deeper than mere generational conflict. The gap had as much to do with the culture and society from which the New Irish came as with the economic and social circumstances they found in New York. Even though both migrant communities originated in Ireland, their cultures, politics, and overall world perspectives were quite different.

I describe and explain the differences between the groups in terms of their lives in Ireland, their reasons for emigrating, and their experiences in New York. The discussion considers the evolution of ethnic identity, as well as the state of modern Irish immigration and the relationship between Ireland and the United States, within the context of the long history of migration between the two countries and the changing dynamic of worldwide immigration to the United States.

For more than three centuries Irish men and women have crossed the Atlantic to make a new home in North America. The five years from 1845 to 1850 are the most important period in Irish American history. In that half decade almost one million Irish entered the United States in the wake of a potato famine that devastated Ireland and eliminated almost two million people from its population. Most of the famine immigrants came through, if they did not settle in, New York City. New York City is a metropolis built by and inhabited by immigrants. In 1850, 46 percent of the population was born abroad; in 1990 28.4 percent of the population was born abroad.[2] The primary difference between the two periods is the origin of the foreign population. European immigrants dominated nineteenth-century movement, while natives of Hispanic and Asian countries outnumbered Europeans at the end of the twentieth century. However, the outmigration of Irish to the United States and to New York City in particular has progressed with few interruptions since before the American Revolution.

The story of nineteenth-century Irish migration to New York covers more than the mass movement of over three million Irish across the Atlantic to a new life, new land, and new culture; it also traces the development of the modern urban community. The story of the Irish is the story of the nineteenth-century American industrial city. The Irish needed New York as a refuge at mid-century, and New York (since before the famine) needed the Irish and subsequent immigrants to build and maintain the complex urban metropolis that was New York City.

The arrival of so many Irish in the period between 1845 and 1850 presented the institutional and political leaders of New York with their first social service crisis. Agencies and commissions that almost certainly would have developed in the course of the city's growth were brought into being at an accelerated pace because of the urgent demand posed by the presence of the Irish immigrant. For example, New York State created the Emigrant Commission in 1847 to monitor the crossing conditions of immigrants and to control the numbers of unhealthy and unfit migrants disembarking in New York City. The first American immigration station at Castle Garden grew out of this program in 1855. The Archdiocese of New York, led by Archbishop John Hughes, himself an immigrant from Country Tyrone, established new parishes and built new churches to minister to the needs of Catholic Irish immigrants. The Sisters of Charity, led by Hughes's sister Angela, opened St. Vincent's Hospital, the city's first Catholic hospital, in 1849. Famine migration stretched the capacity of the Almshouse Department, the Lunatic Asylum, the House of Refugees, and Bellevue Hospital beyond their limits. To alleviate the strain on existing city institutions, the Emigrant Refuge Hospital on Ward's Island opened in 1847. American philanthropy bloomed with a variety of relief programs. The Quakers set up soup kitchens in the city to feed the famine immigrants and ran fundraising drives to relieve the suffering in Ireland. Likewise the General Irish Relief Committee of the City of New York solicited funds and food, which it shipped to the Central Relief Committee of the Society of Friends in Dublin. The committee's work encouraged other organizations, such as the Friendly Sons of St. Patrick and Tammany Hall, to raise money in response to the needs of the Irish abroad.[3]

In the decades that followed, the Irish in New York tested the strength of the nation's largest city as the immigrants and the established American leadership negotiated territory, services, and institutional responsibility. Shut out socially and economically because of their poor skills, Catholicism, and poverty, the Irish carved a place for themselves in two arenas where pedigree, birthright, and money mattered little: politics and the Church. Because of their numbers, need, and concentration, the Irish were recognized first by American-born leaders of Tammany Hall as valued constituents. By the end of the century the Irish controlled city politics in New York and several other major northern and midwestern cities.[4] With the same drive and skill the Irish dominated the hierarchy of the Catholic Church and presided over the development of the institution as it achieved remarkable growth and influence inside a single century. Between 1820 and 1860, the Church expanded from two churches to thirty, and it continued to build more churches and schools through the end of the century.[5]

Perhaps the most dramatic symbol of Catholic and immigrant presence in New York City was the construction of St. Patrick's Cathedral in the upper reaches of Manhattan between 1859 and 1879. Archbishop Hughes boldly decreed to the American native-born community that the cathedral reflected the status, dignity, and permanence of the Catholic ethnics in New York City. In addition the Irish not only controlled the administration of the Church hierarchy, but also registered significant numbers among religious orders.

By the end of the century immigration from eastern and southern Europe, dominated by Jews and Italians, eclipsed the still steady entrance of the Irish to America. The new immigrants entered a city shaped in many ways by the experience and performance of the Irish who had landed before them. In the decades to come, the Jewish population in particular challenged the Irish in the public service and political spheres, competing with the Irish for jobs in the classroom and City Hall, as well as contributing to the political debate in New York. But by the end of World War II, the Irish, the Italians, and the Jews were established ethnic voices in the city. Through the 1940s to the end of the century, the significant immigrant movements would originate in new lands, and after 1965 the immigrants would hail from different hemispheres. Beginning in the 1960s emigrants from Latin America and Asia outnumbered all European emigrants.[6]

The influx of new immigrants buried the persistent stream of Irish who continued to enter America. Slowed by the Depression, World War II, and new immigration legislation, Irish immigration picked up after 1945, and while the number of Irish who entered the United States between 1945 and 1960 was just under half the number who arrived in the 1920s, it was still significant. It demonstrated that after three hundred years America was still a choice destination for the Irish, even though since the 1930s most Irish migrants had been heading for Great Britain. The postwar movement also demonstrated that emigration was still a fact of life in Irish society. And in New York—as well as the other cities to which the Irish immigrated—the introduction of new immigrants into ethnic neighborhoods, shrunk by migration to metropolitan suburbs and marginalized by the presence of different immigrant groups, brought life and energy back into the community.

To the outside observer, the movement of Irish into New York after World War II was all but invisible until the 1980s, when the New Irish made their presence known while lobbying on behalf of immigration legislation. This is not to say that as an ethnic presence the Irish were invisible in America. Ironically, as a group the Irish were very much an accepted presence on the American, and certainly the New York, landscape. Irish Americans were successful political, business, and religious leaders, as well as respected and beloved fixtures on the American stage, movie screen, and television. The Irish were also a strong voice in American literature and journalism. It was because of their success and their presence throughout American society that their immigrant numbers in the late twentieth century did not initially register on the national or, in this case, local consciousness. This was particularly true in the 1980s, when the revelation that the majority of New Irish immigrants were illegal aliens surprised observers who assumed that the undocumented were non-English-speaking foreigners of color. That the Irish continued to find their way to New York City and America and that Ireland continued to produce migrants 150 years after the famine and 300 years after the first Irishman set foot in North America are the issues to confront here. So persistent was the Irish migration to America that in the 1980s, when Irish journalists broadcast the problems of Irish illegal aliens, a sense of Irish entitlement in America permeated the stories. Despite the fact that the undocumented Irish broke U.S. immigration laws, the reports emphasized the rights of the Irish to better treatment because of Ireland's long immigrant tradition in America.[7]

The Irish presence and past in New York were significant to the experience of the postwar migrants. Both those in the wave of the 1950s and those who came in the 1980s entered established and maturing ethnic communities and in some way needed the existing community to facilitate their transition to America. But the relationship of the two groups to Irish America was decidedly different. By the 1980s success within the Irish American community and the progress of Irish society changed the dynamic of the relationship between the host society and the immigrant. Technology changed the landscape as well. Advanced communication, telephones, and travel shortened the distance between Ireland and New York and made the trip to America a commute rather than a final journey. That convenience and their own confidence made the 1980s migrants less reliant on the New York society than their predecessors, because they were never very far from home virtually or in reality. They never felt that New York was their ultimate destination.

The presence of the Irish in New York and their legacy in the city factors into the immigrant experience whether the year is 1880 or 1980. It is necessary to consider that experience in the context of the city at large and the ethnic community into which they settle. Was the relationship between the 1950s and the 1980s generations unusual? How smoothly did past generations of immigrants work themselves into the fabric of the existing Irish American communities they entered? Is the twentieth-century dynamic a continuum or a break from the past?

In chapter 1 I provide a historical overview that puts the Irish American community in perspective in terms of its identity both as an ethnic group and as part of New York City's history. This chapter will establish what should be obvious from the preceding questions: the Irish community in New York has always been a complex and diverse one. Over the course of the last century and a half, the Irish have experienced internal conflicts and clashes as new migrants entered the established networks and institutions of their predecessors and challenged the status quo. Just as the New York community evolved and adapted to social, economic, and cultural change, life in Ireland moved forward as well. The immigrants heading for the United States did not emerge from a static pool. Each generation left Ireland with different experiences and goals, which determined the immigrants' reasons for leaving and affected not only their reception in New York but their overall success as well.

Despite the changes, Irish American identity since the time of the famine (1845–1850) has been defined by two constants: Catholicism and Irish nationalism. At any point in time from 1845 through at least the 1970s, religion and the state of the Republic were the factors that determined Irish immigrant and Irish American culture in New York City. They were the common bonds that held the community together. That changed with the New Irish.

The Irish lived in neighborhoods throughout the city. In the nineteenth century they concentrated on the Lower East Side and in the Five Points section near City Hall. As their circumstances improved, they moved north to the Upper East Side seeking better housing and following the transportation links that brought them to work every day. Through the twentieth century the Irish made their way to the Upper West Side and farther north into Manhattan, the Bronx, and across the East River to Queens, all the time searching for more space, stronger housing value, and a better quality of life for their families. Their neighborhoods were anchored by their churches. Ask any Irish New Yorker, past or present, where home is and the reply will be St. Simon Stock or St. Philip Neri. The parish was home. The neighborhoods thrived through the nineteenth and early twentieth century because the Irish created stable communities on the steady incomes earned from municipal jobs and careers in the utilities and unions of New York and the structure offered by the social and religious life of the Church.

But the Irish in New York also survived on the influx of new immigrants. These new migrants served to enliven and ultimately strengthen the Irish presence in New York City. The neighborhoods have been the nursery of Irish identity. The constant flow of migrants over the past 150 years has kept the Irish identity fresh. But it has been the neighborhoods that nurtured that identity—accepting each successive generation of immigrants and providing the base for family, school, work, religion, and recreation that kept the Irish alive as a community and as an identity. The introduction of new migrants to a neighborhood often brought conflict and some change to the community. The Irish in America are defined as much by their experiences in Ireland as by circumstances in their adopted land. But despite their differences and disputes most migrants ultimately chose to stay in the neighborhoods of New York and make their lives among Irish Americans. In the late twentieth century that scenario changed.

The New Irish were a more transient population than previous generations of migrants. They did not commit themselves to the neighborhoods of New York. They also introduced a new Irish identity to the city—one forged in the modern political and economic era of Ireland, one not defined by the traditional markers of religion and nationalism but determined instead by some future vision as yet undefined. The current state of affairs suggests that, if it is to survive, Irish American identity will take on a new form. The neighborhood will no longer be the nursery of ethnicity it was in the past, fed by streams of immigrants and nurtured by ethnically based institutions. But we need to look at the past to understand the significance of that change and how it will affect the future of Irish American identity.

Within that context this book provides an in-depth look at the circumstances and details surrounding the migration of Irish to America in the 1950s and the 1980s. While smaller than past movements, these two generations are the largest groups of migrants from Ireland to enter the United States in the post–World War II period. The emigrants are profiled and tracked from Ireland to New York—their origins, education, skills, culture, and experience in the "New World." At the same time the postwar period in America brought great economic, social, professional, and academic success to the Irish ethnic community. That success propelled them out of New York City to the suburbs, altering not only city neighborhoods but also the intensity and character of Irish ethnicity. Obviously the Irish experience did not occur in a vacuum. In a nation and a city of immigrants, the Irish entered side by side with other immigrants from around the world. The end of World War II and the United States's emerging position as world leader forced the country to reconsider immigrant policy—not only in terms of how many to admit, but also of who was acceptable.

Statistically, Irish migration to America in the postwar period from 1945 to 1995 was virtually invisible except in the Irish communities the new immigrants entered. The numbers of other immigrant nationalities were so much larger than Ireland's that they attracted more attention. But in the 1980s and 1990s the Irish exercised tremendous influence over the national debate on immigration and immigration reform. Through a strong grassroots effort and powerful institutional connections, members of the young immigrant Irish community negotiated successfully for change. Their effort resulted in special visa programs that facilitated Irish entry into the United States, as well as the entry of more than thirty other nationalities that were "adversely affected" by 1965 immigration legislation.

The late nineteenth century is often considered the era of mass immigration, particularly the years between 1880 and 1920. The popular conception of immigration to America is dominated by the movement of millions of Europeans across the Atlantic as dramatically depicted in black-and-white film footage of families disembarking on Ellis Island. So it may come as a surprise that twentieth-century immigration more than doubles that of the nineteenth century.

Between 1820 and 1900 just over nineteen million men, women, and children, primarily from Europe, entered the United States. Most of these travelers entered through New York City. Between 1901 and 1992 almost forty-one million immigrants from around the world made their way to America, with 56 percent from Europe. But in the nineteenth century Europeans represented 90 percent of all immigrants, Asians 2 percent, Canadians and Mexicans 6 percent, and Africans .01 percent. In the next century, the number of Asians grew to 16 times the previous century's total and represented 15 percent of all immigrants to America. Canadians and Mexicans crossing the American borders totaled almost one-third of all immigrants, and the number of Africans increased from 2,213 to 772,925, just less than 2 percent of total immigration but the largest growth rate of all originating continents. The two decades with the largest numbers of migrants were 1901–10 and 1981–90.[8] In the course of the century the primary points of origin shifted away from Europe, and Los Angeles replaced New York City as the chief port of entry.[9]

In total number of immigrants entering the United States over time, the Irish rank fourth behind the Germans, the British, and the Italians. And like emigrants from several other countries they have experienced uninterrupted migration since at least 1820. But most of the more than four million Irish migrants that the Immigration and Naturalization Service has officially recorded since the early nineteenth century arrived in America between 1840 and 1920. Since the twenties fewer than 500,000 Irish have left home for the United States.

After World War I the United States Congress decided to regulate immigration more closely than it had in previous decades. The threat of international terrorism, the closing of the American frontier, and the popular fear of cultural contamination by foreigners created an unfriendly atmosphere for immigrants in America. As a result, Congress passed the Immigration Act of May 26, 1924, also known as the Johnson-Reed Act. The law established the "first permanent limitation on immigration" and imposed the "national origins quota system" based on the population and the white ethnic makeup of the country in 1920.[10] The Depression in the 1930s and World War II further inhibited immigration.

Between 1945 and 1965 the nation reviewed the immigration question in earnest. Among the major issues considered were the repeal of the Johnson-Reed Act, the validity of the national origins system as the basis for immigrant selection, the threat of Communism to domestic security, and the removal of racist and discriminatory policies that dictated immigration policy. The door for broader inclusion creaked open in 1945 and 1946 with the War Brides Act and the GI Fiancé(e)s Act, which admitted the foreign-born wives and fiancé(e)s of members of the Armed Services. In 1952 Congress passed the McCarran-Walter Act, which essentially kept in place the national origins system of the Johnson-Reed Act. But the new law removed previous restrictions on Asian aliens, allowing limited quotas from nations in the Far East, and eliminated barriers based on race or gender. Subsequent legislation authorized the admission of alien refugees beyond the quotas in place.[11]

The economic realities and labor demands created by World War II and the postwar expansion forced Congress to consider special programs allowing temporary (bracero) workers into the United States. During the war most able-bodied men were serving in the military or working in the factories of the defense industry, as were many women left on the home front to support their families. Agricultural employers, particularly in California and the Southwest, complained that the wartime economy left them short of labor—they could not find enough Americans willing or available to work in their fields. The "bracero" program permitted U.S. growers to hire temporary labor, primarily from Mexico, within certain guidelines and controls. The program remained active until 1964 and had its roots in a short-lived temporary worker program authorized by Congress in 1917. Both projects elicited criticism from several quarters, including Congress and organized labor. First, many critics within the Mexican government and agricultural unions believed that the farmers' complaints that no Americans would work the farm were really a reflection of the compensation offered to the workers. The poorer, more desperate Mexicans would tolerate the working conditions and low pay offered because they had no better prospects at home and were not permitted to join unions under the bracero program. Their compliance, argued organized labor, guaranteed the perpetuation of low wages, prevented the creation of a union, and made them more attractive employees than Americans. Human rights advocates feared that working and living conditions for the braceros were substandard. Social critics and some members of Congress also worried that the bracero program encouraged greater numbers of illegal aliens or *mojados* to cross the border in search of work, again depressing wages and straining local public services for which the undocumented workers did not pay taxes. The issue of illegal aliens became more contentious in the 1970s and 1980s.[12]

Despite the Cold War and the failure to eliminate a national origins standard, the intellectual, political, and economic climate of 1950s America was conducive to a review of immigration law. The economy was strong, most Americans were working, and the outlook for the future was positive. In the wake of the U.S. victory in World War II American confidence soared and the nation felt compassion and responsibility to share its liberty and freedom with victims of international oppression. Unlike the prewar period of economic depression and uncertain international and military political stability, the postwar period was a time of expansion and relative peace and prosperity. Socially and culturally, public opinion toward "aliens" had mellowed as well.

Dramatic increases in immigration followed the end of war in Europe and Asia. The surge can be explained by the end of wartime restrictions, as well as displaced persons and refugee programs, and the opportunities presented by the United States in the expansive 1950s.[13] Immigration and Naturalization figures for 1951–1960 show substantial increases from Europe, Asia, and the Americas. But the countries with the highest numbers of immigrants in the decade were Austria-Hungary, Germany, Italy, the United Kingdom, Canada and Newfoundland, and Mexico.[14]

In the 1950s the country was more tolerant of "foreigners" than it had been in the 1920s, the last time a serious domestic debate on immigration dominated the political agenda. First-, second-, and third-generation descendants of turn-of-the-century immigrants proved to be productive and patriotic citizens. Ethnic Catholics and Jews had achieved remarkable success in politics, labor, business, science, and entertainment, among other areas. They had also served with distinction in World War II and the Korean conflict, as had Asian and African Americans. Restrictions barring and/or limiting Catholics and Jews to certain colleges and businesses were lifted as the children and grandchildren of immigrants proved themselves to be active and eager Americans. Desegregation decisions admitting African Americans to schools in the South and the integration of the military contributed to improved racial, ethnic, and religious tolerance. General economic prosperity and higher national levels of education eased relations as well. In 1960 the nation elected its first Catholic to the White House and was moving toward passage of its first civil rights bill.[15]

In October 1965 Congress approved the Immigration and Nationality Act, which eliminated national origin as the basis for immigration and replaced it with a seven-preference schedule emphasizing family reunification and job skills as the primary standards for entrance to the United States. It abolished the Asia Pacific Triangle, which placed a quota on immigrants from designated Asian countries, even if the immigrant was born outside the country of his or her ancestry.[16] It also limited migration to 120,000 from the Western Hemisphere and 170,000 from the Eastern Hemisphere, but immediate family members were exempt from those quotas. According to historian David Reimers, the objective, as Congress saw it, was not to increase immigration either in total or from any one region of the world. The goal was to eliminate racial and ethnic preferences and grant access to migrants who had previously been denied entry because of the national origins system.[17] What they did not expect was what they got: a tremendous surge in immigration, particularly from Asia, under the family reunification program, which was generous. In the period between 1966 and 1993, total immigration numbered 17,408,177. In contrast, between 1951 and 1965 just under four million (3,965,791) immigrants entered the country. And remember total nineteenth-century migration from 1820 to 1900 was 19 million. To say that the 1965 bill opened the floodgates is not an exaggeration.

In New York City between the periods 1946–1949 and 1970–1979 the average annual number of immigrants more than doubled, from 32,269 to 78,325. In the period immediately following passage of the bill, from the 1960s to the 1970s, the annual average immigration rate to New York City rose 36 percent. According to the New York City Department of City Planning the majority of the post-1965 increase came from the Caribbean, in particular the Dominican Republic.[18]

Also generating debate and headlines was the increase in the number of illegal aliens crossing American borders. For the Irish this debate has multiple implications that will be discussed later in this book. But in order to place the twentieth-century Irish migration situation in perspective, a look at the context of immigration is useful. Fifteen years after the 1965 law was passed the United States revisited the immigration legislation question for a variety of reasons. One of the major issues was undocumented aliens—what to do with those already in place in the country and how to protect national borders from future illegal penetration. Most of the Congressional and editorial discussion related to undocumented immigrants focused on those originating from Central and South America who crossed over United States southern and southwestern borders. Boatloads of Chinese immigrants paying exorbitant fees to risk a perilous ocean crossing at the hands of exploitative smugglers also received dramatic headlines. The popular perception of the illegal alien was that of a non-English-speaking foreigner of color. At the same time thousands of prospective migrants from Europe found themselves inadvertently shut out of the country by the 1965 legislation as well as concurrent economic and political circumstances in their home nations. Others found their way illegally into New York City, and other American cities as well. But in the case of the Irish, the ethnic heritage of the Irish in New York, the established presence of the community, their language, and their color, made them an invisible part of the illegal problem and less obvious targets for detection and/or deportation. It also made their legal status less urgent in the eyes of the establishment.

Following a series of new immigration laws initiated by the passage of the Immigration Reform and Control Act of 1986 and continuing with subsequent changes through the 1990s, European immigration crept upward again. Both Asia and the Americas outpaced it, but the trend that began in the 1970s and 1980s appeared to reverse itself. According to the New York City Department of City Planning, European migration to the Big Apple increased in actual numbers and in its percentage of the total immigrant flow. In the 1970s, 1980s, and early 1990s, Europeans accounted for 21 percent, then 9 percent, then 22 percent of all immigrants to New York. The average annual number of European immigrants grew from 16,200 in the 1970s to 24,400 in the early 1990s.[19] Ireland also moved from 38th place to 12th place in the order of countries sending immigrants to New York City.[20] Of course these figures reflect only the documented aliens entering New York. As will be discussed at length in chapter 4, in the 1980s the majority of Irish immigrants were undocumented or illegal aliens, rendering an accurate count of their presence through that decade impossible. But as this discussion and the available figures demonstrate, the level of Irish immigration began to increase after a significant decline in the 1970s.

Every generation of Irish immigrants, large and small, carries with it the character of the Ireland they leave behind. Each generation is distinguished by a variety of influences and issues that in the past have ranged from famine to civil war to inheritance patterns. The compelling feature of the New Irish population is the mark made by economic and social modernity. Not only did the transformation of Irish society in the 1960s and 1970s influence Irish natives, but because of the links between Ireland and the United States, its repercussions will be felt on present and future generations of Irish Americans.

The parallel and intersecting experiences of the Irish in Ireland and in New York at the end of the century offers an opportunity to observe how ethnicity evolves despite diaspora and in the face of great social and cultural change. In the late 1990s the health of Irish culture and the level of interest in Irish culture and ethnicity were as strong as they have ever been in New York—all this as the ethnic and immigrant community of Irish in the city negotiated who they were, where they lived, how they identified themselves, and how they related to one another. In the 1840s and 1850s the city fathers struggled to cope with the unprecedented numbers of alien Catholic Irish who descended on their doorstep. One hundred fifty years later city leaders still worked at incorporating immigrants into the community and the Irish were still part of the discussion.

The story of the Irish evolves, as it always has in New York City, shaped by the changing social, political, and economic circumstances on both sides of the Atlantic. But to students of the Irish in America, the significance of the relationship of the immigrant and ethnic communities in New York in the last fifty years of the twentieth century centers around the emergence of a new Ireland, one coming to terms with its own identity in a postwar, postcolonial, postmodern era, the impact of which continues to unfold. That is the story of this book.

 **1**

The Background:
When the Irish Ran New York

"The first thing on the agenda is the split."
—paraphrase of Brendan Behan[1]

The Irish have been leaving Ireland to go to America for more than three hundred years. The most significant influx of Irish to the United States occurred between 1841 and 1921, when nearly four million Irish—most of them Catholic—flooded American shores.[2] The migration was notable not only for its numbers but also for the political, social, and cultural impact the immigrants had on the cities and institutions they encountered.

Within fifty years of the famine exodus the Irish had built a complex, diverse community in New York of more than 600,000 immigrants and their children.[3] The total city population in 1890 was 1.5 million, so the Irish were a significant presence. They represented almost one-third of all New Yorkers.[4]

In the latter half of the nineteenth century the Irish typically settled in cities because during this period of industrial expansion the developing urban centers of the United States offered unskilled labor opportunities for both men and women. Although many Irish left rural homes and farms for America, they did not have the capital or experience to buy and/or operate farms in the Midwest as did German and other northern European immigrants of the time.[5] Irish farmers grew potatoes, which required limited agricultural expertise. Young Irish women, migrating alone and at a very young age at the end of the nineteenth century, found work in the homes of middle-class families, keeping house and minding children. They spoke English, had a reputation for being "chaste," and were not prevented from living with their employers by strict parents or cultural codes.[6]

In their essay "The Irish," Daniel Moynihan and Nathan Glazer identified the Irish era in New York City as beginning in the early 1870s and ending in the 1930s.

Symbolically the authors cited the prosecution of William Marcy "Boss" Tweed by Charles O'Conor (1871) and the exile to Europe of ex-mayor James J. Walker (1932) as the bookend events for the era.[7] It is no accident that they chose politics to bracket the period. Except for the Roman Catholic Church, city government was the arena in which the Irish achieved the most power and notoriety as an ethnic group in the late nineteenth and early twentieth centuries. Their success was based on several factors, including numerical strength initially, a common language with the host society, and an understanding of the American political process stemming from their experience fighting for Catholic emancipation, land reform, and home rule within the British system of law and government. The Irish in New York City developed a powerful grassroots base that had its origins in the secret "cell societies" formed by nineteenth-century political movements such as Daniel O'Connell's Catholic Association, the Fenians, and the Irish Republican Brotherhood in Ireland.[8]

As the historian Chris McNickle explained it, the Irish understood that politics was about power and control.[9] They knew how to exploit public office to amass loyalty in order to build and maintain a power base in an alien society. The ballot box was their medium. In 1855, 34 percent of New York City voters were Irish. By 1890, the number of immigrant and first-generation Irish (children of Irish-born parents) still equaled more than one-quarter of the city's population. In thirty-five years the city's population grew from 500,000 to more than a million with the great waves of southern and eastern European immigrants who added to the thousands of workers walking the streets of New York in search of jobs and a better way of life.[10] The Irish were represented by the Tammany organization, which virtually controlled the Democratic Party by the 1880s. When unemployed Irish constituents were faced with "No Irish Need Apply," it was the local ward boss who provided a job or a meal for the price of a vote.[11] According to one source cited by McNickle, the Irish Catholics who ran City Hall controlled 12,000 jobs in 1888. Ten years later, greater New York City Democratic Party officials could place faithful voters in almost 60,000 jobs, from civil service posts to construction crews on municipal building projects.[12]

By the 1950s the Irish political star had waned. Though still active in city politics, as an ethnic force the Irish were relegated to coalition building with ascendant power groups such as the Jews, the Italians, and, in the 1980s and 1990s, African Americans and Hispanics.[13] The Irish no longer had the votes to guarantee victory at the polls. By 1950 the number of foreign-born Irish and native-born Irish of foreign or mixed parentage in New York City had dropped to 5.7 percent of the city's population.[14] In addition, the nature of urban politics had changed. Federally subsidized social welfare and relief programs and civil service reform reduced the impact of local patronage power, as did the growing power of municipal unions to provide jobs and job security.[15]

As the Irish moved up the economic ladder they were no longer seeking the blue-collar and bureaucratic clerical positions that city contracts and civil service offered. As entrepreneurs, professionals, and property owners, the Irish were paying city taxes, not collecting city paychecks, so their political demands were changing. McNickle argues that Irish voters were more conservative than the Jewish party leaders who were beginning to dictate Democratic party philosophy by the 1960s, and the Irish thus found themselves drifting away from the party.[16]

Besides politics, the Irish controlled the Roman Catholic Church in New York, dominating the clergy and the hierarchy of the institution well into the twentieth century. The Irish secured their position as leaders of the Church in New York in the decades following the famine. Historian Kerby Miller estimates that the "vast majority" (almost 90 percent) of Irish famine immigrants were Catholic,[17] in contrast to pre-famine migrants, at least half of whom were Protestant.[18] In the post-famine years, not only did Catholics continue to outnumber Protestant emigrants, but they brought with them a stronger, more formal, and conservative brand of religion—one reinforced by the hardship of famine and reflecting the increased presence of the parish priest in rural Ireland's daily life.[19] The late-century Irish were also more likely to equate Catholicism with Irishness, thanks to post-famine nationalist politics endorsed by Irish Church leaders.[20] And in the United States, mid-century nativism served to further separate and alienate Irish Catholics from Americans as well as Irish Protestants.[21]

The Irish presence in the New York Catholic Church was also obvious in the Church hierarchy. Through the nineteenth century, German and Irish Catholics battled to preserve the religion they carried with them from their homelands, eventually establishing national parishes led by ethnically kindred priests who ministered to their needs in the native tongue. The Irish outnumbered the Germans, as well as other groups, and came to dominate not only the faithful of the New York archdiocese, but also the clergy and institutional leadership. In the 1850s Irish-born Archbishop John Hughes made his mark on the New York archdiocese by centralizing power in the hands of the archbishop and away from the lay leadership within each parish. Jay Dolan describes his tenure as "boss leadership": "he ruled like an Irish chieftain" at a time when the church needed focus in the face of a divergent and rapidly growing immigrant urban population.[22] In the fifty-year period beginning about 1815, the Roman Catholic Church in New York City grew from a minor denomination with about 15,000 members and 2 small churches to include almost half the city's population (400,000) and 32 churches.[23] A solid middle class of Irish and German Catholics contributed to the physical growth and presence of the Church.[24]

Archbishop Hughes's most conspicuous accomplishment was the construction of St. Patrick's Cathedral, a building "worthy of [our] increasing numbers, intelligence and wealth."[25] His sister, Mother Angela Hughes, presided over another institution which symbolized the growing strength and power of Irish Catholics. She established St. Vincent's Hospital as an alternative health facility for Irish immigrants who found the existing public and private health care outlets in the city insensitive to their needs.[26] Hughes was followed in the archbishop's chair by John McCloskey and Michael Corrigan, both of whom shared not only his style of singular leadership, but his ethnicity as well.

For almost a hundred years the majority of the Irish in New York City were Democrat and Catholic. The voting strength and religious presence of the Irish in New York can be easily misunderstood as unity and conformity. But the Irish were not and never have been monolithic. As an immigrant population, their diversity is directly related to the constant influx of new migrants. In the 150 years after the beginning of the famine exodus, emigration to the United States showed highs and lows based on a variety of factors both in the United States and in Ireland. As a result, the Irish who arrived in New York at any given time in those 150 years carried with them more than personal possessions and the addresses of aunts and cousins. They brought with them the expectations and experiences that marked their particular generation in Ireland and influenced the push/pull factors that brought them to America. Conversely, the relatives, family friends, employers, and civic and community leaders who met the arrivals at the docks and airports of New York brought with them their perceptions, prejudices, and expectations of the Irish and Ireland. Quite often these preconceptions clashed with reality.

From 1850 through the 1930s, Ireland's relationship to Great Britain and its struggle for independence shaped Irish migrant identity and nationality. Those emigrants who left Ireland after the famine were raised in a different country from those who left between 1845 and 1850. The post-famine years arguably brought Ireland into the modern era politically, if not economically. At the same time, as the number of Irish in New York grew during this period and they and their descendants achieved power and status, the society into which post-famine emigrants entered changed, as did the host society's perceptions of what was Irish. The Irish in New York were no longer an insignificant ethnic population. Leaders on both sides of the Atlantic valued the votes, dollars, and opinions of immigrants and American-born ethnics.[27]

The dynamic of change and diversity within a community that was growing so dramatically from within, by natural population growth, and from without, by immigration, is instructive. As we look back from the perspective of the 1990s to understand the relationship between late-twentieth-century emigrant generations, that earlier evolution provides a comparative canvas from which to observe and understand the tensions and conflicts that would mark the community a hundred years later.

In the mid-nineteenth century the famine forced changes in the agricultural, economic, and social organization of Ireland. As death, eviction, and emigration emptied family farms and homes through the 1840s, surviving farmers and landlords consolidated, increasing the median size of individual farms larger than one acre from 10.8 acres in 1841 to 15.6 acres in 1851 and to 18.5 acres in 1876.[28] Yet, as Kerby Miller points out, Ireland remained overwhelming agrarian through the nineteenth century. By 1911, nearly 46 percent of Irish farms were under 15 acres, qualifying them primarily as family farms. Between 1861 and 1911, the number of Irish holdings under 30 acres fell by 17.5 percent, compared to 40 percent of French farms in the same period.[29] And while post-famine farmers tended to diversify crop selection and turn more land over to pasture and grazing, most farms were semi-subsistence rather than commercial. Ireland was still a land of small and poor farmers.

The primary significance in the reorganization of farm holdings for Ireland and its population was its impact on social and family relations. The historian Joe Lee argues that prior to the famine, land was subordinated to the people; in the years after, people were subordinated to the land.[30] Before 1845 family plots were subdivided among the children in the family; afterward, the land and dowry resources were provided for one son and one daughter at the discretion of the father. According to Lee[31] and Hasia Diner, a historian who has written on nineteenth-century Irish female emigration, this arrangement created extreme tension and strife within Irish families: jealousy among siblings for the inheritance; hostility between widowed mothers and daughters-in-law who viewed each other as rivals for control of the family economy; and dependence of children on their parents for inheritance or assistance to emigrate. Demographically the changes resulted in later marriages, enforced celibacy, declining birthrates, emigration, and low population growth. Socially, the changes in economic conditions encouraged a conservatism that was reinforced by the Catholic Church. Indeed, following the horror of the famine, the Catholic clergy became more powerful figures locally, promoting the reordered family economy and its emphasis on chastity, obedience, and conformity with spiritual solace and justification.[32]

In general, while Irish society recovered economically from the famine and demonstrated some superficial signs of prosperity and progress in the years after 1850, it remained a primarily rural and agrarian society. What appear to be improvements to the farm management actually stalled the country's industrial and commercial opportunities and growth. By reducing consumer demand and depleting the labor supply needed to develop industry, depopulation in the years after the famine contributed to the dynamic.[33] The dependence of the population on the family farm, the loss of local non-agricultural employment to industrialization abroad, and an increased reliance on imports prevented Ireland from developing a modern, independent economy.

These changes had an impact on emigration. After 1860 migration from Ireland comprised primarily single men and women—young people who were forced out of the Irish economy thanks to changes instituted in the wake of the famine. They differed from the famine refugees in that they traveled alone, they spoke English, and while most still did not have crafts or skills, they were probably stronger and healthier than famine refugees of an earlier generation.[34] This migration trend continued through the end of the nineteenth century, when the number of single young women leaving Ireland actually began to exceed the number of departing young men.

According to Hasia Diner and Janet Nolan, social and economic conditions in Ireland were far more difficult for women than for men. Women were seeking economic as well as social freedom from the strict codes of Irish society, in which a woman's only hope of economic or domestic independence and "adult" status was to join the convent or marry.[35] Ironically, the changes in the economy created idle hours for young girls and women, who in previous generations worked in the field, traveled to factory jobs or domestic work in the city,[36] or did linen or textile work at home. The free time and Compulsory Education Act of the 1870s[37] allowed young girls the luxury of going to school. By 1900 more girls than boys attended school, and the rate of illiteracy fell more quickly for girls than for boys in the last thirty years of the nineteenth century.[38] The national literacy rate in 1911 was 88 percent, compared to 47 percent in 1841.[39] These literate youngsters could read the letters sent to Ireland from America by sisters, brothers, and cousins and learn of the opportunities for work, marriage, and independence.[40] An improved rail system carried newspapers and journals to the rural population of the country, further expanding people's knowledge of the outside world and arguably fueling the ambitions of disinherited sons and daughters[41] on the farms of Ireland. Ireland had changed in the years after the famine, and by definition so had its migrants. The post-famine generation sailed for America carrying with them more than the desire to work and breathe free.

In the late 1870s Ireland was faced with an agricultural crisis reminiscent of the Great Famine. But unlike the 1840s emigration to the United States did not offer a safety valve. An economic slump in America gave prospective migrants little incentive to leave. Instead the crisis mobilized the Irish countryside politically: crop failure and potato blight in the years 1877–79 ignited the three-year agitation (1879–82) known as the Land War.[42] The movement was an attempt by tenant farmers to wrest control of land away from land-owning families and to "abolish the landlord system" by establishing the three F's: fair rent, fixity of tenure, and free sale.[43] The targets of the farmers' discontent were the landlords. About 37 percent of landowners actually lived in Ireland (although not on their own estates), while owners of about one-quarter of Irish farms lived outside the country.[44] The movement, the farmers hoped, would introduce some security to their existence and the opportunity to eventually own their own land. The vehicle created to effect this change was the Land League. The movement was so deep and strong throughout the country that Irish political leaders seized the opportunity to piggyback on the popularity of the Land League. They harnessed the powerful energy of a popular agrarian revolution for tenants' rights to the political, parliamentary movement for home rule for the entire country.

The Land War is significant for its impact on the political awareness and consciousness of the migrants who did go to America and for the political awareness that Ireland's domestic crisis created in the United States. Leaders such as Patrick Ford, an immigrant and publisher of the *Irish World,* used the Land War to demonstrate the similarities between tenant grievances in Ireland and labor discontent in America.[45] The *World* was based in New York City and by the 1880s was Irish America's most influential paper, with a weekly circulation of 35,000 in the United States[46] and 20,000 in Ireland.[47]

Historian Eric Foner argues that the Land League was the first nationalist organization to unite the Irish American community—just thirty years after the famine, most Irish had some memory or direct experience with landlordism, evictions, and famine and so could identify with the abolition of the land system in Ireland and/or separation from Great Britain. The league was also less radical and therefore safer for the middle class to support than other political groups, such as the Fenians or the Clan na Gael.[48] But Foner also demonstrates that the issue of land reform served to highlight class differences within the ethnic community. In America, socioeconomics determined the depth of the league's appeal among the Irish. Labor was more supportive financially of Land League activities than was the Irish American middle class.[49]

By the 1870s New York City was the center of the Irish American middle class or "lace-curtain" society. The community was composed of professionals and entrepreneurs who socialized in fraternal organizations and rarely interacted with the working-class Irish immigrant and second-generation working classes who tended to gather in Irish-owned pubs on the "other side of town." While both the middle and working classes sympathized with the Land League movement, particularly in the wake of Charles Stuart Parnell's fundraising tour of America, the movement appealed to each group on a different level.[50] The downturn in American industry in the 1870s created instability among skilled and unskilled workers that editor Ford exploited to illustrate the bond between the Irish American laborer and the Irish tenant farmer. Thus the labor activism that accompanied the depression of the 1870s could justly be compared to the Land League activism in Ireland, lending the league an American as well as an Irish significance to the Irish American working class.

The *Irish World* was the most radical supporter of the Land League agitation, and Ford's focus on linking the tenant rights platform with an agenda for American social reform had limited appeal. The more conservative ethnic papers, such as the *Irish American* in New York and John Boyle O'Reilly's *Pilot* in Boston, observed no connections between land reform in Ireland and social conditions in the United States. "Landlordism in America, said the *Irish American*, was a thing of the past: 'It exists no longer.' "[51] The primary appeal of the Land League among the middle class was its connection to the issue of home rule and the leadership of Parnell. They could not relate to Ford's complaints about the inequities in America's industrial society. The Irish middle class, institutional leaders in the Church, and major ethnic papers avoided the link of land and labor.

The Land League movement in Ireland arguably radicalized labor in the United States. It was both a model for political action and a training ground for activists who eventually made their way to America and joined the labor movement. Labor action, such as the social boycotting of errant freight handlers, organized by Jeremiah Murphy, the president of the freight handlers union in New York City in 1882, can be traced to the ostracizing and shunning techniques popular among nineteenth-century secret agrarian societies in Ireland. The aggressive and inventive tactics of Irish American labor leaders in this period belie the image so often associated with the Irish at the time as either wild, uncontrollable drunks or lemmings led by local parish priests.[52] The labor movement demonstrated strategic, independent action that was neither endorsed nor condoned by the Catholic Church hierarchy. The labor activity ran counter to Protestant American fears that church leaders were master manipulators of their congregations,[53] but it also contributed to their fears that the Irish were a dangerous race.[54]

The Land League is a good medium through which to illustrate the complexity of Irish American society at the turn of the century. While it united the Irish in its focus on land issues, it set in relief the class and immigrant layers building within the Irish community in New York after the famine. It also demonstrates how the politics, culture, and the economy of both Ireland and the United States interacted and intersected on both sides of the Atlantic and influenced the migrant population before and after it embarked for America.

The life experience of the Irish before and after migration necessarily affected their perceptions of Ireland, New York, and America, as well as their own self-identity. As the Irish continued to migrate to New York in the decades after the famine, the transplanting of the population from one place to another was not static. The migrants were shaped by their home environment. Their experience and success in New York were determined by the emotional, cultural, and political baggage they carried with them. And that baggage was different for each generation of migrants.

The history of any immigrant population must deal with ethnic identity and assimilation. It must consider not only how the migrant sees him- or herself, but also with how he or she is seen by various factions within the host society. The perceptions held both by the immigrant and by the community into which the migrant enters affects his or her behavior, reception, and success in the new environment. Other factors determine the immigrant experience as well, including the push/pull influences that drew the migrant away from home in the first place. The New York Irish community in the last century was a multilayered population divided by class, income, generation, religion, skill, and gender. Fifty years after the famine, the "typical" Irishman could be a priest, a politician, a domestic servant, a public school teacher, a middle-class business owner, a union laborer, or a millionaire.

In a series of articles for the *Journal of American Ethnic History,* a number of historians and sociologists debated the process of acculturation and the development of ethnic or hyphenated identity among immigrant and subsequent-generation groups in America. The sociologist Herbert Gans called ethnicity "people's adaptation of the pre-existing to meet new situations in, as well as opportunities and constraints from, non-ethnic society."[55] A second article described ethnicity as "grounded in real life context and social experience."[56] The authors described ethnicity as a fluid process that is influenced not only by the immigrant group's inherent characteristics and values but by its relationships with the host society and other immigrant groups as well.

In 1896, the American Irish Historical Society was founded in an effort to construct a positive image for the Irish and to construct a favorable history of the Irish in America—one that would elevate characteristic traits of the Irish at the same time it demonstrated their allegiance and loyalty to America and American ideals.[57]

The historian Kenneth Moynihan argues that the society emerged from the frustration middle-class Irish felt at anti-Catholic sentiment in the country and the inability of the Irish to break into the social circles to which they felt entitled by their economic success. He observed that they sought "credibility" in an effort to create "respectability" and gain the country club memberships and social status they were denied because of their race.[58] They were reacting to the social realities all around them. But instead of denying their background, they sought to redefine (or perhaps refine) their image from that of the fighting Irish politician with a smooth tongue to that of the brave and valorous patriot who served his or her country, not only in public office but on the battlefield (e.g., the United States Civil War) as well, simultaneously preserving the ethnic heritage and reinforcing loyalty to the adopted land. The quest for respectability and acceptance continued through the First World War. Catholic leaders and institutions strove to prove the patriotism of their ethnic communicants by urging them to support American neutrality, rather than side with any one of the Catholic countries in the European conflict.[59]

The negotiation of identity existed within the community as well. The most obvious schism within the nineteenth-century immigrant community was religion. The majority of Irish emigrants, particularly after 1845, were Catholic. Protestant Irish, most of whom originated in Ulster, often identified themselves as Scotch-Irish to differentiate themselves from the Catholic population, who suffered discrimination and violence at the hands of American nativists.

"Generational transition" is another serious source of tension in the immigrant culture.[60] The maturing of the children of Irish-born parents in the community represents the transfer of leadership from one generation to the next, including how the symbols and ideals that identify the community's ethnicity are sustained. Timothy Meagher, in "Irish All the Time," an essay about the turn-of-the-century Irish community in Worcester, Massachusetts, follows several generations of Irish families and argues that the exercise of ethnic pride parallels the social and economic security of the group in the larger society.[61]

The display of ethnicity is directly related to the value it holds for the principals concerned at a given time. That value is subject to a variety of intangibles that range from the personal and emotional to the social and economic. For the lace-curtain Irish who founded the American Irish Historical Society, celebration of ethnicity was a protective reaction. In the face of social prejudice they defended and redefined their heritage to garner the respect they felt they had earned in American society. As the children and grandchildren of immigrants, they were comfortable with their place in the American culture as hyphenated citizens. Fifty years later, immigrants from the western counties of Ireland would choose to reject the traditional music and dance of their villages for the more modern, American big-band styles that were considered progressive at home and that they found in the ballrooms and dance halls of New York.[62] They did not want to be perceived as peasants in the New World.[63]

Marion Casey, in unpublished essays on the Irish who migrated in the 1920s and 1930s, offers evidence that the Irish Civil War influenced those who arrived in the twenties, as did the Irish cultural revival initiated by the new Irish government. These immigrants did not share the symbolic ethnicity of Irish Americans that existed in New York in the first decades of the twentieth century. She writes that "not only had America lost any genuine connection with the real Ireland, but Ireland herself was out of touch with the real Irish America." Yet to those outside the community the shift in cultural identity was so subtle that the subculture that Casey argues was formed by the language and music societies of the twenties and thirties went virtually unnoticed.[64]

Casey identifies a pattern of behavior and experience that is recognizable in nineteenth-century Irish New York and will be apparent in the late-twentieth-century community: that Irish identity is not uniform—it is defined by several publics, including the immigrant, the Irish American, the non–Irish American public, and the Irish in Ireland. The only constants in the shaping of their identity have been religion and nationalism. From the famine through the renewal of civil unrest in Ulster in the 1970s, Irish Catholic American culture has been about the Church and the fate of the Republic. Irish political leader Charles Stuart Parnell, on his visit to America in the 1880s, observed that Irish Americans "were even more Irish than the Irish themselves in the true spirit of patriotism." Another visitor to nineteenth-century America observed that "I have met men of the second generation, sons of Irish parents, American in voice and appearance, who have never set foot on Irish soil, with as ardent an affection for Ireland as any native-born rebel."[65]

The Irish immigrants here described developed loyalties and passions in the wake of famine, eviction, emigration, and relocation in a strange land. As refugees and outsiders in a new land their self-identity was built in opposition—first, to a foreign oppressor in their homeland and then to those anti-Catholic and anti-immigrant forces that challenged them in America. Their sense of Irishness is rooted in the time they left Ireland and reinforced by their experience in America. But as late as the 1980s the headlines that dominated the *Irish Echo*, the New York–based national paper, focused on the "Troubles in Northern Ireland." Up to that time the *Echo* targeted an immigrant and Irish American population who were reared on the memories and stories of the Easter Rebellion, the Irish Civil War, and the Irish Republican Army campaign in Northern Ireland. Their Irish identity was defined by nationalist struggle.

In the 1980s the Irish migrant community was not marked by nationalist struggle. They were products of a post–De Valera Ireland. Nationalist struggles were confined to Northern Ireland. Most of the 1980s migrants were from the Republic. Their Ireland was independent—a member of the international community, both economically and culturally. By definition their sense of Irishness was broader than that of their predecessors, and they suffered no colonial insecurities about their homeland.

Immigrant studies are fraught with the tension of identity: are they Irish or are they American? Observers often evaluate and judge a community on the level of assimilation it achieved. Late-twentieth-century observers criticized the Irish community for so readily losing its Irishness in a quest to be American, middle-class, and successful.[66] Subsequent studies have revealed that obituaries for Irish ethnicity were perhaps premature. But without question the definition of what is Irish has changed and continues to change with the immigrant group and concurrent political, economic, and social forces outside and within the immigrant community. It would be impossible for any group of people to enter an urban society like New York and not influence and be influenced by the new environment.[67] But it is not impossible to maintain a sense of self-identity if the immigrants in question wish to hold on to it.

From the late nineteenth century forward, observers found different examples of the tension between self-identity, assimilation, and ethnic perception, as well as layers of diversity within the community—layers that existed prior to migration and layers that were exaggerated as generation after generation left Ireland for New York and other destinations.

As immigration continued through the 1900s the Irish American community was building an identity based not only on its New York society and culture but on the changes and evolution of Irish society through two world wars, its own civil war, political and cultural reformation, and the Great Depression. From this perspective the issues facing the modern immigrant population in New York can be approached with greater understanding.

 2

The 1950s:
"It Was a Great Time in America"[1]

That Ireland which we dreamed of would be the home of a people who valued material wealth only as the basis of right living, of a people who were satisfied with frugal comfort and devoted their leisure to the things of the spirit—a land whose countryside would be bright with cosy homesteads, whose fields and villages would be joyous with the sounds of industry, with the romping of sturdy children, the contests of athletic youths and the laughter of comely maidens, whose firesides would be forums for the wisdom of serene old age. It would, in a word, be the home of a people living the life that God desires that man should live.

—Eamon De Valera, Prime Minister of Ireland, St. Patrick's Day, 1943[2]

America is change, and immigration is one of the great modern dramas of change. So in order to understand the novelty of America, the impulse and momentum that have made America a society of change, we must understand that the people who came here were ready for change.

—Dennis Clark[3]

Between 1946 and 1961, 531,255 people, almost 17 percent of the population, left Ireland.[4] Forty percent of those who were between the ages of 10 and 19 in 1951 were gone by 1961.[5] Most of the migrants went to Great Britain, but 68,151 left for America during and after World War II (1941–1961). It was the largest migration of Irish to the United States since the 1920s.[6] U.S. Immigration and Naturalization Service (INS) records indicate that, in the late 1950s at least, many of those bound for America settled in New York City. Between 1958 and 1961 more than a third of all Irish immigrants admitted to the United States went to New York City, and of those migrants admitted to major cities, at least half chose New York.[7]

The departure of so many Irish from their homeland was devastating for the country. In a land of just under three million people the loss of almost one out of six, mostly single and under the age of thirty-five,[8] reinforced a sense of economic and cultural crisis in the country. In New York, the arrival of the Irish marked a time of great hope and promise for the migrants. "Those were great years for America . . . a joyous period . . . the best period in the life of this country."[9]

Several forces combined to push the migrants out of Ireland. As in previous generations, the economy, or rather lack of a growing economy, made it impossible for many young adults to start an independent life: for many Ireland represented a general way of life that offered little opportunity or stimulation. In the years after World War II, as the world around them moved at a quickening pace, the nation seemed to stand still. It was this stagnation, symbolized most dramatically by the lack of economic growth, that pushed thousands of young Irish off the farms and out of small villages to Great Britain and to the United States.

After the establishment of the Irish Free State and the Civil War of 1922–23, Irish political leaders struggled to create an independent nation. Ireland's political, cultural, and religious leaders, most notably those of Eamon De Valera's Fianna Fail party, were determined to "protect" Ireland from what they identified as the materialistic and unwholesome forces that governed the rest of the modern world, specifically Great Britain and by extension the United States and Europe. The chief exponent of this position, former Easter Rebellion hero Prime Minister De Valera, felt that expansive industrialism exacted too great a spiritual and cultural toll on the country. The price involved foreign intervention and the introduction of "urban" values,[10] both anathema to De Valera's vision of what Ireland should be. Independent of Great Britain and self-governing for the first time in centuries, Ireland's leadership was determined that its people survive without outside, particularly British, assistance or influence. From the 1920s through the years of World War II Irish political parties struggled to create national policies for Ireland that would separate it from its former colonizer and maintain a distinctive national identity.

De Valera in particular cherished the concept of an "Irish Ireland" which permeated all facets of Irish life. That ideal centered on a primarily rural economy, with self-sufficient farms and industry that served the Irish market as its first priority. His Ireland was a pastoral ideal, with farmers providing their families with all they needed to eat from their own land and securing the rest of their needs from local industries. His vision was defined in his "frugal comfort" speech on St. Patrick's Day 1943, part of which is quoted at the beginning of this chapter. The roots of Irish Ireland spread back to the nationalism of the 1890s and Douglas Hyde's Gaelic League. Modernism, capitalism, urbanization, the English language were all equated with the enemy: Great Britain. According to Irish historian Mary Daly, the vision was also heavily influenced by Roman Catholic political and social dogma, which advocated an economy "emphasiz[ing] family rights, widespread property ownership, and the primacy of land."[11] Capitalism was too individualistic, too British, and too Protestant for an Irish Ireland. Echoes of that philosophy can be found in the *Report of the Commission on Emigration and Other Population Problems*.[12] The report commends the honest and "healthy"[13] work and good life that farming offers a family, while it mocks the modern focus on materialism and consumerism. It chides the rural population's desire for greater disposable income that would enable them to purchase "conventional necessities [such] as cigarettes, cinemas and dances."[14]

Ireland's policy of economic and cultural self-sufficiency persisted through the Depression and the war years. A trade war with Great Britain that lasted until 1938 intensified its isolation, while attempts by Sean Lemass, Minister for Industry and

Commerce, to develop national industry within an economy sheltered by tariff and trade barriers achieved only partial success. Without the help of external capital, imported resources, and professional guidance, the task was daunting.[15] Ireland was an inadequate market to develop; with a population of less than three million it offered very little opportunity for diversity or growth. However, Ireland did post some gains in industrial employment, but this did not suffice to provide jobs for all the surplus labor. An international depression and changes in American immigration law kept people from going abroad to find work. Young men and women began to emigrate again once the British economy began to recover in the mid-1930s and especially the 1940s, when the military buildup in Great Britain demanded a steady supply of labor since its own available population was called into the armed forces.

The gender ratio of emigration showed that in the fifteen years between 1946 and 1961 slightly more women than men left Ireland (1,088:1,000). Women outpaced men in the immediate postwar years by almost 30 percent. Ireland's National Economic and Social Council (NESC) speculated that the gap represented a backlog of women who delayed departure because of wartime conditions in Great Britain, and that the number in the second half of the 1940s included the wives and fiancées of men already placed overseas. During the 1950s more men than women emigrated, making the ratio more equitable.[16]

The ratio seems to hold up for those headed for the United States. According to Immigration and Naturalization Service (INS) records for 1955, 1956, 1958, 1959, and 1960, more females than males entered the United States—21,138 to 16,761.[17] The trend is borne out by U.S. census data, which in 1960 counted 16,855 foreign-born Irish females in New York State between the ages of 15 and 44 and 11,657 males in the same age group. Since most emigration occurred after 1945, and most travelers were in their early twenties at the time of departure, those emigrants under the age of 45 were the most likely postwar migrants.[18]

Most of these young men and women can be presumed to be single. Marriage rates hit a low of 5.1 per 1,000 in 1957, and by 1961 the average age for new husbands in Ireland was 30.6 and 26.9 for first-time wives.[19] Since INS data for the late 1950s showed most migrants to be between 10 and 29 years old, most were probably single.[20]

Their departure relieved a growing unemployment problem in Ireland, which Irish leaders feared would intensify with the end of the war and the return of émigrés. The leadership's fears never materialized, however. In fact, in the years after the war, not only did the wartime laborers fail to return as expected, but thousands of others left to join them, to reunite with husbands and loved ones, or to find the material comfort they could not find at home.[21]

Between 1949 and 1956 Ireland's income rose at only one-fifth the rate for the rest of Western Europe. From 1955 to 1957 Ireland was the only country in the Western World in which the total volume of goods and services consumed fell. Unemployment and annual emigration rates reached record levels by the middle of the decade.[22] In the global expansion of the 1950s, when the rest of the modern world was surging forward and emerging from the international depression and world war that had dominated the previous two decades, Ireland was lagging far behind.

Emigration intensified and the population dropped to its lowest level since independence.[23] In 1948 the government created a committee to investigate the reasons for the mass exodus and to offer solutions that would reverse the trend and repopulate the country. The *Report of the Commission on Emigration and Other Population Problems, 1948–1954* (the *Emigration Report*) observed that the danger of emigration was not so much the loss of the migrants but the impact of emigration on those who were left behind:[24]

> More important and far more serious is the effect of emigration upon the national outlook of Irish people at home. The failure of the economy to support and retain a larger population and the fact that, at present, emigration amounts to more than one out of every three persons born weakens national pride and confidence which of itself retards the efforts required for national progress.[25]

A minority report written by R. C. Geary and M. D. McCarthy offered the analogy that emigration was not a disease; it did not need a cure.[26] The authors proclaimed the right of the individual to freedom of movement. Once again, the act of leaving was not the concern, but the consequences of the departure for those left behind. There was a curious detachment from, or acceptance of, emigration as something that existed. The depopulation, imbalance of age distribution, and other consequences of migration were the focus of attention—how does the nation deal with what or who is left.

In the play *A Day in the Life of a Grocer's Assistant*, playwright Tom Murphy deals with the emotional and social struggles of a young man from a small town who chose *not* to emigrate in the late 1950s, not because he felt he could not succeed in America, but because he wanted to stay in Ireland. It is a play about emigration that looks at the motivation and inner turmoil of one who stayed behind and the courage it took to swim against the tide. The work also examines the loss that emigration involves beyond depopulation.

In the play, Pakey returns from England to bury his father carrying a fat wad of money he earned abroad. He is treated as an alien by the townsfolk, all of whom assume he will go back to England. They are eager to avoid him as though his presence is a reminder that they have somehow been left behind. The protagonist, John Joe, who does not run away from the émigré, admits, "I never had any wish to leave." He is fascinated by the emigrant's life aside from what he earns: "But, tell me, tell me this, Pake, apart from the money over there—." But Pakey evades the questions about his personal or social life, or what really becomes an inquiry about his soul: responding to John Joe's phrase "apart from the money," he says, "I'm surprised anyone born and reared in this holy town to make a statement like that. Ah, but they love the dead around here."[27]

Ireland did not offer Pakey the encouragement to dream about the future in his own country. England has given him material opportunity, but he has lost his soul and spirit in exchange. Yet the myopia of his small village prevents Pakey from staying in Ireland. By contrast John Joe constantly struggles with why he stays where he is. He withdraws from family and friends, wondering what is wrong with him.

> It isn't a case of staying or going. Forced to stay or forced to go. Never the freedom to decide and make the choice for ourselves. And then we're half-men here, or half-men away, and how can we hope ever to do anything.[28]

In Murphy's Ireland of the 1950s emigration traumatizes all.[29]

The sense of insecurity and lack of Irish confidence in their country suggested by the play and the report are apparent anecdotally in conversations with migrants of the period; they are significant in understanding the migrants' experience in New York.

To many of the migrants of the 1950s America was a land of wonder. Speaking thirty and forty years later, emigrants recalled the lights of New York City, the tall buildings, the abundance and variety of food, the speed of city life. While these observations may seem the typical ruminations of country youth coming to the big city, comparisons of the impressions and experiences of the fifties migrants with the eighties migrants will show that the former group were generally more humble upon their entry to America and in their response to life abroad. Much of that perception had to do with the individual's socioeconomic origin, but much also stemmed from the individual's sense of the two countries' relative status.

While considering the immediate postwar migration, it is important to note the finality of the emigrant departure. By its focus on those left behind, Ireland's *Emigration Report* implied that once the emigrants were gone, they were not the problem anymore. It became important to look after those who remained.[30] Cynics argued (as they would thirty years later) that the government quietly welcomed the migration because it disguised the true rate of unemployment in the country and rid the electorate of its most malcontent members. The report did observe that emigration relieved the country's unemployment problem. But its argument was somewhat ambiguous. The movement of so many people out of the country, it admitted, reduced the urgency to fully develop Irish resources that would enable Ireland not only to meet labor demands but also to compete with the rising standard of living abroad, which itself exerted a pull on Irish migrants.[31] By siphoning off surplus population, emigration "helped to maintain and even increase our income per head."[32] The report further identified emigrant remittances as a significant component of the Irish economy: "they partly redress the adverse balance of trade, they may stimulate production, or in certain circumstances they may have a limited inflationary effect. Their social effect is to bring about greater equality in the distribution of wealth."[33] The social and economic relief that emigration offered, both by removing the strain on public expenditure and by improving the economy with overseas remittances, reduced apparent official concern with the migrant. The report downplayed the possibility that emigration produced a net brain drain on the country and was reluctant to label those who left as more talented than those who stayed. However, it did suggest that population loss may create an environment that fails to stimulate the remaining populace and does not develop its "latent potentialities."[34] But the report committee did not want to quantify human production or value as it would a "machine" and offered that "in our opinion it is idle to pursue" whether emigration is an economic gain or loss to the community.[35] Emigration was described as an individual's choice, and the government chose to focus on those left behind.

Emigration must also be considered in the context of Irish history and experience. For at least a hundred years, emigration had been such an established feature of Irish life that the rise in the years after the war, while sharp enough to warrant investigation, was neither unusual nor remarkable. Migration was a natural feature of Irish life; it was part of the national psyche.[36]

Irish culture traditionally equated emigration to America with funerals. Farewell parties for those going abroad were called American wakes. In the nineteenth century villages had "professional" mourners called keeners—women whose function it was to wail and moan at death or the departure of villagers to America. Kerby Miller notes that evidence of emigrant wakes predates the famine, but they were most commonly associated with the post-famine culture of Ireland when the trip to America was treated as a death in the family. Unless family members went with them, Irish sons and daughters of the nineteenth century who sailed abroad rarely saw their siblings or parents again.[37] The journey was expensive, and it was grueling.[38]

Later in the nineteenth century, the finality of departure was perpetuated by one of the lowest rates of return of any European immigrant group at the turn of the century. Between 1899 and 1910 only 2.1 percent of all Irish immigrants to the United States went back to Ireland, compared to 18 percent of Swedish migrants in the same period.[39] Among other European migrants, more than 40 percent of Italians, 50 percent of Poles and Hungarians, and more than 60 percent of Greeks who came to America returned to their own country.[40] Even the *Emigration Report* noted that "it has been a characteristic of Irish emigration . . . that few emigrants have returned to their native land."[41]

The trip to America from the west of Ireland was so long, even in the 1940s, that many who left were certain they would never return. One woman remembers that in 1947 the flight to Idlewild was seventeen hours in the air, with one stop in Canada to refuel. It was a long, lonely trip. Once in New York she did not have the money or desire to get back on a plane. She had no choice but to make her way in America.[42]

For many immigrants the flight to America followed what was their first trip off the farm or out of the small towns in which they grew up. There were no taxis to the airport. Jerry Brennan remembered walking off the farm in 1955 carrying his suitcase and traveling alone for two days before he set sail for New York.[43] Another immigrant recalled traveling by bus with his father to Derry, waiting by himself for one day until the SS *Transylvania* was ready to sail, then boarding a ferry that transported passengers out to the deeper water where the ocean liner awaited. The short trip was a festive one, and the party continued until the liner embarked:

> It was quite pleasant for a while. There was, however, one milestone to pass. Inistrahull lighthouse off the coast of Donegal was the last glimpse emigrants would have of Ireland, everyone stayed on deck until it disappeared. They stayed on when they couldn't see it anymore because the more keen sighted kept saying it is still there. When the sharp eyed ones admitted the light had faded all frivolity ceased, handkerchiefs came out and there was much sniffing as we drifted off to our staterooms. The next stop was New York.[44]

The tradition of the wake continued through the twentieth century. Describing the events leading up to her departure in 1947, one emigrant remembered:

> Everybody came with me as far as the cove, you know, and went out on the small ship [the ferry to the ocean liner] with me. I didn't get really lonely till I got on the big ship. And then I realized that there's no turning back. There was callers for two days and nights [before she left], when everybody was coming by, and parties and everything. It's sad, you know, it's sad. To think of breakin' up with all your old chums. I then, well I just got to New York, when I got a telegram saying my father was dead. So I was very lonely, but there was nothing I could do—I was so far away. It's hard breaking away, but when you're young and you have to decide your future you just can't turn back.[45]

Despite the availability of air travel and the improved comfort and reliability of ocean travel, the journey to America one hundred years after the famine was still perceived as a final one for those who chose to leave.

In the 1950s America was clearly a land of opportunity and great wealth to the Irish who emigrated. Before 1960, the Irish Ireland of De Valera's dream was pre-industrial. The report on emigration cited the "desire for improved material standards"[46] as one of the principal reasons for emigration. People wanted the "modern services and amenities"[47] associated with industrialized, urban societies. As late as 1961 four out of five of the homes in County Waterford, just south of Dublin, had no running water. The families drew their water from a well. Government documentaries on the benefits for improved hygiene and farm productivity that in-house plumbing offered were produced to encourage local towns to lay their own pipes in an effort to expedite the delivery of water to as many homes as possible.[48]

Ireland was also culturally isolated from the rest of the world. The country had no national television network in the 1950s; although some homes had televisions that could pick up broadcasts from England and Northern Ireland, it was not a universal commodity. RTE 1 (Irish television) was established in 1961, after a decade of fierce debate that included concerns over the moral and social consequences of the medium.[49] In a dissertation on the public debate that led to the creation of RTE 1, Robert Savage described Ireland in 1953 as "a nation very much secluded from the outside world."[50] The committees formed to analyze the benefits and risks of commercial vs. public television in Ireland wished to "avoid the outside 'foreign' influences that might contaminate what was regarded as the unique culture of the nation." Establishing a state-run network would allow the government to protect Irish society from disruptive "alien influences."[51]

Ireland did have a government-controlled radio network—Radio Eireann, which was founded soon after the Civil War.[52] Irish leaders feared the power of the radio as well and regulated its programming rigorously, offering Irish language shows[53] that audiences found so boring that less than 0.1 percent of the Irish listening audience tuned in to them. Polls conducted by independent and government sources through the 1950s indicated that Irish audiences chose the British Broadcasting Company (BBC), Armed Forces Radio, Radio Luxembourg, and other European broadcasts rather than listen exclusively to the Irish Ireland propaganda that was routinely offered by Radio Eireann.[54]

In dealing with the decision to emigrate, the prospective emigrant faced a myriad of questions, the very least being whether to stay or go. Circling out from that primary personal debate were the arguments presented by family and society— are you too afraid to leave, are you a coward for abandoning your country, where does your allegiance lie (to oneself, one's family, one's country), do you think you're better than those staying behind, what does it say about a country that it must continually export its young talent? Did the apparent acceptance of emigration as a fact of Irish life by the government, society, and the people suggest a national apathy or an inferiority complex born from a colonial mentality?[55]

In the years after the creation of the Republic, Ireland's leaders tried desperately to preserve an Irish Ireland, to prove that Ireland had a unique worth, that there was value in being Irish. Ireland was deliberate in its attempt to shake the perception, founded in recent history, that it perpetually lived in the shadow of England and that some of its citizens' greatest achievements had been executed outside its borders. Yet Irish citizens wasted no time in leaving Irish Ireland for the work, prosperity, and progress of England and America as soon as World War II restrictions were lifted and the postwar economic boom demanded labor.

Kerby Miller calls the mass migration of Irish prior to 1921 an exile, suggesting a less than voluntary, emotionally wrenching departure of people. The emigration of the 1950s did not convey the same sense of tragedy that Miller saw in the earlier diaspora. In a very real sense the Irish voted for progress and modernity with their feet. They chose to emigrate from a land ruled by their own, not an imperial power. An immigrant who came to New York from County Clare as a 13-year-old boy with his family in 1925 wrote to Eamon De Valera in 1961 to tell "him how much I, and thousands of other Irish men and women appreciated all the sacrifices and efforts, imprisonments, etc., etc., etc. he had made for the Irish people and Irish freedom."[56] President De Valera wrote back, closing his letter with the words, "In return for your kind letter I wish you and your children and grandchildren happiness in your new home. How I wish that you and many others such as you could have remained in the old land."[57]

The exchange points to the pain and ambiguity that lay behind the emigration crisis of the 1940s and 1950s. Previous generations could blame Britain for the exodus and its failure to allow Ireland to prosper. Yet in independence, Irish leadership held the country hostage to an idea or concept of Ireland and failed to deal successfully with unemployment and industrial and commercial development. The real grief may have been the realization that Ireland had failed on its own. The lifeblood of the nation—its youth—left for the prosperity and promise of Great Britain and America. They were unwilling to live on ideals. Yet not even emigration could destroy the "idea" of Ireland or the country's pride in having freed itself from England.

The contradictions apparent in the communication between De Valera and the immigrant in America reflected the migrant's complicated relationship with Ireland. In his position as war hero, president, and international figure, De Valera could indulge his romantic vision for an independent, self-sufficient, culturally pure Ireland. The sons and daughters on the farms of western Ireland did not have the same luxury. They had to find work outside of Ireland to support themselves abroad and often their family farms at home.

In 1951 more than half of the population of Ireland lived in rural areas.[58] As late as 1961 at least one-third of the population was engaged in agricultural employment, about 25 percent in industry and 40 percent in services.[59] Between 1951 and 1961, the province of Connaught and the three Irish Republic counties in the province of Ulster suffered the heaviest loss in gross population.[60] In the five-year period from 1956 to 1961, Ulster and Connaught also experienced the greatest rates of migration. The nine counties with the greatest rates of migration in that period were County Kildare and County Longford in Leinster; County Tipperary, SR[61] in Munster; County Leitrim, County Mayo, and County Roscommon in Connaught, and all three Republican counties of Ulster—Cavan, Donegal, and Monaghan.[62] Census records and the government report on emigration show that the movement was out of rural Ireland to cities, either Dublin or urban centers in the United States and England.[63]

How well prepared for city life were these migrants? According to the *Emigration Report*, about two-thirds of the population attended school to the age of 14 (the equivalent of the eighth or ninth grade).[64] Through the fifties schooling beyond the primary grades was a privilege of the financially secure; some scholarships were available, but not on a very broad basis. One historian noted that secondary education was based on the ability to pay entry and tuition fees rather than academic merit. Under the direction of Donough O'Malley (1965–67) the Irish Education Department initiated free secondary schooling throughout the country, with dramatic results. Between 1966 and 1969 the number of secondary students in Ireland increased by almost 40 percent.[65] But until then what schooling was available to rural and lower-income children was administered in facilities with excessively crowded classrooms and primitive plumbing and sanitation facilities. In terms of curriculum, it is interesting to note that the *Emigration Report* criticized the secondary school curriculum for being too focused on "white collar" career training, as opposed to the more "practical" training in agriculture or domestic economy (for girls).[66]

The relatively low level of education achieved by the Irish in America prior to the sixties was borne out by United States census records, which show that in 1960 the median number of years completed in school by the Irish-born 14 years and older was 8.6, with more than half (56.8 percent) completing between five and eight years of school.[67] But the census also showed that younger immigrants between 25 and 44 years old had about two more years of school than Irish-born Irish 45 years and older.[68]

Isolating the 25- to 44-year-old age group provides a clearer picture of the education level of the migrants entering the United States through the 1950s. Irish government sources and the INS annual reports characterized the majority of the migrant population of the decade as younger than 35. Assuming that a typical migrant left between the ages of 16 and 30, and looking back to when immigration numbers were beginning to build in the late forties, by 1960 the majority of the most recent migrant population was 45 or younger. What this suggests in terms of understanding who was entering New York at this time was that the median level of education achieved for this population by 1960 was the third year in high school, which put them on a par with the American and New York population 25 years and older.[69] Of course the Americans included individuals older than 44 who in all probability would bring down the median level of education. But at the very least these numbers suggested that the migrants heading to New York through the 1950s were better educated than those who preceded them and had more years in school than most of their peers in Ireland. Further evidence of the Irish emigrants' education level existed in the percentage of Irish completing four years of high school or the equivalent. In 1960, 15 percent of all the Irish-born 25 years and older living in the United States and New York State had completed four years of high school, compared to 24.6 and 24 percent of the same age category for the United States and New York, respectively. However, if we again focus on the 25- to 44-year-old category, 27 percent of the Irish-born living in the Northeast and 27.5 percent of those in the United States had completed four years of high school.[70] These figures are somewhat surprising given that, anecdotally at least, the fifties emigrants have been compared unfavorably to the New Irish of the 1980s who benefitted from the universal education policies of the 1960s and were hailed as the best-educated generation the country had ever produced.[71] What this evidence suggests is that, while the earlier migrants did not, for the most part, spend as many years in school, and the education may not have been as sophisticated as in later years, the education level of those who came to America was higher than previously thought.

The question left to answer is whether these levels were achieved in Ireland or in America. Historian Joe Lee observes that secondary-level education was out of the question for most lower-class families. Most of the poorer families in Ireland were located in the provinces experiencing heaviest migration: Connaught and Munster. So probably the better-educated migrants from those areas left for the United States[72] or they earned supplementary education in America. The *Irish Echo* throughout the fifties carried a column called "Educational Notes" devoted to the promotion of education. The author repeatedly urged readers to pursue the high school equivalency exam, listing the dates and times for classes designed to help people achieve that goal.

Evidence also exists that mandatory military service for Irish immigrants (indeed all eligible immigrants were required to register for the draft upon entry into the United States) may have helped to advance their education. One migrant offered that he received his high school equivalency degree in the service, and then went on for three years of additional training at the Mechanics Institute in Manhattan, while others attended college on the GI Bill.[73] The educational achievements of the Irish will be discussed in chapter 3, but the significance of the military as a vehicle of assimilation and advance for the Irish in America cannot be overlooked. Marion Truslow, in a dissertation analyzing the American Civil War experience of New York Irish regiments, contends that the army service and the subsequent pension and benefits awarded to the war veterans accelerated the progress of the post-famine Irish in America. By serving their new country, the Irish not only proved their allegiance and loyalty to their new home, but as war veterans they and their families were incorporated into a federal bureaucracy that carried them into the mainstream of American institutional life. The war experience was an Americanizing one for the Irish soldiers who served. It offered the immigrants a crash course in government, culture, politics, and the machinations of American bureaucracy, as well as the acceptance (presumably) of the public for whom they served.[74]

One hundred years later, automatic naturalization was an added reward for all immigrants who served between June 24, 1950, and July 1, 1955, by order of the president of the United States.[75] But the primary benefit, like it or not, of military service was the exposure it offered immigrants to American culture and the diversity of its population. Consider this example. Kevin Morrissey recalled being drafted two years after he arrived in the United States, training in Texas, and then shipping out to Germany with the same unit to which Elvis Presley was assigned. What greater assimilating experience than basic military training and service with the icon of American pop culture?[76]

In terms of the skill levels that Irish migrants brought to America, the INS statistics for the years 1954–56 and 1958–61 bear out the pattern of education levels.[77] Despite the hemorrhage of people from the rural counties of Ireland, only 6 percent of the migrants entering the United States in these years identified themselves as farmers or farmworkers. About one in five through the fifties and then almost one in four in 1960 and 1961 identified themselves as professionals, clerical workers, or sales personnel, indicating advanced levels of education or business training. Those migrants listing no occupation, a category that was clarified to include housewives and children in the later years, included up to almost one-third the migrant population in 1959 and was as low as 21 percent in 1954. It can be assumed that no occupation included the unemployed, which does not necessarily indicate the unskilled or uneducated. Of the 1959 number, 8.5 percent of the total migrant population were children under the age of 10, so the actual number of adult and young adult migrants with "no occupation" was closer to 23 percent or lower in that year, while the number of children in the other years cited hovered around 6–7 percent.[78]

What do these figures tell us? More than half the emigrants leaving Ireland were probably leaving jobs, but for one reason or another the jobs were not meeting their expectations. Kevin Morrissey had a job with the post office in Galway, as he described it, a government position that was the envy of most people in his community. When he announced he was going to emigrate, he was told he was crazy to leave such a secure job. But, according to Morrissey, the pay was so poor that his income had to be supplemented by his parents, who could ill afford the contribution. He lived too far away from the job to commute, and needed help to meet living expenses. Beyond the low pay, he found his situation very unchallenging, with little future or prospects for change. As he saw it, his only choice was to move.[79] Another emigrant from County Limerick left "to work, believed [United States of America] was land of opportunity."[80] One woman from Clare remembers that she had to "make a living. Being the second eldest of eleven gave little choice and to get educated took money."[81] Still another woman left to test the strength of her vocation. She felt the need to explore life and the world beyond Ireland before she returned to begin what she was sure would be a life in the convent.[82] Without a doubt, most emigrants left Ireland for economic reasons: to find a job, to find a better job, to make more money, to pursue a career that was not possible in Ireland. Whatever the reason, work and money were the ultimate goals. But it takes more than just the lure of money to uproot oneself from one's home and culture. Emigrants wanted more from life than what Ireland had to offer. To paraphrase Dennis Clark, they were ready to make a change.[83]

In the 1950s, America was still the land where immigrants went to get rich. The idea that America held the pot of gold had been reinforced by a century of remittances from the New World. Between 1845 and 1854 almost $20 million was sent to Ireland to finance the passage of relatives to the United States.[84] In 1883, the president of the Irish National League of America argued for the end of emigration because $5 million in annual remittances was too great a burden for Irish Americans to bear.[85] And in 1954 the government report on emigration recognized the continued importance of remittances to the gross national product of Ireland.[86] But remittances from America also took the form of material goods. Many Irish tell stories about the wonderful boxes which arrived from America, with postmarks from Dorchester or Queens or Jersey City, filled with clothing and other gifts from cousins and aunts in America. The packages also sent the message—exaggerated or not—that America was a land of plenty.[87] By American standards the immigrants who forwarded these gifts were more often than not working people, of lower- or middle-class standing. But in the non-industrial, non-consuming society that was Ireland, the purchasing power that the cash and material goods represented was staggering. The impression of wealth was compounded by visits to Ireland of well-dressed American cousins who could afford the overseas fare just to vacation.

Letters from America carried the same messages of abundance and plenty in New York. One migrant wrote with wonder that the house he visited in White Plains,

New York, had central heating, as did "every house in [New York] & Canada," as well as shops, train stations, buses, and cars. "Going to bed no hot water bottles needed. To think one has been shivering in the draughts and cold rooms, in England in particular, for the past 10 years!! Central heating is an amazing institution . . ."[88] This same migrant raved about the excellence of the food, as did another young migrant who wrote her mother and brother about the size of a restaurant meal. "We had to sample Chinese food—we had chicken chow mein—so much of it we couldn't get through half."[89]

In the postwar era, it must also be remembered that the United States was the victorious giant—bursting with jobs, opportunity, growth—pacing the future for the rest of the world. David Halberstam wrote in *The Fifties* that the United States was hailed by *Fortune* magazine as having "an economy of abundance." The number of families entering the middle class in America was growing by just over a million a year by 1956—a rate unprecedented in modern history. The growth "reflected a world of 'optimistic philoprogenitive [the word means that Americans were having a lot of children] high spending, debt-happy, bargain-conscious, upgrading, American consumers.' "[90]

Ireland was still clinging to an ideal that was rooted in the past, led by a man whose vision for a happy Ireland was spartan, small, and contained. Irish marriage rates were down, the population was shrinking, and the Irish were aging.[91] Young women in Ireland did not marry until their late twenties. Men waited until after their thirtieth birthday. According to INS figures for 1956, 79 percent of the men and 77 percent of the women entering the United States from Ireland were single.[92] On the other hand, 62.9 percent of females and 66.8 percent of males over the age of 14 in New York State in 1950 were married.[93] The contrast was striking. America was alive with energy and youth and promise.[94] Those who were leaving Ireland wanted to move on—to jobs, to a family, to a future. They wanted to explore and enjoy life beyond "frugal comfort."

The Irish who came to New York City in the 1950s typically went to stay with friends and/or relatives during the initial stages of their migration. These siblings, aunts, and cousins provided food, shelter, and usually a job for the first weeks and months of their stay in America. In 1950 the borough with the highest Irish-born population was Manhattan. With 48,015 immigrants, it had twice as many as Queens, which ranked fourth with 24,741. The Bronx was second with 37,367 and Brooklyn was third with 29,013. Staten Island or Richmond County had fewer than 3,000 Irish and will not be included in further analysis because of the low concentration of Irish living there.[95]

It should be noted that most of the statistical tables in the 1950 census focus only on the Irish-born living in the United States. In 1960, the category for the Irish was expanded to include figures for Americans born of Irish and mixed parentage (only one Irish-born parent). Because the categories are not consistent decade to decade, it is difficult to make straight comparisons between the two census periods.[96] However, given what we know about the migrants and their tendency to live in communities with other Irish immigrants and Irish Americans, we can use the data from both censuses (with other sources) to make general observations about neighborhoods and lifestyles.

In terms of numbers and political clout, the Irish in New York in the 1950s were an ethnic power on the wane. In the late nineteenth century they had represented more than one-third of the city's population; sixty years later they had dropped to 10 percent.[97] In 1950, 40- to 54-year-olds represented 39 percent of the foreign-born Irish living in the New York–Northeastern New Jersey Standard Metropolitan Area and were three times the size of the 20- to 39-year-old group.[98] The immigrants coming into the city through the fifties were entering an aging immigrant community.

These older migrants were primarily veterans or refugees of Ireland's most traumatic political period: the years between the 1916 Easter Rebellion and the Irish Civil War, which pitted Irish citizens against one another in the wake of the 1922 Anglo-Irish Treaty. Lines formed behind Michael Collins and the acceptance of the Free State or Eamon De Valera and the ideal of the Republic. Families, friends, and communities were torn by the debate. The Irish were at war with each other until 1923.[99] During the 1920s more than 200,000 Irish left the troubled island for America, carrying with them the emotional and cultural baggage of seven years of political and social upheaval. Many were advocates of the Irish Ireland philosophy that the leaders of the newly independent country encouraged. They participated in the Golden Age of Irish music which peaked in the 1920s,[100] and they led the United Irish Counties Association, which organized the first feis in the early 1930s to celebrate Irish music, dancing, sports, and games.

Father Sean Reid, a Carmelite priest, is not atypical of his generation. He grew up in a "Republican household" in County Kilkenny and remembers hating the green uniform of the Free State soldiers. The Carmelites were also a fiercely political order. The rectory at 28th Street in Manhattan hid Eamon De Valera after his escape from an Irish jail in 1919.[101] According to Reid, backing De Valera was an asset within the community of the order. His first assignment as a young priest in New York City was to judge the step dancing contest at the 1933 feis (a festival of Irish dancing, sports, music) because it was known that he had danced as a child in Ireland. Politically, culturally, and religiously Reid symbolized the 1920s migrant.[102]

Through the 1930s the immigrant and first-generation Irish American community declined in gross numbers through death, migration out of the city, and the decrease in immigration. The Irish in this period were well represented among the working-class and union occupations in the city. They made up 33 percent of workers at Consolidated Edison Co., 60 percent of the International Longshoreman's Union, 70 percent of the Transport Workers Union, 50 percent of the police department, 75 percent of the fire department, and 25 percent of the New York Telephone Company.[103]

Historian Robert Snyder describes working-class life in the 1930s and 1940s as quite stable for the Irish in Washington Heights in northern Manhattan. Married couples centered their lives around children, the local tavern, family gatherings, church socials, the activities of the Ancient Order of Hibernians Division 3, and impromptu music sessions in neighborhood homes. Single adults attended Irish dances at the Innisfail Hall or Leitrim House, frequented neighborhood bars, and watched Irish football games in Gaelic Park until they formed their own families.[104]

By 1960, the younger foreign-born segment of the population in New York State was gaining ground: 15- to 44-year-olds made up 21 percent of the population, but 45- to 75-year-olds represented more than two-thirds of the population and 55- to 64-year-olds were a solid quarter of the population. The census also indicated that in 1960 second-generation Irish outnumbered immigrants by almost three to one. The second generation was also younger than the immigrant population: 37 percent were between the ages 15 and 44, compared to 21 percent of the immigrant population; 48 percent of the foreign-born were between 45 and 64 years of age, compared to 36 percent of the second-generation Irish.[105] Since the census only isolated the foreign-born and native-born Irish by state, we must guess how those numbers translate to New York City.[106] But almost two-thirds (63 percent) of the foreign-born Irish in the state lived in New York City.[107] And since the INS data suggest that many Irish who were coming to the United States through the fifties went to New York and most were younger than 40, it is likely that the percentage of young immigrants in New York City was rising as well. One young immigrant wrote her mother: "I thought New York was a big place, but whatever street, whatever locality, you meet someone from Kilgarvan or Kenmare."[108]

Using the census tract data for 1950, we can track clusters of the Irish-born and identify the Irish neighborhoods of the time.[109] Northern Manhattan was the region with the most concentrated representation of foreign-born Irish. Inwood and Washington Heights represented about 18.5 percent of the Irish population in Manhattan.[110] The tracts which ran between Amsterdam Avenue and Central Park West from 74th Street north to 114th Street, expanding west to the Hudson River above 98th Street, represented 17 percent of the Irish population in Manhattan, and on the East Side the borough's largest concentration of Irish, 24 percent, ran north from 49th Street to 99th Street between Third and First Avenues, stretching all the way across to Fifth Avenue and the East River north of 63rd and 79th Street. In 1950 Washington Heights was a working-class neighborhood, whose Irish and Irish-American population has been estimated at 27,000, or about one-fifth of the total population for the area.[111] Family, church, and ethnic organizations dominated community life among the Irish. Mothers typically stayed home to rear large families, and the fathers found jobs as policemen or transit workers. The parish to which one belonged—in this case, St. Rose of Lima, Church of the Incarnation, or Good Shepherd—typically defined social and neighborhood boundaries.[112] Northern Manhattan became an attractive area for the Irish in the 1920s and 1930s. It offered spacious, economical housing for family living; it was located near parks and recreational facilities; and the completion of subway lines connecting northern Manhattan to the business districts in midtown and lower Manhattan made the daily work commute very easy.

One Irish American, born in 1924 to Irish immigrant parents, grew up just south of Washington Heights, in a four-family house at 540 West 133rd Street between Amsterdam Avenue and Broadway, a section of northern Manhattan known as Vinegar Hill (presumably after a battle that took place in eighteenth-century County Wexford). His father worked for the Fifth Avenue Bus Company, and his mother raised five children. One of his sisters and an aunt were nuns. The family moved to Stuyvesant Town in 1949.[113] It was into these kinds of neighborhoods and families that the migrant population of the 1950s moved.

Like this immigrant's family, the great majority of the immigrants and Irish American families that made up the Irish community in New York were Roman Catholic, as were the major institutional and fraternal organizations that are associated with the Irish in New York. However, the Irish Protestant population should not be overlooked. One second-generation Irish American who grew up on the Upper West Side of Manhattan in the 1930s and 1940s remembered that the Protestant community enjoyed an active social and cultural life that revolved around the Orange Lodges and neighborhood churches.

This woman was born in 1929 to parents from County Antrim and County Fermanagh.[114] She lived with her mother and father on West 83rd Street in a neighborhood she recalled as made up of "Irish Catholic and Italian families." Her father was a parcel post driver for the United States Postal Service, and her mother "worked at various jobs over the years including a private school on West 93rd Street."[115] She lived in a five-family brownstone; two of the other families who lived there were Irish Catholic. Religion was not an obstacle to friendship, and she played with two Catholic girls in her building who attended Holy Trinity elementary school across the street from her building. She attended Public School #9 on 82nd Street.

She remembered that the Irish Protestants at the time were spread out around the city, "unlike their Irish Catholic counterparts. . . . However, they still remained loyal to their Orange Lodges and traveled distances to attend meetings, dances, committee meetings and social affairs. They also traveled distances to visit each other and gathered together regularly in each other's homes."

Like that of the Catholics, her Irish identity and culture were manifested and reinforced through church activities. She recalled attending church services in the Bronx in the 1940s led by a Reverend Mr. Megaw "in a strong Irish brogue" for the members of different Orange Lodges. "I remember lining up with my mother and her lodge members on the sidewalk a block or so away from the church. The lodges all walked in their own groups, the members wearing their Orange sashes and some carrying banners then marched into church." These special joint services were discontinued when Mr. Megaw died.[116]

The family's local church was the West Park Presbyterian Church on 86th Street and Amsterdam Avenue. She attended Sunday School regularly and a variety of weekday activities such as Bible and gym classes, and dances that the "church authorities [designed] to keep the young people off the streets." As a teenager in the 1940s she joined a Fife and Drum Corps made up of members from different lodges. They met downtown in a Protestant church on East 23rd Street. She actively participated in the cultural and religious activities of her lodge and church until 1951 when she married and moved out to eastern Long Island.[117]

Heading north into the Bronx, the major clusters of the Irish-born population were found in Mott Haven, which extended from just north of the Major Deegan Expressway all the way up to East 149th Street, running east and west along St. Ann's Avenue. In the East Bronx, smaller clusters could be found north of 162nd Street, west of Jerome Avenue, up to 168th Street and north along Ogden Avenue, as well as in the tracts north of St. Simon Stock Church at 182nd Street and Valentine Avenue to Belford Boulevard, just west of Webster Avenue.[118]

In Brooklyn the most significant concentrations of Irish were clustered west and north of Prospect Park, between Sixth Avenue and Prospect Park West, and running north along Eastern Parkway to New York Avenue.[119] Writer Pete Hamill, who was born in 1935, grew up in this neighborhood in the 1940s and 1950s. He recalls his childhood in a primarily working-class neighborhood in his autobiography, *A Drinking Life*.[120] Hamill's parents were Catholic immigrants from Belfast. His early years as the eldest of seven children were defined by his religion and his poverty. He went to Holy Name grammar school at 245 Prospect Park West,[121] which he attended with other ethnic Catholics, many of whom were Irish, and then Regis High School in Manhattan as a scholarship student. He dropped out before graduation. The family went to nine o'clock mass on Sunday, and in the sixth grade Hamill was picked to be an altar boy. His father was an embittered, disabled man who had difficulty maintaining a steady job, and his mother often worked outside the home during his father's periods of unemployment. While Hamill's family did appear to be less prosperous than his friends' families, the chief occupations in the neighborhood were blue collar. Neighborhood families owned the local shops and bars, and he recalls rumors about families in the area going on relief after the war.

In 1950, Queens had only fairly small concentrations of Irish throughout the borough, but clusters of foreign-born Irish could be found around the Woodside area.[122]

The 1960 census included data on second-generation families, providing a clearer sense of Irish immigrant and Irish American neighborhood outlines. The total Irish foreign-stock population of New York City, which included native, foreign or mixed parentage, as well as foreign-born, residents, was 311,638 or 4 percent of the city's total population. Of that total, 131,764 were foreign-born.[123] The INS reports that between 1951 and 1960 48,362 Irish immigrated to the United States.[124] As noted, by the end of the decade we know that one-third of all Irish immigrants were going to New York City, and that they were predominately single and between 16 and 35 years old. Using the census data we can create socioeconomic profiles of the neighborhoods into which these migrants moved and create a foundation for understanding the lifestyles and culture of the New York Irish as they moved into the 1960s.[125]

The Bronx was the borough with the largest number of Irish (first- and second-generation), followed by Queens, then Brooklyn and Manhattan. In Queens, the

Irish were most densely concentrated in three areas: three tracts near Woodside, between 46th and 58th Streets, along Queens Boulevard; the area just east of Woodside Avenue from 73rd Street to Junction Boulevard, between Roosevelt Avenue and Northern Boulevard; and finally the area west of Northern Boulevard over to Triboro Boulevard along either side of 38th Street. Starting near the Woodside neighborhood, the area into which Kevin Morrissey moved in the late 1950s, and focusing on three tracts with the highest numbers of Irish, we can make these observations. The Irish represented the largest group in what appeared to be multi-ethnic communities. In tract 235 they totaled almost one-quarter of the population, followed by Italians and Germans. Germans were second with Italians third in the other two tracts. The median level of income for families and unrelated individuals in these tracts was between $5,261 and $5,777, below that for the borough, which was $6,443, but higher than that for the whole city at $5,103 and well within the range of middle-class status for the time.[126]

Most of the children of elementary-school age attended private school, which, given the ethnic mix of the neighborhood, was probably a Catholic school. High school students were divided evenly between public and private schools. This trend is consistent with anecdotal evidence and immigrant interviews, which suggested that many Irish immigrant and Irish American families of the time sent their children to parish schools.[127]

In Manhattan, large concentrations of Irish still lived in the Washington Heights and Inwood sections of the city, but the Irish enclaves were creeping north as African American and Hispanic families moved northward out of Harlem into the southeastern sections of Washington Heights, as had the Jews in the 1930s and 1940s.[128] In the most heavily Irish-populated census tracts of the Heights, the Irish totaled 12–15 percent of the population, the largest ethnic group per tract.[129] Germans, Russians, Poles, Austrians, and Italians, the majority of whom were probably Jewish according to studies done by Ira Katznelson and Ronald Bayor,[130] are included in the ethnic mix as the next most populous groups. The median income for families and unrelated individuals in these tracts ranges from $4,311 to $4,763, below middle-class standards and city income for the time, but above the borough's median income level of $3,923 in the same category. Just under half of the elementary and high school students, 46 percent and 44 percent respectively, attended private school.[131]

Farther north in Manhattan, in the Inwood section, which ran east and west of Broadway, north of Dyckman Street, about one in five of the residents in the community[132] were Irish. The median income in this community was almost $1,000 higher than in Washington Heights, ranging from $5,166 to $5,813, which put it in a middle-class category and was about 25 percent higher than the median income for the borough. Of the 2,282 children in elementary school in this neighborhood, 66 percent were in private school, as were 56 percent of the 1,234 high school students, more than likely in the schools attached to the parishes of Good Shepherd and St. Jude's.

As a youngster, Kareem Abdul-Jabbar remembers going to St. Jude's (class of

'61) and being the only African American in a class full of Irish children.[133] In fact, in the two tracts sandwiching St. Jude parish, 196 "Negroes" and 3,854 first- and second-generation Irish lived among a total population of 17,988. The Irish outnumbered the African Americans by almost 20 to 1.[134]

Several studies have been done on the ethnic transition in the neighborhoods of northern Manhattan. According to observers such as Bayor, Katznelson, and Snyder, the insularity and strong ethnic solidarity that the tight Irish clusters in Washington Heights and Inwood represented also reflected the insecurity they felt in having to share their neighborhood with other ethnic groups. In the 1930s and 1940s the Jews began moving into the Washington Heights neighborhood. Despite the similarities apparent between the two groups—both were family-oriented, middle-class Democrats, with strong religious beliefs and often working on the city payroll—they were separated by their ethnic difference and by territoriality. Each saw the other as an opponent. The tension escalated to violent physical acts of anti-Semitism through the end of World War II, when the ceasefire and the termination of other political issues which divided the groups eased outright conflicts.[135]

By the mid-century, the Irish found themselves and their neighborhoods vulnerable to the incursion of new ethnic groups. They were often outnumbered where they lived and where they worked. The newcomers challenged Irish leadership and tenure in political offices and civil service jobs, such as education and safety.[136] A detective who was also president of one of the city's major fraternal organizations offers a surprising example from the period. The Emerald Society of the New York City Police Department was founded in the early 1950s. According to him, despite the popular belief that "the Irish run the police department," the society was organized to rectify what the Irish officers of the time considered inequities in the treatment of Irish officers compared to other ethnic groups.[137] Feeling that they were being squeezed out of where they belonged, the Irish organized. This vulnerability at work and at home came at a time when the Irish were losing their presence at City Hall. Bill O'Dwyer was elected mayor in 1945 and 1949, but the Irish hold on the Democratic Party was weakening as early as 1945. And by 1961, it was virtually gone.[138]

The east side of Manhattan, in the neighborhood of Yorkville, also boasted clusters of Irish, from 74th Street north to 99th Street, and from Third Avenue over to the East River and then narrowing between Third and First above 89th Street.[139] Four of the tracts are good references because they have the highest number of Irish—about 13 percent of the total neighborhood population.[140] Germans slightly outnumbered them at 14.5 percent, but its German restaurants, bakeries, and specialty shops have traditionally identified the Yorktown neighborhood. Median income for families and unrelated individuals in this part of the Upper East Side range from $4,009 to $4,411, about 20 percent lower than the middle-class standard for the time, as well as the city standard, but slightly above the standard for the borough. One caveat to note in this neighborhood is that the number of unrelated individuals present in these tracts is significantly higher than in the Inwood neighborhood—25 percent vs. 9 percent—which suggests a larger proportion of single individuals and may also account for the lower income levels. Fifty-seven percent of the elementary-school children in these tracts attended private school, as did 43 percent of high school students.

In the Bronx, the most densely Irish neighborhoods were Mott Haven, Morrisania, Fordham, and an area in the eastern half of the borough that was bounded by Tremont Avenue to the north, Rosedale and Castle Hill Avenues to the west and east, and Wood Avenue and McGraw to the south.[141]

Mott Haven, like Washington Heights, had a significant nonwhite population, as more and more minorities pushed their way north. In tracts 27.1 and 33, the ethnic ratio was about 14 percent Irish, 36 percent Puerto Rican, and 8 percent African American. The median income ranged from $3,878 to $4,417 for families and unrelated individuals, placing Mott Haven below the middle-income range. In contrast to the other neighborhoods examined, these two tracts in Mott Haven show that only 26 percent of elementary-school children and 30 percent of secondary students attended a private school, perhaps reflecting the lower income and racial and ethnic makeup of the community.

Farther north in the borough the incomes were higher and the Puerto Rican population was almost nonexistent. In tracts just north of St. Simon Stock parish, the Irish made up 17 percent of the population and were the largest ethnic group in the area, followed by those from Italy, the USSR, Poland, and Germany.[142] Median incomes for families and unrelated individuals ranged from a low of $4,901 (in the southernmost tract, number 383) to a high of $5,641 (in the largest tract, number 405).

Just about half of the elementary- and high-school-age children attended private school (52 percent and 48 percent, respectively). The census data demonstrated that the farther north one moved in Manhattan or as families moved out of the borough, they entered more prosperous, family-oriented, middle-class neighborhoods. These communities in northern Manhattan and the outer boroughs were also inhabited by other white ethnics, often typically Catholic nationalities such as Italians or Poles, or foreign stock from the USSR, Germany, Poland, and Austria, many of whom can be assumed to be Jews.

Two migrant families were representative of the population just detailed by the data in the Bronx tracts[143] 383, 399, 405, and 407. Both had children who attended St. Simon Stock School, and both had lived in different parishes in the Bronx and Manhattan, including St. Helena's on Olmstead Avenue in the southeast Bronx, Holy Name of Jesus at West 96th Street near Amsterdam Avenue in Manhattan, and St. Simon Stock at East 182nd Street and Ryer Avenue (near Valentine Avenue) in the Bronx.[144] One man who emigrated in 1956 said that he and his wife had left Ireland to get work in New York.[145] They were both the children of farmers. He worked as a carpenter in the city and his wife was a housewife. In the second family, both spouses had also left Ireland to find work, the woman in 1961, the man in 1956.[146] Like the former family, both husband and wife had been raised on farms in Ireland. However, in New York, the wife had a job with Guardian Life Insurance as a filing clerk, while her husband worked as a carpenter. It is important to note that in conversations with migrants from the period, the occupations reported by these two families are typical of the work found by the Irish of the 1950s. Many of the young women were office workers in large insurance firms such as Metropolitan Life or the telephone company; others served as nurses in city hospitals. More often than not, the men worked in blue-collar positions, such as construction, and belonged to unions, such as the Transport Workers Union, which boasted a large Irish membership. To find a job in transit it helped to have a friendly cousin or acquaintance who would facilitate the process of obtaining a union card.[147]

Across the East River in Brooklyn the largest clusters of Irish immigrants and second-generation families identified by the 1960 census were found along three sides of Prospect Park in Park Slope. They were found along Prospect Park West back to Sixth Avenue, north to Atlantic Avenue on one side and south to Prospect Expressway on the other side. A total of 10,888 Irish lived in these communities.[148] Two other major clusters of Irish can be found on either side of the Gowanus Expressway, in the Bay Ridge and Fort Hamilton sections of the borough, numbering 4,125 and 4,859 respectively. While neither cluster was as populous as the Park Slope neighborhood, in several of the tracts in Bay Ridge the Irish account for as much as 10 percent of the total population and were the largest ethnic group represented.[149]

Another cluster significant in terms of concentration rather than number was an area on the other side of Prospect Park sandwiched between Avenue N and Church Avenue, east of Flatbush Avenue toward 46th Street. Seventeen tracts identified in the area totaled 6,366 Irish or 9 percent of the total Irish population in Brooklyn. In some tracts, such as numbers 824 and 838, the Irish made up 15 percent of the total population; in others, such as 830, the Irish represented only 7 percent. What is striking about this area is that the median income in some areas is 20 to 50 percent above middle-class standards, ranging from $6,000 to $7,412, the highest seen in any of the neighborhoods discussed so far.[150]

To summarize the socioeconomic profile of the Irish, the data showed the first and second generations to be middle- to lower-middle-class people who liked to live in predominately white, multi-ethnic neighborhoods where significant numbers of school-age children attended private schools. Given the Catholic Church's building boom in the 1950s and the preponderance of anecdotal evidence suggesting that "everybody sent their children to Catholic school," it can be assumed that a substantial proportion of the Irish children in these neighborhoods were going to parochial schools. The Irish also appear to be upwardly mobile and able to move to northern Manhattan and the outer boroughs—neighborhoods with steadily higher incomes.

In the immediate postwar period, the first- and second-generation Irish community in New York comprised emigrants from the 1920s and 1930s and their children and grandchildren. A slowdown in migration rates during the international depression of the thirties and World War II aged the immigrant population of the Irish in the city. The community was given an infusion of youth through the 1950s with the entry of thousands of single migrant men and women in their twenties who found work as nurses, clerks, city employees, contractors, and union laborers. The young Irish were leaving a country suspended in time by economic stagnation and cultural paranoia, perpetuated by national leaders who were too indecisive and insecure about the new republic's national future and identity to bring the country into the twentieth century. The migrants arriving in New York demonstrated their frustration with Ireland's paralysis by their flight to America.

They were more often than not rural people, many of them having grown up on or near farms. Most attended school at least to what would be the middle years of an American high school, and about 25 percent completed four years of secondary education. Many had jobs in Ireland, and while the Irish government claimed that the majority of emigrants through the fifties were unskilled, nearly a quarter identified themselves to INS officials as professionals, clerical workers, or sales personnel. Interviews with emigrants of the time suggested that migrants were basically dissatisfied with the opportunities and lifestyles available to them in Ireland. Personal ambition or family economic pressure pushed them to find a better life in New York.

The fifties migrants found a place for themselves in established Irish communities throughout the city. They married, joined the army, raised families, supported the local parish church, and sent their children to the parochial schools. What they brought to America and how they contributed socially and culturally to the ethnic legacy and history of Irish New York is discussed in the following chapters.

 **3**

The 1970s: The Interim

When the immigration laws were changed in the 1960s the
old social and benevolent organizations began to die. The
Irish moment was over.

        —Pete Hamill[1]

... the best of decades.

        —Fergal Tobin[2]

The 1960s and 1970s were decades of transition for the Irish in Ireland and Irish
Americans in New York. In order to understand the relationship between the New
Irish of the 1980s and the emigrant and Irish American community that survived
in New York from the end of World War II, it is necessary to look at that twenty-
year period. Social, legislative, religious, demographic, and cultural changes in Ireland and New York in the sixties and seventies had a profound impact on the daily
lives of Irish on both sides of the Atlantic. These changes also affected immigration, in terms of both number and perception. For Ireland and the ethnic community in New York, the exodus and presence of Irish in New York had been a fairly
constant phenomenon for generations. Late-twentieth-century politics and society
interrupted that continuum, with specific consequence for the generation of migrants who left Ireland in the 1980s.

  In the 1960s and 1970s European ethnic communities throughout New York
emptied out as upwardly mobile second- and third-generation families left for jobs,
better housing, and less crowded schools in the metropolitan perimeter counties
of New York, New Jersey, and Long Island. As these families left, they drained the
strength and vitality of their respective immigrant communities in New York.
This was particularly true of the first-generation (the immigrant) and second-
generation (native of foreign or mixed parentage) Irish who by 1970 represented
only 2.8 percent of the city's population, compared to 4 percent in 1960.[3] Pockets
of strength and solidarity remained in Inwood in Manhattan; in the Bronx neighborhoods north of Tremont Avenue, running east and west along the Grand Concourse and University Avenue; in Prospect Park in Brooklyn; and in the Woodside

area of Queens, but these communities were aging, populated primarily by people aged twenty-five years and older. Less than 20 percent of these neighborhood inhabitants were elementary and high school age children.[4]

Consider Inwood, one of the strongest ethnic communities left. In the neighborhood which ran north from Dyckman Street to West 218th Street between Inwood Hill Park and 10th Avenue, the Irish made up almost 18 percent of the population.[5] They represented the largest designated ethnic group, with the exception of people who identified themselves as persons of Spanish language. The latter was dominated by immigrants from the Dominican Republic.[6]

As Robert Snyder observed in his study of ethnic transition in Manhattan's Washington Heights neighborhood during the 1970s, Irish communities like the Heights and Inwood became increasingly insulated ethnically as they watched their peers in surrounding parishes and neighborhoods leave for the suburbs. They "gathered the wagons" against the new immigrant groups who replaced their neighbors.[7] Despite the migration of Irish out of upper Manhattan through the sixties, Inwood remained, demographically, a community of immigrants. In 1960, 61.5 percent of the total population was foreign stock—either born abroad or born in the United States to immigrant parents. Just under 30 percent of the total population was born outside the United States. Ten years later 61.8 percent of the population was still foreign stock, including the 33.5 percent of the total who were born abroad. The difference in 1970 was the place of birth.[8]

Comparing the population of Irish in the Inwood census tracts 291, 293, and 295 in 1960, examined in an earlier chapter, with the same tracts in 1970, the population of Irish was still close to one in five.[9] However, in 1960, 99 percent of the population was white, and just about 2 percent were either born in Puerto Rico or had parents who were born in Puerto Rico. By 1970 almost one-quarter of the neighborhood population consisted of people who identified themselves as persons of Spanish language, most of whom, Snyder reported, came originally from the Dominican Republic.

In terms of other population characteristics, a smaller, though significant, number of schoolchildren still attended private school in 1970: 52 percent of elementary students and 38 percent of secondary students, compared to 66 percent and 56 percent respectively in the previous decade. (Private or nonpublic schools could include Catholic schools, those affiliated with other religious institutions, independent schools—any school that is not "controlled and supported primarily by a local, State or Federal agency.") Despite the drop, the level of attendance at nonpublic institutions was still more than twice that of schoolchildren statewide. For the 1959–60 school year, 23.4 percent of all New York State students attended nonpublic schools. Ten years later, fewer than 20 percent (19.6) were enrolled in nonpublic institutions. The comparison undoubtedly reflects the concerns of urban parents with the safety and quality of city schools, as much as it does the importance to ethnic families, particularly Irish Catholic families, of parochial school education.[10]

Education levels for adults improved slightly. In 1970 just over 41 percent of those aged 25 and older graduated high school; for the three tracts, the median number of years spent in school was 10.7, compared to 10.2 years spent in school and a high school completion rate of 37.6 percent in 1960.[11] Comparative income levels for the neighborhood appear slightly higher in 1960 than in 1970. In the beginning of the decade Inwood's median income for families was $6,304, which put it just ahead of the $5,338 median income for families in Manhattan borough and $6,091 for families citywide. At the end of the ten-year period, income levels for families in the three tracts cited were slightly below those in the host borough and throughout the city. For all families, Inwood's median income was $8,853. Median income for all families in Manhattan was $8,983 and $9,298 throughout the city. However, the number of families below poverty level was lower in Inwood than in the borough or the city: 9.7 percent for tracts 291, 293, and 295, compared to 10.6 percent for the city and 13.1 percent for Manhattan.[12]

Except for the color of the inhabitants, their language, and their country of origin, it appeared that very little had changed in the socioeconomic background of the Inwood neighborhood. In fact, Robert Snyder quoted a local parish priest who observed that the Irish and the Dominicans were "so alike, it's uncanny."[13] But Snyder also observed that increases in crime, which the Irish blamed on the newcomers, different languages, and the ultimate goal of the Dominicans to return to their homeland, prevented the two ethnic groups from coming together in any meaningful way as neighbors rooted in the community. As a result the Irish who remained in northern Manhattan felt alienated and besieged on their home ground, creating an environment of fear and hostility that was aggravated by visits from families and friends who had left the neighborhood.[14] Snyder quoted Inwood residents who recalled family conversations ultimately punctuated by the question, "When are you going to get out of there? Why subject the kids?"[15]

The urban pressures and ethnic transition facing Inwood occurred throughout the city. As the 1960 census showed, the Irish continued to move north out of Manhattan and the Bronx. Comparisons of population figures between 1960 and 1970 indicated that while the whole number of Irish in the city declined in that 10-year span, the boroughs with the largest drops in population were Manhattan (46 percent), Brooklyn (39 percent), and the Bronx (25 percent).[16] By 1970, former Irish neighborhoods like Morrisania and Mott Haven in the East and South Bronx, respectively, were vacated by the Irish. In 1995 Father Gerald Ryan, pastor of St. Luke's parish on East 138th Street since 1966, observed that "within a few months [of my arrival] there were no Irish families left. We are an Afro-Hispanic community at present. St. Luke's was an 'Irish' parish up to 1966."[17]

At St. Nicholas of Tollantine parish in the Bronx, the alphabetized baptismal register for 1953–1959 under "O" includes the family names, O'Hara, O'Connell, O'Hee, O'Leary, O'Connor, O'Reilly, and O'Sullivan. Fifteen years later, in the baptismal records for 1977–1985, the names inscribed under "O" reflect the ethnic changes in the neighborhood: Oily, Oliveros, Otero, Onofre and Ojar.[18]

Woodside, Queens, experienced similar demographic transitions. An Irish American raised in Woodside owned and operated a bar on 65th Street with his mother from 1949 to 1979. When he sold it to a Spanish buyer in the late 1970s, he did so recognizing that the sale cemented what was already obvious after years of declining offers from Irish buyers. The community had changed. "The Spanish language and music could be heard coming from windows on every block."[19] Putting the property on the market in 1978, the Irish owner waited fifteen months before closing a deal with a Spanish buyer who wanted to open "the first Spanish bar in Upper Woodside."[20] Some of the seller's customers viewed the transfer as a "sellout."

But the reality was that the European immigrants and their children who moved into Woodside and raised their families between the 1920s and 1950s were dying, aging, or leaving the city to raise the next generation in the suburbs. New immigrants with families and futures in the city were taking their place. In 1995, the bar owner observed, "Where there were 14 Irish bars in Woodside in the 1960s and 1970s, now empty stores or non-alcohol-related businesses fill [the] locations."[21] In the earlier decades of the century the Irish left lower Manhattan for upper Manhattan, the Bronx, and Queens. The selling saloon owner observed that Germans from Yorkville and the Irish from Greenwich Village and upper Manhattan were literally carried to Woodside and the adjoining Sunnyside neighborhood by the elevated railroad, as well as the IRT train, the Long Island Railroad, and interborough buses. Public transportation ferried workers back into Manhattan for their daily commutes to work.[22] Just as the expanding subway system drew the Irish, then the Jews, then the Dominicans from the Lower East Side to the Upper West Side of Manhattan, expanding interborough connections facilitated the development of ethnic neighborhoods on the opposite side of the East River. But by the sixties, the Irish were leaving the city altogether. The gross number of foreign-stock Irish, which included the foreign-born and natives of foreign or mixed parentage, fell from 311,638 in 1960 to 220,622 by 1970, a drop of almost 30 percent.[23]

While most of the depopulation was due to internal migration within the tri-state area, Irish census records through the 1970s also showed an unprecedented return migration to the home country. Several factors can account for the in-migration. Anecdotally return migrants cited a preference for raising their families in Ireland.[24] Indeed, Ireland's National Economic and Social Council (NESC) in an emigration study published in 1991 stated that in-migration through the 1970s reflected the return of former emigrants and their families.[25] Education and social policies which improved academic opportunities for children of all classes, as well as massive public spending programs intended to upgrade Ireland's standard of living, were attractive lures for parents.[26]

It was easy enough to keep abreast of developments at home. News of the changes in Ireland was chronicled weekly in the *Irish Echo,* the ethnic paper of choice for Irish America. The *Echo* boasted on its front page every week (at least in the sixties) that "The *Irish Echo* Is the Largest Circulating Irish-American Newspaper—Guaranteed."[27] Headline stories from the sixties into the eighties focused primarily on news from Ireland. In a given year, everything from Ireland's proposed entry into the Common Market, election results, and the death of prominent political leaders was carried to emigrants living in the United States.[28] The news coverage as well as letters and visits to and from home kept the migrants informed of social and economic change in Ireland.

By the early 1960s, improved transatlantic travel, paid vacations, and a burgeoning tourist industry made it easy for non-emigrating immigrants in America as well as Irish and non-Irish American natives to visit Ireland.[29] In 1965 the United States Department of Commerce reported an increase of 43 percent in the number of American visitors to Ireland in 1964 over 1963, compared to a 13 percent increase for all of Europe.[30] The popularity of Ireland as a destination could just as easily be measured by the ad space in the *Echo* filled by travel agencies and airlines boasting the cheapest fares and tour packages to the island.

Despite the increase in traffic, fares to Ireland in the 1960s were certainly not bargains for the average family. An ad for the Grimes Travel Agency in July 1965 listed a 14- to 21-day jet economy ticket to Dublin for $277; a one-way tourist class steamship ticket to a British port was listed at $203 in the off-season; a one-way cabin-class ticket to an Irish or British port was $244 in the off-season.[31] Median incomes in New York City were listed at between $6,000 and $9,000 between 1960 and 1970, translating to gross weekly paychecks of between $115 and $173, probably making annual visits to Ireland out of the question for most migrant families in New York City. But if they could afford the air or sea fare, living expenses while visiting relatives would probably be minimal. Among four migrants who ultimately returned to Ireland in the late 1960s and 1970s, one visited Ireland twice between 1961 and 1976, one visited "many times" after emigrating in 1952, one visited once in 1961 after emigrating in 1956, and another visited "every year" after emigrating in 1959.[32] So it could be done.

Immigration and Naturalization Service records show that through the 1950s into the early 1960s the number of aliens traveling to Ireland increased steadily, reflecting both the attraction of Ireland as a tourist destination and the ability of migrants to visit home as they became more secure financially. In 1954, 22,086 travelers left the United States for Ireland—4,956 aliens and 17,130 citizens.[33] In 1961, 14,362 aliens and 30,623 citizens traveled to Ireland.[34]

The changing ratio of sea to air travel is particularly interesting in this period. Within a decade, air travel had become the preferred method of transport for citizens and aliens. In 1954 more passengers traveled to Ireland by sea than by air: 12,404 vs. 9,682. Both aliens and citizens were more likely to take a boat than a plane: of the aliens 3,305 went by sea and 1,921 by air; for citizens the figures were 9,369 and 7,761.[35] By 1961, not only had the total number of travelers to Ireland increased by nearly 40 percent, but airlines were preferred more than three to one (34,025:10,960) over passenger ships. And aliens were more likely than citizens to fly: 11,338 aliens traveled by air, vs. 3,024 by sea (3.74:1), and for citizens it was 22,687 vs. 7,936 (2.85:1).[36] Several reasons can account for the change, including the greater accessibility of air travel to the average consumer, the increased prosperity of the Irish immigrant and Irish American population over time, and the naturalization of immigrants, which added to the numbers of citizens traveling to Ireland.[37] Migrants returning for home visits may also have welcomed the increased time in Ireland that flying allowed them. They also faced lower land costs when visiting relatives.

While not all visitors to Ireland ultimately returned to the land of their birth, the visits certainly highlighted the differences between the two countries. For some migrants, social and economic change in Ireland would not be enough to induce them to return. Others would be drawn to the slower pace and pastoral beauty that life in a small Irish town offered. Most would be struck by the contrast between memory and reality. Consider these observations from a letter to the *Irish Echo* editor in 1965 and correspondence between friends in 1952:

> Dear Mr. O'Connor:
> Your letter from the reader—"Wants to Go Back" prompted me to write this letter. He states both he and his wife are opposed to the American man on almost all subjects: "the deity of money, the monarchy of the business executive and the great American dream."
> One might ask why he came, why he wants to stay.
> He came for what all of us did: for opportunity and a chance to develop the best that is in him, and for money too. What land gets along without it? Surely you cannot overlook the significance and meaning of the great lady of steel when you enter New York harbor:
> "Keep ancient lands . . ."
> Yes this great land opens doors to all and tolerates the many who accept the advantages and privileges, meanwhile stuffing their bankrolls—avoiding very knavishly the responsibility of citizenship or interest in government and its welfare—awaiting instead for their return to the isle of their birth or perhaps to a memory, that to many is found wanting, because the great freedom in America has already developed in them a personality that cannot fully tolerate the slow pace of the "old country." They instead feel warped and discontent. . . .
>
> Wants to Stay, Bronx[38]

> [Ireland] is lovely country when one can appreciate it, and I can see from some of your written observations that you do. But M., never think of leaving it to come to this man's Country:
> It takes one half a life time to become accustomed to [the] U.S. and by that time one is grown so old that the enjoyment is gone from Life. . . . [39]

> You know M. I think if you could manufacture or get the feelings of a returned Irishman who had seen life in U.S. coming back after building up in his mind's eye what Ireland should be for 30 years or so, then return to find his God had feet of Clay, both in (sociability?) and in bigotry. Did you happen to see the article in the *Tyrone Constitution* a few weeks ago, "Tyrone man's suggestions, after 30 years in U.S." Boy what a furore, and the usual "out," "he's a communist."
> But M., the fields, mountains, the old haunts, what memories, especially when one had never expected a couple of years ago, to ever lay eyes on them. . . . [40]

Other migrants chose to leave "for the children," unable to tolerate the realities and difficulties of urban life in the 1960s and 1970s. When asked "why did you return to live in Ireland," respondents to a questionnaire wrote: "To get out of City and a better [life] for children."[41] "The Bronx was changing, busing children to our school and ours out. The young coloured in NY expected too much at least the older ones were just like ourself, willing to work and live like everyone else."[42] "I wanted to rear my family in Ireland."[43] "Always did plan to return and when the family arrived 5 [five children]. We said, Now is the time to go back."[44] A contributing, if not deciding, factor in the immigrants' decision to return to Ireland permanently was the income workers could carry with them to Ireland. Older return migrants could collect American pension and Social Security benefits in addition to whatever incomes they secured when back in Ireland.[45] Workers were "fully insured" or eligible to collect Supplemental Security Income (SSI) benefits after working forty quarters or ten years in the United States.[46] Immigrants arriving in America in the early 1950s as young twenty-somethings could have worked, married, begun a family, and returned to Ireland in the seventies with a monthly check from Uncle Sam at retirement.

According to the United States Social Security Administration, 6,528 Social Security beneficiaries lived in Ireland in December 1994. Included in this number were 4,383 retired worker beneficiaries. Of these beneficiaries, only 19 percent were Irish citizens; 75 percent were American citizens. What the data did not show was how many of the U.S. citizens in this group were Irish-born immigrants who returned to Ireland after living and working in America for a time. However, if we look at the annual distribution rates for SSI benefits from the late 1950s on, the number of recipients living in Ireland more than triples from 1955 to 1977, when the most checks were sent to Eire. Consider these numbers of individual beneficiaries receiving monthly supplements and living abroad in Ireland at the end of each calendar year, taken from the "Annual Statistical Supplement" of the *Social Security Bulletin*:[47]

Year	Number of Recipients	Year	Number of Recipients	Year	Number of Recipients
1955	1,463	1968	4,705	1983	6,170
1956	1,542	1969	5,212	1984	6,179
1957	1,703	1970	5,613	1985	6,207
1958	2,189	1971	5,911	1986	6,203
1959	2,438	1972	6,246	1987	6,097
1960	2,843	1973	6,548	1988	6,022
1961	3,141	1974	6,652	1989	5,963
1962	3,484	1976	6,736	1990	5,996
1964	3,764	1977	6,798	1991	6,039
1965	4,015	1979	6,721	1992	6,114
1966	4,164	1980	6,429	1993	6,230
1967	4,368	1982	6,386	1994	6,528

The number of recipients rose steadily through the 1960s and 1970s, peaking in 1977. Coincidentally the peak period of return migration to Ireland was between 1971 and 1979,[48] suggesting that many of the SSI recipients were return migrants. The Social Security Administration estimates that 30 percent of all legal immigrants emigrate, although the Irish have traditionally posted the lowest rate of return migration of all nationalities. Of that 30 percent, only 17 percent leave the country after ten years, or after working the required amount of quarters to be eligible to collect SSI benefits.[49] SSI recipients between 1955 and 1977 would have had to be in the United States at least between the years 1945 and 1967—ten years before 1955 and 1977 respectively. The INS counted 101,117 immigrants from Ireland entering the United States between 1941 and 1970.[50] Of those 30,335 or fewer can be assumed to have emigrated, presumably back to Ireland. Seventeen percent, or 5,156, of these latter emigrants probably worked enough quarters to qualify for SSI benefits. The difference between the number of SSI recipients in Ireland in 1955 and 1977 is 5,335. While return migration cannot account for the entire jump in beneficiaries, the availability of the pension and the improved standard of living and opportunities for young families in Ireland certainly provided incentive and certainly accounted for a significant proportion of new beneficiaries.

Not all those who did go back to Ireland were received as welcome prodigals. Often they were referred to pejoratively as returned Yanks. In interviews with return migrants and their families, episodes were recalled in which the migrants were chastised for everything from their Americanized accents and vernacular to their clothes, their supposed wealth, and the apparent sophistication they gained from traveling and living abroad. The reception seemed to be one of jealousy and intimidation on the part of the Irish who stayed behind and who were now receiving the emigrants back into their community. At the most extreme level an Irish American recounted the experience of a cousin who returned to a town in the west of Ireland and attempted to start a business, only to be thwarted at every turn by a hostile local bureaucracy that seemed to be deliberately attempting to ensure the failure of the "Americans." The returned migrants ultimately went back to the United States, embittered and disillusioned. Another family recalls a chilly period of reception when they first arrived in Dublin. The couple and their family sensed that their neighbors felt that because of what they had experienced and achieved living in New York they were somehow superior to the Irish. The family overcame these perceptions and remained in Dublin to raise and educate their children.[51]

John P. McCarthy, an Irish American commentator on things Irish and American, wrote in a 1983 column, "The Dilemma of the Returned Yank," that

> As for the younger returning immigrants, the difficulties they confront are different but also derivative from certain images they have or seek to impose on Ireland. Some believe they had been shortchanged by Ireland in the unavailability of educational and other advancements opportunities in their youth. In spite of such educational shortcomings, most of these immigrants to America have done extraordinarily well in their adopted country. Their American success has emboldened them to return home and

demonstrate their competence and manifest their success. . . . Whatever they return to, whether it be pursuit of a job, the opening of a business, or if it comes to it, the receipt of public welfare or the dole, it is bound to be seen as taking something away from a resident, as opposed to a returned, native. When that narrow jealousy meets the assertive confidence of the returned Yank, hostility is bound to result. Not surprisingly a substantial number abandon their attempt to settle in Ireland and return to the United States in a relatively short time.[52]

The reaction of the Irish to the returned emigrants suggests an identity crisis among the Irish that is borne out in contemporary literature. As discussed in an earlier chapter, Thomas Murphy's *A Crucial Week in the Life of a Grocer's Assistant*[53] focused on a young man torn by his decision to stay in Ireland and the fact that he did not want to emigrate, as did many of his village peers and friends. In the course of the play, the audience is introduced to a visiting emigrant from England, too proud to admit his failure abroad and feigning the wealth that all emigrants were supposed to earn outside of Ireland. In Patrick McCabe's *Butcher Boy*, the lead character is a preadolescent boy growing up in the "New Ireland" of the 1960s. His Uncle Alo, who migrated to England, is not as prosperous as the family claims him to be.[54] In both stories, the migrant who left Ireland because he was unable to create a life for himself in his native land, and who did not find happiness, success, or security abroad, could not return home because emigrants were supposed to discover the pot of gold. Uncle Alo also left unresolved personal issues in Ireland that could not be forgotten upon his return. Unwanted at home and out of place abroad, the failed migrant was suspended between two cultures and became unsettled, unsatisfied, and unhappy. As much as the local Irish community bemoaned the loss of its emigrating young people and held wakes at their departure, they did not want to witness their failure or feel threatened by their success.[55] The message in the literature seems to bear out what Kerby Miller described regarding the nineteenth-century migrant: that he or she was essentially dead to the community and to the family. His or her presence was too vivid a reminder of the many failures of Ireland.

Historian Joe Lee described the Irish character in the immediate postwar years as that of a begrudger. In a "stunted" economy that had little or no real growth or capacity for growth, the individual could only get ahead at the expense of others. The result was often the castigation of anyone who strove to succeed because that person's rise necessarily kept a neighbor down. On the other hand, Lee argued, the success of immigrant sons and daughters was acceptable, because it was not achieved at the expense of local talent. Indeed the entire town could and did share in the glory of a neighbor's child abroad. But for those who stayed behind the frustration of waiting one's turn for promotion, raises, and recognition, combined with the political and cultural insularity and isolation that choked Ireland in the 1950s, encouraged jealousy and pettiness at all levels of Irish society.

The inter-related combination of economic, marital and mobility patterns meant that Ireland had more than her fair share of individuals suffering from thwarted ambition, disappointed dreams, frustrated hopes, shattered ideals. The society was too static for the begrudgers to be able to diffuse their resentments on a wide circle of targets. Day after day, year after year, a stunted society obliged them to focus obsessively on the same individuals as the sources of their failure.[56]

Ironically, as the economic stress of the country lifted for a time in the 1960s and 1970s, the practice of begrudgery intensified, as the prosperity of the period was made manifest in conspicuous consumption. Lee called it an ethos of "If you've got it, flaunt it."[57]

The economic policies inaugurated as the "First Programme for Economic Expansion" in the late 1950s, based on the recommendations of secretary of finance T. K. Whitaker's *Economic Development* report presented in 1958, began a ten- to fifteen-year period of hope and growth in Ireland.[58] The program acknowledged the economic and social damage that perpetual emigration had inflicted on Irish society. The proactive stance of the government to improve education and encourage economic growth resulted in a slowdown of emigration that eventually led to a period of in-migration through the seventies, rising marriage and birth rates, and an increase in population. Most significantly, the period of growth was a time of great expectation, energy, and promise, a marked contrast from the stagnation of the immediate postwar period and a nonquantitative aspect of Ireland's perception of its own past that should not be underestimated. Fergal Tobin's book title describes it simply: the 1960s was "the best of decades."[59]

Not surprisingly, Ireland's outward migration slowed as it opened itself up economically and socially to international influences. Ireland joined the European Economic Community (EEC) in 1973.[60] The Irish Development Authority (IDA), created in the late fifties, aggressively courted foreign investment in Ireland through the 1970s with the goal of attracting jobs and capital to the country.[61] While the relative success of Irish entry to the EEC and of IDA's business development program is open to criticism, Ireland emerged from the isolationist position it had assumed in the 1950s and was a participant, however small, on the world stage, which broadened the perspective of its people.

The intrusion of electronic media into Irish homes was arguably responsible for the wider worldview of Irish citizens. By 1980, 92 percent of Irish homes had television. Dublin had the highest rate of ownership with 96 percent of homes claiming a set, but even the provinces with the lowest percentage of televisions— Connaught and the three Republican counties in Ulster—at 87 percent represented a significant majority of homes.[62] In a recent film set in the late 1980s, even a family of "travelers"—Ireland's indigenous itinerant class and a group strongly resistant to "modern" ways—played the television while they danced around the campfire to traditional Irish music.[63]

The prediction of television's opponents that the Irish would be corrupted by the medium in the 1950s might have been correct—Irish people were certainly exposed to a variety of non-Irish culture through the available programming. Whether they were "corrupted" is a matter for debate, but it is clear the people were eager for more than what they had. The poor audience ratings for Irish-language radio programming and the popularity of the British television offerings received on the east coast of Ireland in the 1950s signaled the demand for diversity, if nothing else. The Irish culture may be unique, but it was not enough for the general population. One historian observed:

> The service made an enormous and almost immediate impact on Irish life. While bringing to Irish homes the vulgar triviality of "canned" Anglo-American programmes, it also relieved the drabness of much of Irish life and shattered the cosy complacency of traditional Irish attitudes. Subjects which had been virtually taboo—the place of the Church in Irish society, for example—were widely aired in popular programmes, and received with pleasurable shock by the viewing public. It is difficult to conceive of a more radical force in the maturing of Irish society.[64]

The approval of the state-sponsored industry in 1960 followed years of debate in which Irish-language advocates (such as Gael Linn), the airline and tourism industry, and the Church presented arguments which if nothing else recognized the power of television. This power was perceived not only in terms of the messages television could send, but how easily those messages could reach isolated parts of the country.[65] In a speech introducing Irish television to the country, Eamon De Valera warned of the dangers of the new medium as well as its potential for good:

> Never before was there in the hands of man an instrument so powerful to influence the thoughts and actions of the multitude. A persistent policy pursued over radio and television, in addition to imparting knowledge, can build up the character of a whole people, including sturdiness and vigour and confidence. On the other hand, it can lead, through demoralisation, to decadence and dissolution.[66]

Just as De Valera could not prevent the flow of Irish people leaving the country through the 1950s with the concept of "frugal comfort" and the virtue of an Irish Ireland, neither could he or the Church keep the rest of the world out of Ireland by denying television to its citizens. Ireland's isolation was coming to an end.

Of the total program hours broadcast by Radio Telefis Eireann (RTE) in 1972, 57 percent were acquired or non-RTE-originated programming.[67] How many of the acquired hours were U.S. programs is not available. But a quick review of RTE programming guides in the late seventies and eighties indicated that the Irish could watch such American programs as *Little House on the Prairie, Different Strokes, Wonderful World of Disney, Dallas, The Fall Guy, Mork and Mindy,* and *Nurse,* as well as *Brideshead Revisited* from England.[68] How many Irish were actually watching the American shows is not known, but what is clear is that their choices had broadened since the 1950s, and the opportunity to view what others around the world were watching was available to the Irish. Television also represented a symbol of modern consumerism in Ireland that previously was enjoyed only by cousins in Queens, not those in County Cork.

In the United States, a change in immigration policy coincided with Ireland's improving quality of life. While it had little immediate impact on Irish emigration at the time, Congress passed the 1965 Immigration Act to correct what was considered preferential treatment of traditional European migrating nationalities. The act focused on family reunification, requiring prospective migrants to have a close family member living in the United States to secure entry. The new law, coupled with increasing prosperity and growth in Ireland, dramatically decreased the numbers of young people boarding emigrant ships or transatlantic flights to America. INS figures show that through the 1970s, Irish migration to the United States dropped to about a thousand a year.[69]

As the rate of emigration slowed in the late sixties and seventies, and the migrants who could transmit the changes in Irish society to America stayed home, the gulf between the reality of Irish society and the perception of it in the United States deepened. The immigrant community in New York through the seventies consisted predominately of veterans of the 1922–23 Civil War or their children who emigrated in the years before or just after World War II. Their memories of Ireland were of a largely agricultural economy and a society still coming to terms with its newly won noncolonial status and the unresolved issues inherent in the separation of Northern Ireland and the Republic. As John McCarthy observed, the leaders of the Irish American community and ethnic groups "have not realized that history has moved on and that contemporary Ireland is more concerned with economic development, fiscal stability, European integration, community reconciliation, and the various strains imposed on individual and familial harmony in the contemporary world than with the irredentist cause [a unified Ireland]."[70]

The ethnic community in New York City in the 1960s and 1970s was shrinking, and it was aging. The big band dances at City Center stopped in the sixties, and bandleader Brendan Ward ran a travel agency.[71] By the early eighties, the Irish Institute had closed its doors on West 48th Street in Manhattan. The building, a popular meeting place for county organizations and other Irish societies, shut down for lack of use. The institute sold the property and committed the proceeds to its support of Irish culture. County organization membership dwindled as members dispersed geographically, aged, or passed on, and the need for networking died as immigrant numbers declined. Attendance and team membership at Gaelic Park dropped off as the population which traditionally filled the park on Sunday afternoons disappeared. The most visible symbol of the Irish in New York remained constant during this time: the St. Patrick's Day Parade. In his history of the parade in New York, John Ridge made this observation about the 1980 event:

> The extravaganza of the St. Patrick's Day Parade assumed more significance than ever before in the 1970s and 1980s as declining immigration from Ireland and a dispersal of the Irish population of the city made the Irish community less visible. The city's Irish were slowly being submerged or replaced by new immigrant groups. Judge Comerford [Irish American leader and chairman of the parade since 1966] observed that "without the parade many people wouldn't think there were any Irish in New York."[72]

But the parade marched only once a year and drew many Irish Americans and other spectators from the suburbs. What was left of the Irish in New York was often only symbolic. Without the direct tie of immigration to keep the connection with Ireland fresh, the Irish American experience became less real, more emotional, and more strongly rooted in that less than reliable source—memory.

Mary Ford, an Irish American who grew up in the Bronx surrounded by immigrant parents, aunts, and uncles, wrote that Irish habits, Irish food, and stories about "home" never left her relatives despite more than half a lifetime in America. They socialized, lived, and often worked only with other Irish migrants. "[They] were as unassimilated as immigrants could be."[73] When the immigrants died (and their children and grandchildren dispersed to the suburbs), so too did the "Irish-only" family gatherings. "Many of the last parties [at her aunt's house] were funerals."[74] Ford's experience is significant for a couple of reasons. The first is the significance of the immigrant generation to disseminating ethnicity, which was responsible for introducing and sustaining the Irish culture and traditions to the American-born descendants.

But the other point to note is one that repeats itself in many forms among this population. The traditions and experiences that forged Irish identity were not necessarily framed by the formal transmission of culture through music and dance lessons or language classes. The conventional cultural carriers, such as language, dancing, Celtic instruments, and Gaelic sports, enjoyed tremendous popularity in the postwar period, and many families routinely participated in these rites. But Ford's primary sense of being Irish came from being with her family. Her family came from Ireland, but now they were in America, a distinctly different place. Their closeness, as much as their origin, was a bond they carried that kept them connected in a new world. It helped them make the transition from home, by keeping some part of home with them.

Pete Hamill, son of a Belfast immigrant, had similar experiences as a child. "There were never major pronouncements, no manifestoes issued, no statements of purpose. You were born in America but you were Irish. You were Irish because your parents were Irish and all their friends were Irish."[75] Being Irish was not a self-conscious exercise among the generations born and raised in the Irish neighborhoods of the 1940s, 1950s, and 1960s. Many of those interviewed never attended a ceili (dance/party) or a feis, never enrolled in an Irish language course or learned to step dance, yet all were raised with an Irish identity. Their fathers may have played football in Gaelic Park or belonged to the Emerald Societies of New York's police and fire departments, but with the exception of the Catholic Church and its educational system (which is not to be underestimated), one's sense of being Irish was not necessarily transmitted institutionally. It came from growing up among other Irish families and relatives and belonging to an Irish community. When the tie of immigration broke and the immigrants of previous generations disappeared, the strength, solidarity, and importance of being Irish weakened. But as these writers and the anecdotal evidence show, the sense of identity that came from being Irish did not die. The sense of belonging to a larger tradition or community is difficult to break; it may fade or mellow like childhood memories, but it is held in reserve, in expectation of the appropriate trigger to renew it and pass it on. As the writer from the Bronx hopes for her children: "that sometime in their lives they will know a place like Monahan's [the writer's aunt from Ireland], where there were stories told and stories made and the backyard was paved over so that everyone could dance."[76]

An active member of Gaelic League, an Irish-language society, in the 1940s and 1950s noted in a recollection of his years in the league that with the increase in immigration after World War II the language societies expected a growth in membership, which never happened. "The majority of the young Irish," he wrote, "favored the dance halls," where thousands of young Irish and Irish Americans from around the city met each week to socialize. But, he commented, the immigrants who rejected the Gaelic League as young adults looked, thirty and forty years later, to enroll their children and grandchildren in step dancing classes.[77] Historians and sociologists have documented the surge in ethnic awareness and identity that usually occurs among some third-generation ethnics. Comfortable socially and economically as Americans, the third generation has the interest and confidence to explore the family's origins. It may just be that after years of struggling to achieve and succeed in America, the grandchildren of immigrants can afford to take the time to look back at where they started. But beyond the actual exercise of culture, be it language, dancing, music, or literature, the exploration of ethnicity through formal instruction or group membership offered contact with other people with the same interest, background, and ethnicity. While it can never replace the "neighborhood" or "parish" community that gave the Irish immigrants and their children identity and belonging and nurtured their ethnicity during the first years in America, the pursuit of ethnic culture creates a bond and awareness among the members that they belong to a larger community of people who share a common background.

The 1970s were a fallow period in Irish life and culture in the city. With no emigration to keep the neighborhoods thriving, and the dispersion of the middle class to the suburbs, there were few Irish left to keep the social and ethnic organizations of the city alive. The lack of emigrants also denied New Yorkers the opportunity to learn firsthand about the social and economic change that Ireland had experienced in the 1960s and 1970s. The local New York image of the Irish was that of an unsophisticated migrant who left a premodern society in the 1950s. Jim Carroll, an Irish American who spent his teen years in Inwood, described the people in his neighborhood in the fall of 1963: "Hallways in my new building and each park bench filled with chattering old Irish ladies either gossiping or saying the rosary, or men long time here or younger ones right off the boat huddling in floppy overcoats in front of drug stores discussing their operations, ball scores, or the Commie threat. Guys my age strictly All-American. . . ."[78]

The image of the Irish as rural dwellers from a quaint countryside was not undermined by increased American travel to Ireland. The tourist industry in Ireland and America profited by promoting the image of Ireland as a pastoral ideal. "Ireland is represented as a place of picturesque scenery and unspoiled beauty, of friendly and quaint people, a place which is steeped in past traditions and ways of life. In short, it is represented as a pre-modern society."[79]

Luke Gibbons, an Irish film historian, explained that "the absence of a visual tradition in Ireland, equal in stature to its powerful literary counterpart, has meant that the dominant images of Ireland have, for the most part, emanated from outside the country, or have been produced at home with an eye on the foreign (or tourist) market."[80] Those images were encouraged by tour operators who bused groups of Americans around the Irish countryside stopping at preselected pubs, hotels, and bed and breakfasts, making sure that the tourists saw exactly what they paid for: friendly people, green pastures, dark pubs with singing balladeers and beer, and lots of castle ruins. To be sure, there were individuals who navigated their own tours of the country and others who visited relatives that might have brought them closer to the "unpackaged" Ireland, but the prevailing image of Ireland at the time was shaped by marketers appealing to consumers eager to escape the real world.

Films such as *The Quiet Man* and *Ryan's Daughter* reinforced the visual image of the tourist's Ireland. Made in or about Ireland by non-Irish moviemakers, they were screened widely to American audiences.[81] And despite Gibbons's observation that the film tradition of Ireland did not share the strength or stature of its literary history, the Irish literature most popular in America, on college campuses at least, was that of pre–World War II authors, which, as suggested earlier, also focused on premodern Ireland. The urban contemporary realism of such authors and filmmakers as Roddy Doyle, Patrick McCabe, and Neil Jordan was several decades away.

In short, the 1970s created a reality vacuum between Ireland and New York. Irish Americans in the metropolitan area, migrants and natives alike, held an image of Ireland that was frozen in time at about 1950. Even the resumption of violence in Northern Ireland, the most compelling news stories to come across the sea from that island, centered on an issue that was neither new nor modern to the Irish in America: it was just the sorry resurrection of a centuries-long battle. Many of the immigrants left in the city were veterans of the 1920s Civil War struggle that ultimately divided the country into the twenty-six and six counties of the Republic and Northern Ireland, respectively. "The troubles" were no indication of great change in the country.

In Ireland, economic promise, as well as the cultural and social freedoms brought on by the country's few steps into the international marketplace, the introduction of television, and the Vatican II reforms in the Catholic Church (to be covered in chapter 5), kept young people in Ireland and created an environment that encouraged a generation to look to Ireland as the place to build a future. For the first time in decades, Irish youngsters entered adulthood believing that they did not have to leave Ireland to do well. The changes in Ireland and its exposure to American and British music, television, movies, and fashion via electronic media destroyed the cultural isolation that the fifties generation carried with them to New York. The Irish raised in the sixties and seventies were arguably more confident and sophisticated than previous generations of Irish thanks to the global awareness that television encouraged as well as a universal education system that cut across class lines.

The political, social, cultural, and economic events on both sides of the Atlantic that informed the respective societies and shaped a new generation in Ireland created a gap between the two countries that would not be recognized until the international recession of 1979–80. The economic downturn reversed Ireland's good fortune and pushed thousands of young Irish back on to emigrant ships and planes. After fifteen years of sharply reduced emigration and positive net immigration to Ireland, the traditional trend of more people leaving than returning to Ireland resumed. But the dynamic between Irish immigrants and Irish Americans, as well as between the immigrant and America, was different. The new immigrants represented the contemporary evolution of Irish society, which was unrecognizable to many Irish Americans. The migrants' presence in New York reflected the distance that had grown between Irish America's perception of Ireland and the reality of contemporary Ireland.

 **4**

The 1980s: The New Irish

Ar scath a cheile a mhaireas na daoine.
                                    —Berna Brennan[1]

After two decades of stability and growth, which included a net inward migration of people as well as a natural population increase due to higher birth rates, Ireland lost about 10 percent of its population between 1981 and 1991.[2] In those ten years, almost 360,000 Irish citizens left their homeland, most in the second half of the decade, in numbers the country had not witnessed since the end of World War II. (The net migration figure was 208,000 after calculating for deaths and births.)[3]

While many parallels exist between the migrations of the immediate postwar period and the 1980s, the irony for Ireland of the latter exodus is that the government responded too well to many of the unrequited demands that pushed the earlier generation out of the country. Yet despite improvements in government services and the standard of living, Ireland still could not satisfy the ambitions of its school graduates. In the 1960s and 1970s Ireland modernized to such an extent that the Republic in 1982 would have been unrecognizable to a young Irish person of 1952. The country was a member of the European Economic Community (EEC); it had one of the best-educated populations in the EEC; 92 percent of Irish homes had television, with broadcasting that included selections from at least three Irish-based networks;[4] 47 percent of its people were under 25;[5] and fittingly, it could boast of international rock music stars like Bob Geldoff and U2. In thirty years Ireland had opened itself up literally and figuratively to the rest of the world.

But Ireland could not sustain the promise it offered to the emerging generation raised in the "good times" of the 1960s and 1970s. Sean Minihane, an eighties emigrant and founder of the Irish Immigrant Reform Movement (IIRM) in the United States, said that his generation was to be the one that "did not have to emigrate."[6]

For more than a hundred years emigration had been the expected route for those unable to survive in the Irish economy, particularly residents in the rural counties of the west and north. The attempts of the Irish government to expand the economy with the goal of full employment were successful until the international recession of 1979–80 exposed the frailty of the Irish program. The government had bought its expansion on credit, offering generous subsidies to foreign companies and investing in expensive social welfare programs that it could not carry after the worldwide fiscal crisis. Ireland did not recover from the economic downturn of the early 1980s. Inflation soared as high as 23 percent and unemployment rose steadily into the high teens, hitting 19 percent by 1986. Just as they had thirty years before, thousands of Irish people in their twenties left Ireland for a better life abroad.

As had been the case since the Depression, most of the migrants left for Great Britain—about 70 percent by most estimates. Ten percent headed for the United States, and the rest went to continental Europe or Australia.[7] Unlike previous generations, however, the migrants entering the United States were illegal aliens. The 1965 Immigration and Nationality Act reordered the priority of entry to favor family reunification, which required aliens to have immediate family in the United States to sponsor them.[8] This change in the law, coupled with the return migration of Irish through the 1970s, made emigration to America difficult for the Irish because they did not have the close relations they needed to gain legal access to America. As a result, most of the Irish who emigrated through the 1980s entered the United States as tourists, overstayed their visas, and lived and worked as undocumented aliens. In 1978, 43,000 Irish residents entered the United States as non-immigrants, of whom 34,000 were tourists. In 1987, when Irish unemployment stood at 19 percent, 105,000 non-immigrants entered, 81,000 listing "pleasure" as their objective.[9] To further emphasize the exodus from Ireland, *U.S. News and World Report* reported that in January 1987 the U.S. Embassy in Dublin received 250,000 requests for visas.[10] Just exactly how many Irish arrived to stay during the decade was debatable at the time and remained vague ten years later.

Conservative estimates put the figure at about 40,000. Immigrant advocates, including the IIRM and the *Irish Voice,* claimed the population to be as high as 150,000–200,000.[11] Official United States data show Irish immigration rising through the eighties, but to nowhere near the high-end levels reported in the popular media. The INS recorded that only 949 immigrants were admitted to the United States from Ireland in 1982. That number had doubled to 1,839 by 1986.[12] The Irish census for the years 1981 to 1986 shows an average annual net migration of 14,377, but that number takes into account total population change, including deaths and in-migration to the country.[13] The National Economic and Social Council (NESC) in Ireland estimated that while the net population loss in the 1981–90 period was 208,000, the total outflow of people was closer to 360,000 (or 10 percent of the entire population).[14] If we use the estimated ratio that 10 to 14 percent of migrants headed to the United States, then we can conclude that in the 1980s anywhere from 36,000 to 50,000 Irish entered the United States. In fact, the INS reports that from 1982 through 1990 31,921 Irish immigrants were admitted to America.[15] However, this latter number must be tempered by several factors. Almost all (25,412) of the

Irish immigrants reported by the INS were admitted in the years 1987 to 1990,[16] one year after Congress enacted the first in a series of special immigration laws that were ultimately quite favorable to the Irish.

Many of the recipients of the special visas awarded to the Irish were already living in the United States illegally when they applied for and received their green cards. Therefore, the data presented by the INS for much of the 1980s do not accurately reflect the Irish immigrant population in America. Through much of the 1980s the majority of the population lived underground, working "under the table" and socializing primarily with each other in ethnic neighborhoods in the Bronx and Queens. While we cannot assign an exact number to the population, based on census and INS estimates from America and Ireland, we can assume that it was much lower than 150,000 and probably closer to 50,000.

A word here about the visa programs: beginning in 1986, a series of non-preference visa programs were established by Congress to provide immigrant access to America for thirty-six countries identified as "adversely affected" by the 1965 Immigration Act. (The Republic of Ireland was one of the countries.) The first of these were known as the Donnelly, Berman, and Morrison Programs for the congressmen who sponsored each bill; the two most significant to the Irish were the Donnelly and the Morrison. The Donnelly Program distributed 40,000 visas (called NP-5 visas) over three years starting in 1988. Applicants could apply as often as they wished to this program. The Irish won 40 percent (16,000) of the Donnelly visas. The Morrisons were basically an extension of the Donnellys; the Irish were allocated 40 percent (48,000) out of 120,000 visas made available over three years beginning in 1992. Applicants could apply only once for this visa, and improperly filed applications were rejected. In fact, Vice Consul James MacIntyre of the Irish consulate said in an April 6, 1995, interview that 450,000 entries were disqualified overall from the general pool for wrongful application.[17]

In 1994 the Schumer Program, or Permanent Diversity Program, began. Each year it makes available, on a permanent basis, 55,000 visas to citizens of those countries whose citizens received the fewest green cards during each preceding five-year period. The list is revised each year and will not include visas won in the lottery programs. No one country can receive more than 3,850 visas per year. Applicants must have a high school education or the equivalent, or have two years' experience in an occupation within the five-year period prior to application.[18]

In 1999 the INS reported that almost 88,000 Irish legally immigrated to the United States between 1981 and 1997. About 46,000 of those immigrants entered in the years 1991 through 1994, probably on the non-preference visas offered in the late 1980s and early 1990s.[19]

Looking at United States census figures for 1980 and 1990 to identify Irish population growth in New York by immigration or internal migration is problematic because, as discovered in earlier census reports, questions and data organization are not consistent from decade to decade. However, the numbers that do exist offer general information about the immigrant and ethnic population and community that the New Irish were entering through the 1980s.

For example, the 1980 figures for foreign-born in New York City clearly demonstrate how small the immigrant population had become and how immigration had slowed since 1960. The numbers of foreign-born for each borough were as follows: Bronx, 12,599; Brooklyn (Kings County), 6,572; Manhattan (New York County), 7,260; Queens, 13,590; and Staten Island (Richmond County), 1,333, making the total for the city 41,354 foreign-born Irish.[20] For the New York–New Jersey Standard Metropolitan Statistical Area (SMSA), which encompassed the New York City and northern New Jersey metropolitan area, the census identified 52,496 foreign-born Irish, almost 80 percent of whom had migrated prior to 1960 and 60 percent before 1950.[21] Since the New York City population constituted the bulk (79 percent) of the SMSA number, it can be assumed that the great majority of Irish immigrants in the city were well into middle age.

In 1980 the United States census introduced a category called ancestry. The questions asked for this category were open-ended, and respondents could submit single- or multiple-identity entries. For example, in response to the question "What is your ancestry?" a citizen could reply Irish or Irish-Italian or Irish-Italian-German. For multiple entries, answers such as Irish-Italian or German-Irish were included in the totals for Irish, Italian, and German ancestries. In the census tract tables, the total for all the ethnic identity figures were larger than the population totals for a given area, because one entry could be counted more than once.

The 1980 census defined ancestry as a "person's nationality group, lineage, or the country in which the person or the person's parents or ancestors were born before their arrival in the U.S."[22] However, the bureau did not request the date of original immigration among the general population, making it difficult to track immigrant neighborhood size and migration from earlier census reports. The "responses to the ancestry question reflected the ethnic groups with which the person identified and not necessarily the degree of attachment or association the person had with the particular group(s)."[23] The 1990 census kept the ancestry category, with the same qualifiers. "For example, a response of 'Irish' might reflect total involvement in an 'Irish' community or only a memory of ancestors several generations removed from the individual."[24]

While the 1980 and 1990 reports provided interesting data on ethnic identity among the population, the ancestry question made it very difficult to accurately quantify immigrant neighborhoods. Combined with the undocumented status of most Irish migrants after 1980, it was necessary to look at other evidence to place the New Irish population.

In 1980 the number of New Yorkers identifying themselves by the single ancestry of Irish, the category most likely to be immigrant or first-generation, by borough, was as follows: Bronx, 56,673; Brooklyn, 74,180; Manhattan, 51,603; Queens, 106,982; and Staten Island, 28,163.[25] These ethnics represented 4.5 percent of the city's total population.[26]

By 1990, the numbers claiming single Irish ancestry by borough were as follows: Bronx, 40,956; Brooklyn, 53,081; Manhattan, 47,344; Queens, 86,117; and Staten Island, 26,653.[27] In ten years the percentage of single ancestry Irish within the entire city population had dropped one percentage point to 3.5.[28] If we look at the population totals for single- and multiple-ancestry ethnics from 1980 to 1990, we see that the Bronx drops from 88,628 to 64,884 (27 percent), Brooklyn from 148,390 to 113,912 (23 percent), Manhattan from 114,793 to 108,543 (5 percent), Queens from 219,312 to 175,058 (20 percent), and Staten Island from 76,610 to 72,731 (5 percent).[29] So the New Irish were entering shrinking, diluted, and arguably aging ethnic communities. In terms of the mobility of the Irish in general, these numbers suggested that the Irish continued their migration out of the city, and within the city they preferred Brooklyn and Queens to the other boroughs.

A variety of sources provide evidence that a significant number of New Irish immigrants entered the United States during the 1980s, even though their exact number is difficult to pinpoint. But what can these or other sources tell us about who the migrants were, where they came from, and how they compared to previous generations of migrants? To profile the population we will look at conventional data sources such as the INS annual reports and census studies from Ireland and the United States, and the emigration study completed by Ireland's National Economic and Social Council in 1991,[30] as well as surveys conducted by the *Irish Voice* and the author[31] of truly random segments of the population, anecdotal evidence, and interviews with immigrants, community leaders, and institutional service providers who worked with the population.

By all accounts, the majority of emigrants who left Ireland for America through the 1980s were single, employed men and women in their twenties, who had at least a secondary-level education[32] and represented all social categories[33] and counties in the country.[34] Unlike previous generations of emigrants, who overrepresented the unskilled, lower socioeconomic segments of Irish society and hailed from counties in Connaught and Ulster, late-twentieth-century migration was a fairly universal exodus. And as in the 1950s, more men than women emigrated. The NESC put the ratio of emigration since 1980 at 736 women per 1,000 men.[35] How this translates to gender flows to the United States is difficult to tell because of the migrants' legal status. However, according to INS figures for 1992, 55.3 percent of the 12,226 Irish who immigrated to the United States were male and 44.7 percent were female.[36]

As the NESC report pointed out, Irish migration, with the exception of famine migration that incorporated the movement of entire families, has traditionally been dominated by young people concentrated in the 15- to 24-year-old age category.[37] The New Irish conformed to this pattern. In the period 1981–1986, 67 percent of the net migrating population were in the 15- to 24-year-old category.[38] The Kerry Emigrant Support Group reported that 72 percent of emigrants were under 30 years of age.[39] The New Irish survey found that the average age of the respondents was 29 for men and 27.5 for women at the time the survey was conducted in 1990. Almost 60 percent of those surveyed emigrated in the years 1985–87. The average age of all respondents at the time of arrival in the United States was just over 23, which falls within the range of the NESC profile, although it is among the "older" migrants leaving.

Regarding the survey, most of the contacts with the New Irish community were made through the Emerald Isle Immigration Center (EIIC). The center needed data to service its population, and as an Irish American academic I needed credibility among the predominately undocumented population to gather the information. The New Irish were understandably reluctant to share personal information about their migration and employment history with someone outside their community, despite promises of anonymity. The EIIC was an organization they trusted, and they were assured that the information they disclosed would be used not only for academic research, but to create data pools from which the EIIC could draw to advocate on their behalf for grants and funding.[40]

Those who answered the survey were members of the EIIC and were arguably among the more focused and responsible of the New Irish community. They were aware of or at least interested in what affected them politically and what they needed to do to improve their status economically and academically in the United States. More than 60 percent of them lived in Queens or the Bronx, where many of the undocumented New Irish neighborhoods were located.

Contrary to NESC findings, more women than men answered the survey: 54 percent to 45 percent. And many of the migrants who participated in the New Irish survey waited a few years after completing their education before leaving home. But in results similar to the NESC findings, the number of years between graduation and emigration was determined by the level of education achieved. Those who left school at the secondary level tended to try the local job market a little longer than those with more advanced degrees. In other words, university graduates left soon after school, compared to intercert or leaving cert candidates. (In Ireland, intercert and leaving certs are secondary-school diplomas. An intercert [intermediate certificate] is achieved after four years. A leaving cert [leaving certificate] requires one more year of school and qualifies the student to go to the university level. It is generally agreed that a leaving cert holder has had the equivalent of one year of an American university education.[41])

Several reasons could account for this migration trend, not the least being the age and maturity of the emigrant. University graduates were older, perhaps more secure and confident than 16- to 18-year-olds just out of secondary school. Higher-level graduates may also have found fewer jobs commensurate with their skills in Ireland and more opportunity to find both a job and advancement abroad.[42] They may simply have had more ambition than lower-level graduates, although one should be reluctant to measure ambition solely on the number of years spent in school.

In terms of the actual educational level of the New Irish, the Kerry Emigrant Support Group agreed with the NESC characterization of the emigrants as having "at best a second level education." According to its data, the Kerry group reported that 51 percent of migrants had a second-level (secondary) education, 31 percent had a first-level (primary) education, and almost 10 percent had a third-level (university) education. The New Irish survey respondents followed that pattern fairly closely, although fewer arrived here with just a primary-level education. Forty-nine percent had leaving certs, 19 percent had reached the intercert level, 6 percent had undergraduate-level education, and 9 percent had graduate experience. So about 85 percent had at least a secondary-level education, almost half were qualified to enter the Irish university system, and 15 percent were actually in the university. Compared to the general Irish population, in which at least half of secondary-school graduates went on to third-level education, the New Irish were not as well-educated as their peers at home.[43] Compared to the migrants of the 1950s, whose median level of education was put at the third year of high school and of whom 27 percent had completed four years of high school, the New Irish had a higher level of education when they entered New York.[44]

The Department of Labour in Ireland conducted surveys and follow-up studies of second-level school leavers (secondary-school graduates) and third-level school (university) entrants between 1980 and 1989 to determine the migration characteristics or "intent to migrate" tendencies among the population. The studies were based on national stratified random samples of all school leavers from about two hundred schools. The respondents, or their parents or guardians, were interviewed each May at least a year after leaving school.[45] The survey revealed that fewer than 5 percent of school leavers emigrated within one year of graduation.[46] Among other characteristics, the study found that the higher the level of education, the greater the actual emigration and internal migration rate, as well as the intended migration rate of the respondents. Using income level and occupational options ranging from unskilled laborer to professional as measures of aspiration, the study found that the higher the level of aspiration, the greater the tendency to migrate—with occupational aspiration being the more predictive variable.[47]

The New Irish survey reflects the Department of Labour results and the NESC conclusions. The age of the respondents varied according to the educational level they achieved. The average age upon arrival for those with leaving certificates was 24.25 years, for those with some undergraduate experience it was 23.7 years, and for those with graduate experience it dropped to 22.7 years. These results suggest that for the better-educated respondent the decision to migrate came soon after or upon entering the labor force. The more years a respondent spent in school, the less time he/she spent pursuing occupational options in Ireland. American and European firms visiting universities in Ireland not only offered much more attractive employment packages in terms of salary and positions to the graduates, but they offered the opportunity and adventure of living abroad which many graduates found irresistible.

Animator Don Bluth, who had been with Disney Studios in the United States, opened Sullivan Bluth animation studios in Dublin in the late 1980s. His studio created 300 jobs. In a November 8, 1988, interview with the *Irish Times*, Bluth expressed delight with the quality of his Irish employees' work, but dismay "at the poor self image many people have here and why it is so many young people assume the natural thing to do is leave." Even for those working at Sullivan Bluth, the article claimed that once the trainees acquired their skill, they still felt that they had to go abroad to pursue ultimate success.[48]

The inevitability of emigration in modern Irish culture must be considered in any discussion of the push/pull factors forcing young people out of Ireland. In the 1980s it was complicated by the promise of the 1970s and the belief that the emerging generation had that "they did not have to emigrate." When they reached maturity and were ready to take their place as the "New Europeans" their government boasted they would be, a certain resentment and resignation that little had changed in the country surfaced among emigrants and their families. (Fifty-nine percent of the undocumented surveyed by the *Irish Voice* accused past and present Irish governments of being responsible for the emigration problem.[49]) The betrayal was compounded when the migrants' status in America forced them into jobs that many felt were beneath them.

So while migration had been a part of life in most Irish families, after the economic renewal and the birth of the modern Irish nation in the 1960s, emigration was supposed to belong to the past. (The NESC report offers statistics showing that up to 40 percent of Irish aged 10 to 19 in 1951 had emigrated by 1961.[50] Some migration continued through the seventies, but great numbers of emigrants from Great Britain and America returned alone or with families to participate in the new, stronger Irish economy. The seventies were the only period up to that time in modern Irish recorded history that experienced a net inflow of people.[51]) And if emigration could not be avoided, then the New Irish felt entitled to better than the typically menial migrant jobs in unskilled manual labor and domestic service they found.

Oddly enough, it was job status, security, and opportunity rather than true unemployment that pushed the majority of migrants out of Ireland. Two-thirds of the respondents in the New Irish survey had jobs when they left Ireland, but a third came to New York for a better future and a quarter came to look for work. So while their reasons for migrating were technically economic, unemployment was not necessarily the issue, as much as underemployment. In this way the late-century migrants were not that different than mid-century emigrants, in that they saw greater opportunity outside Ireland, in spite of the country's twenty-year modernization effort.

The NESC argued that the migrants' "personal and occupational aspirations" were not being met at home.[52] Just under 20 percent of the employed New Irish surveyed had a job in skilled trade when they left Ireland, 9 percent were professionals, 9 percent were in construction, 16 percent worked in offices, and almost one-third (31 percent) were employed in miscellaneous positions ranging from bar/restaurant/hotel service to fishing and factory work. Some among the New Irish, including twenty from the New Irish survey, were civil servants who were released from their jobs for extended periods as part of a government cutback program. Those who accepted the release were guaranteed jobs at a commensurate level after an agreed-upon absence. Many of these bureaucrats migrated—seeking adventure and opportunity abroad, secure in the knowledge they could return if their sojourn failed.

It must be remembered that the New Irish were not a monolithic group. The population was stratified by class and education as well as legal status. NESC data identifying the socioeconomic background of migrants through the eighties showed that those leaving the country were fairly representative of the broad cross-section of Irish society. No one group or class dominated the outflow in the 1980s, although professional and nonmanual workers left at a slightly higher rate than skilled manual and unskilled workers. Using the occupation level of the head of household as the indicator of background, the male migrant who left in the 1987–88 period was just as likely to be the son of a professional as the son of an unskilled laborer. Overall farmers were the least likely to emigrate (just as in the 1950s), as were women from lower socioeconomic backgrounds.[53]

Emigrants with higher levels of education were more likely to have green cards than the rest of the population. These graduates had a better chance of entering the country through the legal channels of corporate recruitment than their less-educated peers.[54] The New Irish survey showed that 25 percent of the documented population had at least some undergraduate education, compared to 7 percent of the undocumented population. Although more than half (53 percent) of the undocumented had leaving certs, almost one-quarter (23 percent) had just reached the intercert level compared to 14 percent of the documented population. Anecdotal evidence suggests that the more educated, documented emigrants tended to live outside the New Irish ghettoes of Woodside and the Bronx. These young professionals preferred to live outside the clannish, traditionally Irish neighborhoods.

Still another segment of the population chose to live apart from the New Irish population, and these migrants were more correctly identified by lifestyle rather than status. Shane Doyle, owner of the Sin é Cafe on the Lower East Side of Manhattan, was an undocumented migrant who came to New York in the 1980s. He opened a number of small businesses and when interviewed in 1990 was operating Sin é, a restaurant/bar/nightclub that attracted contemporary Irish rock groups such as Black 47. Sin é became a trendy hangout for popular Irish celebrities such as Sinead O'Connor; Gabriel Byrne and his American wife, Ellen Barkin (they are now divorced); and U2, among others. Photos of events and guests at the club were often featured in the *Irish Voice*. Mr. Doyle employed New Irish as waiters and waitresses and claimed that many of his Irish clients and employees lived and worked outside the traditional New Irish communities deliberately, opting instead for a New York lifestyle over the sameness of "little Ireland" communities in the outer boroughs.[55]

While the hard data on the population are vague, anecdotal evidence that Irish immigration to America increased significantly through the 1980s was quite strong. Advocacy and support groups for the Irish began to surface soon after the passage of the 1986 Immigration Reform and Control Act (IRCA). The law offered amnesty to aliens living illegally in the United States prior to 1982, imposed fines on employers who hired undocumented aliens, and included a provision offering 40,000 nonpreference visas to thirty-six countries "disadvantaged" by the Immigration and Nationality Act amendments of October 3, 1965. Ireland was among those thirty-six countries and won 40 percent of the allocated visas in a lottery. The Irish Immigration Reform Movement (IIRM), a lobbying and social support group founded by the new immigrants themselves, was organized in May 1987. Project Irish Outreach, a social services office of the Archdiocese of New York, opened in September 1987, and in February 1988 the archdiocese assigned its first immigrant chaplain from Ireland to a Bronx parish ministering to the Irish community.[56] The *Irish Voice*, an alternative to the older, more established *Irish Echo*, produced its first edition in December 1987, with a promise to be "forthright in its attempts to win for the estimated 135,000 Irish illegals, their proper places as full members of this society."[57]

The popularity of the *Voice* forced its chief rival not only to update its look, but to refocus its editorial content. In the early eighties, as the population of New Irish began to build, the *Echo* devoted little if any news coverage to the issue of contemporary immigration. The "troubles" in Northern Ireland dominated its headlines. Yet if a reader or editor turned to the classifieds in the *Echo* between 1981 and 1985, clues to the changing community were quite clear.

On January 13, 1981, the *Echo* had just one page of classifieds with two listings seeking child care and three for domestic agencies.[58] In the December 18, 1982, issue, twenty-two help-wanted ads for babysitters appeared in two and a half pages of classifieds, along with six domestic agency ads and four ads for immigration attorneys.[59] Three years later, the October 12, 1985, issue (one year before IRCA was passed) carried three and a half pages of classifieds, with eighty listings seeking child care, including one for a family in Chelsea, Vermont. At least twelve boxed ads for domestic agencies were in the same issue.[60] The November 2, 1985, issue contained four and three-quarter pages of classifieds with fourteen listings for lawyers, seven of whom were identified as immigration specialists.[61] The expansion demonstrated not only a growing demand for domestic help, but indicated that a growing number of readers, most likely undocumented Irish immigrants, were reading the paper in order to find work and legal advice.[62]

Other evidence that the Irish immigrant population was growing included an increase in phone calls between the United States and Ireland. Between 1982 and 1988, overseas calls to the Emerald Isle rose from 1.7 million per year to 5.1 million per year, a threefold increase. Phone call costs on New York Bell during that period dropped from a minimum of $4.29 for a five-minute call to $3.88 during economy hours on AT&T International lines.[63] The New Irish survey conducted by the author and Emerald Isle Immigration Center (EIIC) in 1990 confirmed the popularity of the phone as the preferred medium of communication among the New Irish.[64] Fifty-five percent of the 257 respondents admitted to phoning home (to Ireland) more than once a month; another 30 percent called Ireland once a month. Only 13 percent called less than once a month.

Institutional services aimed specifically at the New Irish reflected not only the growing numbers of immigrants but the concern of community, political, and religious leaders over their legal and underground status. On September 24, 1987, Irish Deputy Prime Minister Brian Lenihan appointed James Farrell to the new post of new immigrant liaison officer for the consul general's New York office.[65] Farrell had been with the consulate since 1985, when he was assigned as liaison with the New York Irish American community. Farrell was the logical choice for the new post. He was young—in his mid-thirties at the time of his appointment—so he could relate well on a personal level to the new immigrant population and identify with the social and economic forces that pushed them out of Ireland. He had also lived in New York for a number of years, so he was familiar with the city and the ethnic community and was well-known and respected by Irish and Irish Americans alike.

Farrell was a very visible fixture outside the consul's Manhattan offices on Madison Avenue—he regularly attended IIRM meetings and could be seen on many Sunday afternoons at Gaelic Park sporting events. Consulate hours were expanded to include three hours on Saturday from 10 A.M. to 1 P.M. Farrell's tenure was a marked reversal from what New York Catholic Charities executive director Monsignor James J. Murray qualified as the "stand-offish" attitude of the consul staff prior to 1986, which Monsignor Murray felt "trickled down" from the Dublin government.[66] He recalled seeing an interview on American television with James Flavin, who was consul general during Prime Minister Garrett Fitzgerald's administration, in which Flavin said that those who were currently coming to New York came of their own free will and knew what they were doing.[67]

While Farrell improved the communication and services offered to immigrants by the consulate, he also cultivated the consulate's ties with Irish American leaders and local institutional representatives. The most obvious networking body he supported was the Irish Immigration Working Committee, which was a regular gathering of officers of the Ancient Order of Hibernians (AOH), Catholic Charities, the Irish American Labor Coalition (IALC), and the Irish American Business Coalition (IABC).

The IABC joined the working committee in the spring of 1988. At the time it was a small organization which drew its membership from professionals in the securities industry and the business world. An attorney with the Securities Industry Association founded the coalition and represented the group at the committee meetings in the late 1980s. He lived in Woodside, Queens, and came into contact with the New Irish on a daily basis. He said his impetus for creating the coalition was a sense that some white-collar professionals were feeling removed from their ancestry, but were nonetheless interested in Irish American causes. Immigration was an issue people like himself could embrace.[68] IABC contacts in Washington kept the coalition informed of action on immigration legislation and the position of legislators who were critical to its passage. That information was passed on to the working committee in an effort to share knowledge that would enable it to sway or reinforce the position of key lawmakers.[69]

The Irish American Labor Coalition joined the Irish Immigration Working Committee at its creation. It was also known under its original name, the American Labor Committee for Human Rights in Northern Ireland. The group organized in the early eighties in response to the MacBride Principles campaign and at the height of the hunger strike protests in Northern Ireland.[70] The MacBride Principles were a set of fair employment guidelines aimed at ending anti-Catholic labor discrimination in Northern Ireland; they were launched in the early 1980s in the United States. Supporters worked to raise awareness and to gain support for the program among companies with operations in Ulster, as well as the shareholders of companies with investments in Northern Ireland and government employees with pension portfolio holdings in companies engaged in Northern Ireland.[71] The Irish Immigration Working Committee was a network of about a hundred people representing longshoremen, the AFL-CIO, the teamsters, and other unions. It met formally about four or five times a year. Joe Jamison of the Transport Workers Union (TWU) represented the group on the working committee. He was appointed by the late John Lawe, international president of the TWU, to provide a point of view for labor on Irish immigration efforts.[72]

Jack Irwin was the AOH representative on the working committee during Farrell's term. Irwin had been involved in the immigration issue as the national chair of the AOH immigration committee. In October 1988 he addressed the IIRM at the Towerview Ballroom in Queens. He read to them the resolution unanimously adopted at the AOH national convention in July 1988:

> We, the AOH, will actively pursue and assist the Irish Immigration Reform Movement in pursuing immigration reform which would lead to an independent immigrant visa category and to corrective legislation which would legalize the undocumented Irish and which would correct the injustices of the 1965 Immigration and Nationality Act.

The AOH had strengthened its position on immigration reform since the 1984 convention's rather generic resolution calling for "fair and equitable immigration from all countries in Europe."[73] This change may have begun in 1986 when newly elected national president Nick Murphy appointed himself chairman of the immigration committee to draw attention to the problems of the undocumented.[74] But it was the dissatisfaction of the New Irish themselves with the pace of reform action that mobilized the community to pursue real change. At a 1987 meeting of the County Cork Association, the issue of immigration reform surfaced and a committee was appointed to investigate just what the national immigration committee of the AOH was doing. The committee included Mae O'Driscoll, who later became the first woman president of the Cork Association; Pat Hurley and Sean Minihane, both New Irish immigrants; and Father Matthew Fitzgerald, a parish priest on Long Island. They created the Irish Immigration Reform Movement (IIRM).

The group's first meeting was held on May 20, 1987. Six committees covered crucial areas of concern at each meeting—New Irish Action Group, the Irish American Action Group, the Irish Government Action Group, the Fundraising Action Group, the Public Relations Action Group, and the National Report. The movement grew nationwide and by 1989 had chapters in seventeen cities with about five thousand members. The annual membership fee was $10. In New York the group met monthly, rotating venues in various locations in Queens, the Bronx, and Brooklyn.[75]

The two most vocal and visible representatives of the group in the late 1980s were Minihane, national chairperson of the IIRM, and Hurley, chair of the Irish

Government Action Group. These men, both in their mid-twenties, were very effective in gaining national attention for the plight of the New Irish. The strategy of the group was to bring the New Irish out of the "shadows," and take the risk of exposing their undocumented status. The thinking was that without a vote in the United States and with no political voice in Ireland,[76] the New Irish could do very little about their status by remaining silent. The IIRM appealed directly to those with power and sympathy for their cause—the Irish American voter and Irish American leaders in Congress, the Catholic Church, labor, and the press.

In his written testimony before the House subcommittee on immigration on September 19, 1988, Don Martin of the IIRM, an Irish American, played on the representatives' emotion and patriotism to press for immigration reform on behalf of the Irish. Referring to the fact that the average annual immigration rate from Ireland since 1965 had been about 800, he said:

> That number is less by 120 the number of Irishmen who died storming Marye's Heights in Fredericksburg on December 13, 1862, in defense of this union.[77]

In its early stages the group was criticized for its brash and aggressive behavior. Observers complained that it alienated other ethnic political lobbies, as well as established Irish American groups and Irish and United States government leaders. Observers suggested that the new immigrants would do better to join forces with them, rather than alienate them.[78] In its 1988 list of superlatives, the *Irish Voice* called the IIRM the best and worst group of the year.[79] As time passed and legislative victory was achieved, the IIRM lost its rough edges and found a balance in style between aggression and compromise, and eventually became a part of the establishment it had earlier set out to challenge.

While early critics may have had reason to object to the infant group's strategies and lack of tact, its achievements were remarkable for a group new to the American system of politics and legislative reform. Within two years of its inception the IIRM had met with representatives of the Irish government to lobby for funding and assistance in the United States; it won approval for grants totaling $89,000 from the city and state of New York, sent Pat Hurley to speak at the AOH convention in Cleveland in July of 1988, hired a Washington lobbyist to press for immigration reform on behalf of the New Irish, testified at the September 1988 House subcommittee hearings on immigration reform, sent a delegation to Washington to personally meet with members of the immigration subcommittees in both the House and the Senate to press their case during the September hearings, appeared in national media such as *The New York Times Magazine, Newsweek,* and *Irish America Magazine,* and marched in the 1989 New York St. Patrick's Day Parade behind its own banner.[80]

In its early years the New York chapter operated a hotline every Tuesday and Thursday night from 6:30 P.M. to 9:30 P.M. from its Woodside office to counsel and advise the New Irish on everything from employment, homesickness, health care, visa applications, housing, banking, and civil rights. Every month members received a mailing with an agenda for the upcoming meeting, news releases and updates on immigration bills, and issues of importance to the immigrant community. For example, the March 1989 mailing included an application for the Berman visa with instructions for completing and mailing the form properly.

The Emerald Isle Immigration Center,[81] the 1990s descendant of the IIRM, which focused on mainstreaming the aliens once the IIRM succeeded in documenting them, continued to issue regular newsletters. It updated members on center-sponsored seminars on education and job fairs, visa material, and general news of interest to the New Irish immigrant community, which in the nineties was predominately documented and seeking information on surviving and succeeding in the American labor market. Newsletters from October 1992 and December 1994 offered information on the center's first job fair, which was held on October 26, 1992, at the Manhattan Club on West 52nd Street. Among the companies listed as expecting to attend were "UPS, Equitable Life Insurance Company, New York Mercantile Exchange, Merrill Lynch, and representatives from the hotel and health-care industries"—all of which offered migrants more security and career opportunities than the domestic and table waiting jobs many held as undocumented aliens. The same issue offered advice on how to conduct oneself in an interview, excerpted from the center's booklet *Market Yourself.* Two years later, the EIIC newsletter was providing information on filing a tax return and planning tax seminars in February and March in anticipation of the Internal Revenue Service filing deadline of April 15. The end-of-year mailing also offered information on the latest visa lottery, how to secure financial aid for advanced education, on an Irish club at La Guardia College, and on a hotline for immigrants who face emotional and social stress as they adapt to life in America.[82]

The style of the IIRM leaders and the attendant criticism of them reflected the generally tense relationship between the New Irish and the older generations of Irish who emigrated in the 1920s, 1930s, and 1950s and who led the Irish American cultural, social, and political institutions that the New Irish in New York defied and/or rejected by their outspoken behavior. The older Irish Americans, either immigrants themselves or the children of immigrants, in many instances employed the New Irish on construction sites and in restaurants and bars around the city. It was not uncommon to hear older, established Irish Americans complain that the New Irish were unwilling to work from the bottom up, as they [older migrants] had had to,[83] or that the New Irish expected a lot for a little bit of effort. "They [the New Irish] think the world owes them a living just because they have degrees. This is what I get from talking to some of them. It's not prove yourself first, they want to start at the top."[84]

Others complained that the younger generation was not appreciative or respectful of the help offered by family and friends already here in the States. A letter to the editor in the September 1987 issue of *Irish America Magazine* lamented the poor behavior of recent migrants who abused the hospitality of Irish Americans and documented Irish immigrants.[85] Two months later another reader shared a similar story about cousins from Ireland who ran up phone bills, watched television instead of going to job interviews arranged by the family, and were finally "deported" by their hosts. "I thought that our family had been the only ones duped by the young Irish lads and lassies," the second reader confessed.[86] One young woman who emigrated from County Cavan in the early eighties and worked as a waitress in New York said in an interview that she would not help any more people from home. "If you don't find them jobs for $400 a week, they think you haven't done anything. It's possible to do well in America but you have to work for it."[87]

On March 10, 1989, the Irish American Business Coalition hosted a reception in honor of Representative Brian Donnelly at the South Street Seaport in New York. An open invitation was extended to all Donnelly visa recipients to attend the party and thank the congressman.[88] Few New Irish responded to the invitation. Don Martin, an Irish American, who was political coordinator for the group, represented the IIRM.[89] The sponsors of the event were disappointed. The $75 admission price may have kept some migrants away, but as one IABC member pointed out, the price was far less than the legal fees accrued in the normal visa application process.

On the other hand, some in the New Irish community suggested that the establishment exploited their undocumented status. Sociologist Mary Corcoran interviewed men in the construction field who argued that their Irish American employers could push the New Irish harder and pay them less with the implicit threat of exposing their undocumented status. She quoted one worker who described the tight controls and supervision of the construction site: "In Ireland the lads show up on the construction site five minutes late, here the workers are there half an hour before they are supposed to start. Coffee breaks are taken standing up."[90] Her informants contended that working in these construction crews was akin to slavery and that the New Irish had no leverage because they lacked work permits. She also argued that they accepted high-risk tasks because they feared being fired. While that may have been true, working "under the table" also freed the new immigrants from paying taxes, which allowed them more disposable income than if the government's deductions were taken from their pay. For some of the immigrants interviewed in the course of this study, taxation was a real concern. A green card was considered a convenience that would allow them easy access into and out of America, but it also represented a probable cut in pay that some were reluctant to take. Mary Corcoran also cited high tax rates in Ireland for driving many migrants from the country. She observed that "early aversion to excessive taxation [in Ireland] develops into a pattern of tax evasion in the host country."[91]

The "implicit" knowledge of status as a weapon may have been used against the New Irish, but the lack of a green card almost certainly inhibited their security or promotion on the job. Being "illegal" characterized them (however unfairly) as unreliable because of their potential transience. Employers might not have been willing to invest training, time, and money in a worker if that person was likely to leave without notice or be deported as an illegal alien.

Prior to 1986, obtaining a green card was not a problem for most Irish. The economy in New York was strong, and contractors, restaurants, and families were eager to hire young Irish with or without documentation. As a result few New Irish made any effort to file for a resident visa. James Farrell said that before 1986 there was no impetus for the green card. Among other reasons, he said, the Irish were fearful of lawyers and did not want to pay the legal fees involved in processing the application.[92] Rates for green card applications at the time ranged from $1,600 to $3,000 and the waiting period for an unskilled worker's permit was eighteen months to two years,[93] requiring a commitment to a sponsor and the United States that most Irish were unwilling to make. Before IRCA the Irish were seemingly happy enough to work outside the American mainstream, which may have betrayed their reluctance to make a long-term commitment to the United States.

That environment changed with the passage of IRCA, which imposed fines on any person or agency hiring or placing an undocumented worker. It also sanctioned tighter INS screening procedures at points of entry to discourage visa overstays. In Ireland this included the establishment of a visa control station at Shannon Airport in Limerick to check foreign travelers before they boarded flights to America, so that suspected overstays were never allowed to leave Ireland.

The new system had greater consequences for those migrants already in the United States who wanted or needed to return home for visits or emergencies. Stories swirled around the Irish community in New York about migrants who could not attend a parent's funeral or who missed the births of siblings, nieces and nephews, or cousins.[94] Going home was easy. Returning was the problem. Undocumented migrants risked refusal at the boarding gate if they attempted re-entry and could not satisfactorily prove they were tourists. The INS became quite adept at recognizing the "nontourist." Many emigrants were denied re-entry when baggage checks revealed uncashed New York State lottery tickets, New York Bell phone bills, forged Social Security cards, or frequently stamped passports. On the other hand, frequent flyers between both countries learned to arrive at the airport with letters from the local police and priest verifying that the migrant had a steady job to return to in Ireland, or that he or she was just on a visit to a cousin in Queens. Forty-four percent of the undocumented respondents to the New Irish survey ranked the inability to travel to Ireland as their number one problem in New York, compared to 5 percent of documented respondents.[95]

Yet in spite of the problems moving in and out of the country, only 22 percent of the New Irish respondents admitted to having applied for a Donnelly visa by 1990. Indeed in 1995, the new immigrant liaison officer at the New York consulate office said that Irish demand for the nonpreference visas made available to them under a subsequent visa program was below the number allotted for Ireland.[96] In 1994, the last year that visas were available under the Morrison Program (AA-1) of the 1990 immigration act, which allocated 16,000 visas for the Irish for each of three years, 22,524 were available to the Irish because the target for the previous two years had not been claimed.[97] An emigrant support group in Kerry alerted prospective migrants of the availability of Morrison visas in 1994, claiming that in the early years of the program response to the lottery had been as low as 40 percent and urging those interested to take advantage of the available visas.[98]

What can explain the lack of interest in the visas? Perhaps the number of illegal Irish aliens presumed to be in the United States was lower than previously thought,[99] or the undocumented Irish living in America who really wanted and needed the visa were shut out by Irish in Ireland who received the visas but were not using them,[100] or Irish migrants simply had no long-range plans to stay or live in America, so the visas were of no use to them. Whatever the reasons, the response rate was curious.

The New Irish survey confirmed the apparent ambivalence to America: 40 percent of all respondents to the New Irish survey were not sure if they would be in New York in five years' time and 16 percent said they would not be. (Forty-one percent of all respondents did plan to spend the next five years in the Big Apple.) Status undoubtedly affected the undocumented population; as one 24-year-old woman wrote, "It is difficult to plan your future here [New York] when you don't know if you can stay or not."[101] But it should not have been the concern for the 43 percent of documented respondents who were not sure where they would be in five years' time either.

Unhappiness with the urban environment in New York was certainly a factor in the respondents' ambivalence. For many in the community it was their first time living in a large city. Crime was identified by 47 percent of all the respondents as their number one fear in New York.[102] The city was described variously as "a quagmire"[103] or riddled with drugs. A 26-year-old documented man from Connecticut who had lived in the Bronx for four years wrote that he felt happier, safer, and more relaxed in the suburbs. "I will never—and I mean never—live in New York City again."[104] As documented aliens, visa holders could live and work anywhere they chose in the United States—which probably accounted for some of the doubt expressed about a future in New York. However, even with the green card, some New Irish were reluctant to give up on Ireland. A 27-year-old Offaly man with a visa wrote that "New York is a wonderful city to come and work in and earn money. But New York is not the place to raise a family and grow old in. There is no place like home, after all."[105]

The disparity between "home" and New York for the Irish permeated almost every aspect of their adjustment to life in America. The issue raised earlier regarding exploitation in the workplace provides a good example of the differences between the two. Without denying that abuse exists, the complaints cited previously must also be considered in the context of contrasting work ethics in Ireland and America. Undeniably the pace and the culture of work in America, particularly New York, is much more demanding and aggressive than in Ireland.[106] The disparity in style and pace most likely contributed to what Irish workers in New York considered exploitation or harshness. American bosses, on the other hand, would be likely to perceive the Irish as lazy or sloppy in their work habits. The contrast in attitudes and expectations could easily create tension on the job.[107] So, while the New Irish construction workers, by virtue of their status, may have been targets of abuse, they may also have had trouble adapting to a much more exacting American workplace.

Irish women had their own stories of abuse, within and without the Irish

American community. A great number of New Irish women worked as care givers for children and the aged (nannies and granny minders). Their employers were typically one- or two-income middle- and upper-middle-class families from across the ethnic and religious spectrum, who in the booming eighties had the income to pay for domestic service. Surveys conducted by the author and the *Irish Voice* show that 28 percent and 54 percent of immigrant women were employed in child or elderly care, respectively.[108] Those women who "lived in" were the most vulnerable to employer abuse, because they never left the work site. If, for example, the employer parents called the nanny at the end of her workday to say they would not be home on time, she had no choice but to stay on the job. Many young women lived with families in the suburbs and did not have a car or access to public transit that could bring them in contact with their peers in the New Irish neighborhoods of New York City. Naturally, these young women felt isolated and lonely, by themselves with children all day and dependent on the goodwill and fairness of their employers. One young woman who lived with a family for eighteen months was unhappy with her situation and decided to leave. She had been giving her employer money every week to save for an immigration lawyer.[109] When she resigned her position and asked for her savings, the woman for whom she worked denied having ever received it.[110]

Of course, for every nanny's tale of abuse, employers presented corresponding complaints of negligence: high unpaid phone bills to Ireland; au pairs who left the suburbs for the weekend and showed up to work Monday morning in a cab from Queens, bleary-eyed and obviously too tired to care for toddlers and infants; or live-ins who walked out without notice and left the family stranded for help.[111]

Nannies were vulnerable because of their isolation both at work and where they lived. The immigrant men and women who lived and worked in New York, and/or outside the domestic service sphere, could network with their peers on the job, with their roommates, or with others in their neighborhood pub to exchange information on housing, work, home, friends, and other topics. Live-ins created their own networks outside the immigrant community in New York. Typically nannies and au pairs would meet other women in the same position in the parks and schools where they brought the children in their care. These women would meet socially on the weekends, if they could, in the Irish pubs and neighborhoods of Queens and the Bronx or in the suburbs where they lived. One migrant who arrived in 1985 and worked as a live-in nanny in a New Jersey suburb met regularly with other au pairs in a local bar. "The first thing we talked about was 'how much money do you make?'"[112] Sharing the information gave the young women the information and confidence they needed to negotiate with their employers or change jobs, and to alleviate the isolation they felt living with a strange family away from home.

Undocumented mothers shared the same day-to-day experience of being alone with small children, but as mothers they were responsible for integrating their children into schools and other American institutions. R. H., a New Irish mother with two young children living in the Bronx, formed a support group called the Bronx Women's Group in 1987.[113] She asked a friend who worked at the *Irish Voice* to write an article about her, describing her loneliness and isolation and desire to meet other women in the same situation. As a result, twenty-two women and thirty-six children attended the first meeting of the women's group in December 1987. Most of the women were undocumented and most had children. Like the nannies, the women were isolated at home with children most of the time, which removed them from the New Irish networking systems at the workplace and at the bar. Ms. H. said that the mothers always told new friends, even other Irish, that their husbands were documented or American, because they did not trust anyone with the knowledge of their true status.

As undocumented new mothers in a strange culture they shied away from joining such parents' associations as the Parent Teacher Association (PTA), which offered not only social outlets but an introduction to American education and family culture. Ms. H. worried that her silence and the silence of women like her prevented them from understanding their rights and the rights of their children in American society. They could not address the needs of their children by remaining in the shadows. Social workers familiar with the community explained that mothers in Ireland typically relied on extended family networks to help with child care, explain health care requirements, and introduce them to the local educational system.[114] New Irish mothers in America were on their own. While many lived in ethnic neighborhoods, they tended not to live with or socialize with their American relatives, unlike their counterparts in generations past. R. H.'s group, and mother-toddler groups formed at the New Irish community centers established by Catholic Charities in the Bronx and Queens, filled the gaps left by the absence of extended family.

By far one of the most difficult aspects of being undocumented in America for the New Irish was the high cost of medical care and the fear of having to pay for catastrophic illness or injury. Patricia O'Callaghan, director of the Archdiocese of New York's Project Irish Outreach, said that nearly one in five calls to the archdiocese's counseling and referral service in 1988 were about medical problems.[115] The Irish were raised in a country with a health and medical services system that provided free care for all citizens. Unable to afford insurance on their own and ineligible for group employment coverage because of their legal status, they feared illness and the minimum expense of $40 or $50 for an office visit or up to ten or twenty times that amount in the case of severe injury or a hospital stay. In some instances the New Irish were eligible for Medicaid, and Cardinal John J. O'Connor instructed all New York archdiocesan hospitals to treat the New Irish and all undocumented immigrants regardless of their status.[116] Mayor Edward I. Koch also announced in an October 15, 1985, memo that all city services, including health and medical facilities, were open to all undocumented aliens.[117] More often than not, however, in the event of a severe accident or illness, the community hosted a fundraiser or organized a simple collection to help the victim meet the expense of medical treatment. It was not unusual through the eighties to see an ad in the *Irish Voice* or a poster in the bar at Gaelic Park in the Bronx for a benefit dance.

For many New Irish the decision to migrate was motivated by a desire to escape what they felt was a restrictive and suffocating culture and lifestyle in Ireland. In the New Irish survey, 25.5 percent of the respondents cited a "restrictive life style, culture" as a reason for leaving Ireland.[118] One 32-year-old woman who emigrated to New York in 1985 wrote, "I like the USA. Am very glad I left Ireland, hated the weather and the way of life."[119] Another respondent, a 30-year-old woman, confessed that after living in New York she could never be as "narrow-minded" as she was when she left Ireland.[120] Still another 25-year-old woman from Kilkenny wrote that "the biggest thing about New York for me is that nobody cares what you do."[121]

Ide O'Carroll argues in her book *Models for Movers* that young women in Ireland left the country because of the legal, religious, and cultural codes that inhibited their reproductive and marital freedoms. In the late 1980s a series of referenda on abortion, contraception, and divorce in Ireland were defeated. This defeat, says O'Carroll, was the "last straw" for many women who had held out hope that what they perceived as patriarchal and sexist standards of morality could be reformed democratically.[122]

Indeed, within the community there was a very vocal and active homosexual population whose activities in New York were as much culturally motivated as politically conscious. The targets of the Irish gay activism were quite deliberate. For example, the Irish Lesbian and Gay Organization's (ILGO's) most visible act of consciousness raising and defiance was its effort to march in the New York St. Patrick's Day Parade behind its own banner. Choosing the parade as a medium for protest was calculated, selected as much for what it represented symbolically as for the exposure it offered the gay community in New York and in Ireland.

The parade is organized by the Ancient Order of Hibernians, a Catholic fraternal group. AOH leaders banned the overt participation of ILGO because the homosexual lifestyle violated church doctrine. AOH leaders said they had no objection to the ILGO members marching in the parade with other groups, but they felt that marching as openly gay men and women insulted the Church.[123] Members of the established Irish American community could not understand the "fuss" made by ILGO and its insistence on marching behind a sign announcing their sexual preference. But that was the point. The behavior and motivation of the group was precipitated as much by a desire to participate and express themselves freely in an Irish American event as by a desire to openly defy and protest against the cultural repression and bias they had experienced in Ireland. The Roman Catholic Church is an influential political and cultural force in Ireland that until the sixties and seventies was virtually unchallenged (in public anyway). Events in the 1980s regarding abortion and birth control and charges of clerical child abuse and sexual misconduct shattered the authority and confidence of the Church in Ireland.[124] A 1991 poll by the Augustinian Order showed that "attitudes towards the Catholic Church in Ireland are characterized by a feeling of 'anger, frustration, and disillusionment.'" The poll results showed that many felt the Church's leadership was "out of touch with what its members need."[125]

Who or what was the real target of ILGO's protest? The mobilization of the gay community in America and the fight for civil rights and cultural acceptance was a battle not unknown to the general public in the United States, and one that could not claim complete victory. But the challenge presented by ILGO went deeper than a generic protest for acceptance of alternative lifestyles. It was more likely an extension of the push factors that drove the homosexual migrants out of Ireland and into a more liberating environment. Writing in 1996, Anne Maguire, an ILGO leader, admitted that she had no real interest in the parade itself. "Those of us who are most actively involved, have no inclination to be associated with, never mind march in, the parade. This, very simply, is where our 'coming out' took place in Irish America."[126] Many American Irish saw the protest as an insult to their own institution, but the two groups spoke from different cultural experiences.

The influence and pervasive presence of the Roman Catholic Church in the everyday lives of the Irish cannot be overlooked in analyzing the culture and society the emigrants left behind. From the nineteenth century, when the parish priest ran the local villages, through the mid-twentieth century, the Church's impact on the society has been immense. Until 1972 the Irish Constitution included language recognizing the "special position of the Catholic Church."[127] The institution's positions on reproduction and family life can be characterized as conservative at best, misogynistic to its critics, and intolerable to the men and women who spoke out against them.

The power of the Church has not gone unnoticed in Ireland in the past. It has been criticized by observers, including expatriates such as James Joyce who complained of a paralyzed Irish society repressed under its strong thumb. But the 1980s arguably saw more overt social protest than in previous years, and more disaffection among young people in the practice of their faith.

In the United States, while Catholics disagreed with the Church, its doctrines did not dictate the dominant or popular culture, and American Catholics chose to pick what they liked from the religion.[128] An Irish immigrant who arrived in New York in the late 1940s said that the Church in America made her a better Catholic because she was freer than she was in Ireland to explore her faith and practice her religion as she felt comfortable. The impact of the Church and its significance in the lives of different generations of immigrants in Ireland and America will be explored in chapter 5.

Arriving in America, the New Irish tended to move into traditionally Irish neighborhoods like those in Woodside, Queens, and Bainbridge in the Bronx. Forty-one percent of New Irish survey respondents lived in Queens, while almost a quarter (22 percent) lived in the Bronx. The immigrants settled in the neighborhoods of their predecessors and undoubtedly revitalized stagnant and aging communities, but they tended not to socialize or mix with the older migrants or Irish Americans. Unlike previous migrants who "came out" to live with aunts, uncles, cousins, and other relatives and friends, the New Irish lived with their peers in dormitory-style living arrangements. Often five or six migrants would share an apartment to save on rent and living expenses. They typically chose buildings run by Irish landlords. One priest sent to live with the New Irish said he would determine who the Irish landlords in the parish were, then visit their buildings in search of young Irish who might want counseling or to hear a friendly voice from home.

The ghettoes created by the community perpetuated the isolation of the community. Eighty-three percent of those surveyed in the New Irish study claimed to have Irish friends. Only 18 percent claimed to have American friends. And 65 percent identified the pub as the place where they spent their leisure time, suggesting that the majority of those surveyed preferred to stay among their own and socialize locally in the neighborhood pub.

But in a city that offers so much cultural, sporting, and sight-seeing diversions, the dominance of the bar and the clannishness of the Irish social life, as well as the low pickup rate of visas, force us to consider other issues in the lives of emigrants. Forty percent of all New Irish respondents were unsure if they would spend the next five years in the New York area. An equal number (41 percent) planned to be in the area for the next five years. Clearly the population was unsettled. Forced out of Ireland because of dissatisfaction with opportunities and job security at home, they traveled to America and labored in unskilled, futureless positions outside the economic and social mainstream of New York. For many the one source of common bonding and dependability in their lives was the camaraderie and Irish context they found in the neighborhood bars of the New Irish communities.

The New Irish of the 1980s were twenty-something unmarried men and women from all over the country with at least a high school education who were dissatisfied economically and unchallenged professionally at home. The majority left Ireland for America only to be barred from "the American Dream" by the structure of American immigration policy. They were essentially suspended in time, circling the periphery of economic and cultural participation in both American and Irish society. With arguably more talent, education, and sophistication than past generations of Irish immigrants, they had the least chance of success of any generation of Irish because of their legal status and their ambivalence about being in "the Land of Opportunity."

Not all in the population congregated in the "ghettoes" of the outer boroughs. Some chose to explore the unconventional lifestyle and freedom of the artistic and avant-garde in lower Manhattan; others pursued professional and academic careers complete with proper documentation. The common bond within the population was their failure, inability, or reluctance to assimilate into the established Irish American community.

The New Irish were raised in a "modern" society, with "modern" expectations, and could not relate to the social, cultural, or political views of Irish immigrants and Irish Americans whose perception of Ireland, Irish people, and emigration to America was grounded in a premodern society.

 5

The Catholic Church:
What Parish Are You From?

We are all tattooed in our cradles with the beliefs of our
tribe; the record may seem superficial, but it is indelible.
—Oliver Wendell Holmes[1]

It is impossible to overestimate the significance of the Roman Catholic Church in
the daily lives and identity of the Irish and their descendants in Ireland and Irish
America in the fifty years after World War II. Whether as a spiritual leader or as a
target of rebellion and attack, the Church was a central institution in the lives of
its people on both sides of the Atlantic. The ability of the Church to command and
expect absolute obedience and acceptance of Catholic dogma passed soon after
Vatican II, but its influence over the lives of its people remained, whether that
influence generated respect or hostility. Lapsed practitioners and daily communicants alike were shaped by the religious, cultural, and social tenets learned in an
Irish Catholic childhood.

Niall Williams, a Dublin-born diarist who with his American-born wife returned to her great-grandfather's farm in County Clare in the 1990s to raise their
own children, described his boyhood church:

> I remembered the church as part of my growing up and adolescence. Although I had
> never quite forgiven the church building itself for replacing the old stone one, I had
> taken my thoughts there at several key times in a most natural and free way, kneeling
> under the high vaulted roof to ask for good examination results or a football win, or
> when my grandfather was ill, to pray. It was part of me, as I suppose churches were of
> all those children who grew up in my generation.
>
> And so, that evening, going with my father back down to Kilmacud church for
> mass, I felt more forcibly than I can say a deep sadness on seeing the church more than
> three-quarters empty. I sat there and kept waiting for the crowd to come in. . . . There

were no teenagers in the pews. Coming from the older people who made up the congregation, the prayers seemed to take on the quality of melancholy.[2]

Pete Hamill, a second-generation Irish Catholic New Yorker born in the 1930s and educated in Brooklyn and Manhattan parochial schools, remembers the power of the Church as a less than positive influence:

> This was part of the most sickening aspect of Irish-American life in those days: the assumption that if you rose above an acceptable level of mediocrity, you were guilty of the sin of pride. You were to accept your place and stay in it for the rest of your life; the true rewards would be given you in heaven, after you were dead. There was ferocious pressure to conform, to avoid breaking out of the pack; self-denial was the supreme virtue. It was the perfect mentality for an infantryman, a civil servant, or a priest. And it added some very honorable lives to the world. But too often, it discouraged kids who aspired to something different. The boy who chose another road was accused of being Full of Himself; he was isolated, assigned a place outside the tribe. Be ordinary was the message; maintain anonymity; tamp down desires or wild dreams. Some boys withered. And the girls were smothered worse than the boys. They could be nuns or wives, brides of Christ or mothers of us all. There were almost no other possibilities.[3]

The formative power of the Church in the development of the character of its faithful was compounded by the Church's role in influencing local political and social action. In Ireland the Church was conspicuous in its involvement in legislation and government policy, most aggressively in the fifties and sixties and less so in the eighties. Among the more controversial issues in which the Church asserted its authority were the Mother and Child Scheme proposed by Dr. Noel Browne, the *Commission on Emigration and Other Population Problems 1948–1954 Reports*, and the government commission called to consider the development of Irish television. The Church opposed the health care program proposed by Dr. Browne which would have established free (voluntary) pre- and postnatal care for mothers, as well as free medical care for all children under 16, without a means test. The Church raised moral and religious objections to the exposure of Catholic women to the advice of public health officials whose treatment and counsel might run counter to the teachings of the Church. The medical community also objected to the loss of income the plan could inflict on doctors. Scholars debate who had more influence on the scheme's fate, but it was ultimately defeated.[4]

It is important to understand just how influential the Church was during the fifties. While it was not unusual for priests and nuns or religious institutions in the United States to participate in public debates on legislative and social issues, or to sway government or public opinion one way or another, America also enjoyed separation of church and state, and no one religious institution had a monopoly on the moral voice in public debate. But in Ireland, until 1972 at least, the Irish constitution included a reference to the "special position of the Catholic Church,"[5] which gave the Church no real power but reflected its central presence in Irish society. Tim Pat Coogan very ironically entitled his chapter on De Valera's relationship with the Church and its hierarchy "When Bishops Were Bishops." "Those were the days [the

1950s] when bishops were bishops in Ireland—when their lordships could pronounce it a mortal sin for Catholics to attend Trinity College, Dublin."[6]

The influence of the bishops at the highest levels of the Irish government made the moral and spiritual voice of Irish political leadership a very Roman Catholic voice. Various historians and observers have noted that "from its early days, the government proved willing to use the power of the state to protect Catholic moral values" and that "the Irish state from the beginning was self-consciously Catholic," particularly regarding individual rights.[7] In the *Emigration Report*, at least two clergy wrote addendum opinions to the government study: the Rev. Thomas Counihan, S.J., and the Rev. E. J. Coyne, S.J. But aside from the participation of these representatives of the Church, within the body of the majority report exist clear examples of the impact of Catholic teaching and thought on government policy:

> Side by side with the improvement of economic and social conditions there should be a strong complementary attack on the "secondary" cause of emigration—the too ready acceptance of emigration as inevitable, the tendency to attach too high a value to the monetary aspects of employment abroad and too low a value to employment and life at home. This attack should be designed to bring about a better balance between the relative values of employment at home and abroad and hence a set of values in which purely monetary standards would play a smaller part than at present.[8]

Much like De Valera's call for "frugal comfort," this observation encouraged the "sacrifice" of the people to resist the purely physical rewards of a materialistic society. Another passage, criticizing the delayed marriage trend and low birth rates of postwar Ireland, was more specific in its spiritual and Catholic tone:

> The primary purpose of marriage, in the natural order of things, is the birth and bringing up of children. The principle which rightly guides the normal Christian married couple in this matter is to have as many children as they can reasonably hope to bring up properly, assuming the practice of Christian virtues in their lives and the readiness to make certain sacrifices. Married couples may of course, "plan" or "space" or "limit" or "control" their family, that is, may decide the number of children they want and when they will have them, if their decisions are based on morally good motives and their actions and methods of controls do not violate the moral precepts of the natural law. But today these words, and such terms as "family-planning," "family-spacing," "family-limitation" and "family-control" are frequently and widely used to mean arranging to have a small family of one or two children, or indeed no family at all, either from selfish or purely materialistic motives which are morally indefensible, or by the use of contraceptives or artificial means, or by other methods which are contrary to the natural law.[9]

Again the official government message here, despite passing recognition to economic and material hardship, was that the absence of Christian goodwill and adherence to Catholic social policy were contributing factors to the social and cultural malaise of the country.

The Church even weighed in on the advisability of television. As previously noted, church leaders were concerned with the breakdown in Irish culture and morality that the introduction of television would mean to Irish society. But according to one historian, the value of the medium as a proselytizing tool for the Church in Ireland and Europe was not lost on the Vatican.

The geographical position of Ireland provided clear access to Europe, which the Vatican felt was unduly influenced by broadcasting systems that were at best "not greatly concerned with moral issues" and at worst, "as in the case of communist controlled stations . . . actively hostile to Christianity and the Catholic Church in particular."[10] Papal interest was so great that Eamon De Valera agreed to allow review copies of the final report of the Television Commission to be seen by the Pontifical Commission on Radio and Television before the Irish government acted on it. In explaining Pope Pius XII's interest in the medium, his emissary Monsignor George Roche confided in Irish Minister for Health Sean MacEntee that

> they [Roche and Monsignor Andrea Deskur, the Assistant Secretary of the Pontifical Commission on Cinema, Radio and Television] had been charged to express informally the great personal interest which His Holiness had in the matter, because of the great service which he believed a television service under the auspices of an Irish Government could render in combatting irreligion and materialism.[11]

In the years after Vatican II, the improved education, quality of life, and general exposure of Irish society to other ways of life through television and international business and marketing influences (as well as the 1972 referendum that removed the Church's status in the Constitution) caused the bishops to lose much of their overt power and influence on the Irish government. However, the power of Catholic dogma cannot be underestimated. Major legislative referenda regarding marital and abortion rights in the middle of the 1980s collided head-on with the Vatican's moral opposition to birth control and divorce, and generated much public controversy both in Ireland and in immigrant communities in the United States.

According to some women's advocates and social workers, the defeat of the referenda was the final straw for many women who could not abide the "misogynist message" of Irish society. While conceding that the primary push factor behind emigration was economic, these advocates argued that social forces in Ireland, particularly female issues such as domestic violence, reproduction, and sexuality, created an intolerable environment from which some women needed to escape.[12] According to the New Irish survey, 26 percent of all respondents and 22 percent of the women surveyed claimed that a "restrictive lifestyle/culture" was one of the reasons they had left Ireland.[13]

The moral rigidity of postwar Ireland, which was shaped by strict Catholic dogma, was soundly rejected by the young adult population of the 1980s and 1990s. Their rejection was all the more significant because as a demographic group they formed almost half of the population in 1980.[14] Their voice and their actions had a serious impact on Irish society. The change in social attitudes and morality represented on contemporary film between the fifties and the eighties fairly reflected the evolution of real Irish society.

Two popular movies made in the 1990s but set in the fifties and sixties presented a country and social atmosphere in which sex was a sin, to be enjoyed, or rather exercised, only within the bounds of marriage and then only to procreate (according to Catholic law). Female characters who became pregnant in *Circle of Friends* (1995) and *The Playboys* (1992), both set in the late 1950s, were stigmatized by local society. One eventually left her community with the child; the other traveled to England for an abortion.

By way of contrast, *The Snapper* (1993; "snapper" is Irish slang for a baby) is set in the 1990s and tells the story of the oldest daughter of a large Catholic family who becomes pregnant. Like the characters in the other two films, she tries to hide the identity of the father. However, while the young woman's condition and ultimate decision to keep the child bring turmoil and confusion to her family, the experience is ultimately a liberating one for the family, particularly the young mother's father, who participates more in the prenatal life of his grandchild than he ever did with his own children. The film was scripted by Roddy Doyle, a writer born and raised in Dublin in the 1950s and 1960s, who also wrote the novel on which the film is based; he is best known for the novel and film *The Commitments*.

In 1993, nearly one in five births in Ireland occurred outside marriage.[15] This is six times the rate of illegitimate births in the early 1970s.[16] As the public debate surrounding the divorce and abortion referenda demonstrated, the moral hegemony of the Catholic Church had clearly eroded. The Irish, at least urban Irish, were no longer paralyzed by the presence of sin or destroyed by the shame or indiscretion of a family member's sexual activity.[17]

The issue of choice and reproductive freedom produced a dramatic and tragic confrontation in the early 1990s when a 14-year-old girl who had been raped by a classmate's father was prevented by the government from having an abortion in England with the threat of prosecution under Irish law. The girl's case was ultimately appealed, but she miscarried the child before an abortion could be performed.[18] Her struggle personified the debate and brought great visibility and "unprecedented" public protest to the issue of reproductive freedom in Ireland.[19] Throughout the eighties examples emerged of young Irish throwing off the yoke of Catholic rigidity in very public ways that might not be understood outside Irish society, but can be seen as radical behavior in the context of Catholic Ireland.

In October 1992, Sinead O'Connor ripped up a photo of the Pope on the late-night American variety show *Saturday Night Live*, calling John Paul II the "real enemy." Her protest met with severe criticism in the United States from Catholic and non-Catholic groups alike.[20] But however extreme or objectionable her action, if it had been understood in the context of her position as a modern Irish Catholic woman, denied the right to birth control, abortion, and divorce in her own country, her behavior might have been greeted differently in the United States.

When the New Irish came to New York, they carried their religious attitudes with them. As discussed in chapter 4, the disruption of the St. Patrick's Day Parade is perhaps the most extreme example of the Irish working through their anger at the Church. On a more local level, a young migrant mother living in the Bronx with two young children formed a support group called the Bronx Women's Group in December 1987, as discussed in the previous chapter.

R. H. wanted to create a place where women could meet with their children to bond and network as new parents in an unfamiliar environment, but she also wanted a place where the women would be free to discuss and explore their feelings as women and immigrants. Part of that exploration involved their Catholicism. She felt strongly that part of Irish women's developing self-awareness involved confronting their relationship with the Church.[21]

In New York, Irish clergy from Archbishop John Hughes to John Cardinal O'Connor have dominated the administration of the Archdiocese of New York since the late nineteenth century.[22] (The New York archdiocese includes Manhattan, the Bronx, Staten Island, and seven counties outside the city: Sullivan, Ulster, Dutchess, Orange, Putnam, Westchester, and Rockland. The Diocese of Brooklyn comprises the boroughs of Brooklyn and Queens.) And until the 1960s and 1970s, when vocations generally declined,[23] Irish and Irish Americans made up a significant proportion of the parish priests and teaching religious in the city.[24] For most Irish in New York, their religion was as much a cultural qualifier as their ethnicity. To identify someone as Irish Catholic would seem a redundancy.[25] The culture we identify with the Irish immigrant community in New York is predominately Catholic.

In fact, scholarship in the 1970s suggested that the declining power and authority of the Catholic Church in the wake of Vatican II and the dissolution of the neighborhood parishes as ethnics left for the suburbs were among the primary factors responsible for what some historians and observers saw as the loss of Irish identity as the second and third generations assimilated into American society.[26] More recent scholarship and evidence suggest that Irish identity did not disappear. While it may be more appropriately defined as Irish American identity, the ethnics' connection to their immigrant and ancestral past did not die.[27]

The Church played an important role in the maintenance of that identity. The Irish parish and parochial school overlapped with the Emerald Society at work, the upstairs neighbors from Mayo, and Sunday afternoons at Gaelic Park. Ethnic reinforcement existed all around families in the fifties. Whether that intensity could be sustained after the move to the suburbs is debatable. At the very least, the move to the suburbs by ethnic Catholics did not diminish church attendance. According to Father Andrew Greeley, American Catholicism was alive and well in the late twentieth century. In a 1995 interview he said that "in 1990, as in 1960, about 85 percent of those who were raised Catholic continue to practice their religion throughout their lifetime." He also believed that parish life continued to be important in the lives of Catholics. While they no longer represented the "refuge" of the past, "American Catholics like their parish communities and support them . . . because they choose to do so."[28]

Greeley noted that the sharpest decline in church attendance occurred between 1968 and 1975. He attributed the fall to the issuance in 1968 of *Humanae*

Vitae, the papal encyclical which denied birth control as a method of family planning for Catholics.[29] But the fall also coincided with the drop in Irish immigration to America, the diaspora to the suburbs,[30] and the premature eulogies for Irish ethnicity by contemporary scholars, all of which combined to suggest the disappearance of the Irish as an ethnic presence. Note too that the oldest of the baby boomers—those born between 1945 and 1967—were entering their twenties at the time of the encyclical. At that age many practicing Catholics typically drift away from the Church, only to return when they begin to raise families. And for the oldest boomers that would be about the time Catholic Church attendance ascended.

The tie between church and ethnic identity needs to be explained. For centuries the Irish have lived in the shadow of England. They battled physically and morally to maintain the independence of their land, their culture, their language, and their religion from England. Despite its political and economic control of Ireland, the British were never successful in fully eradicating either the native Irish religion or language. Because of the struggle to maintain Irish identity, the Catholic religion and the Irish language have been indelibly tied to Irish nationalism and therefore to Irish identity.[31]

Much of Irish and Irish American literary and cultural symbolism has been Catholic. In his speeches, Patrick Pearse, leader of the 1916 rebellion, invoked images of blood sacrifice and redemption that were undeniably Catholic in origin. James Joyce, as expatriate, always wrote about Ireland. His collection of short stories, *Dubliners,*[32] introduced the reader to "everyday" people in turn-of-the-century Dublin, people whose daily lives were influenced, and in his view inhibited, by the moral guidelines of the Church and the not always reliable example of the priest.[33]

Irish American writer Elizabeth Cullinan wrote of New York characters in the 1950s and 1960s whose lives were literally and figuratively dominated by the Church. Her primary characters are women, many of whose mothers and aunts wanted to be or were nuns, were educated by nuns in Catholic schools, and whose lives were forever marked by their Irish Catholicism. One not so subtle image that occurred at least twice in a book of short stories was that of a woman who lived across the street from her parish church, "in the shadow" of the building and all it represented.[34] In fiction and in fact the religion and the institution of Catholicism were the reality for the Irish, in Ireland and America.[35]

John Grimes, who was appointed general manager of *The Irish Echo* in 1957 and who served as publisher in 1978 until his death in 1987,[36] wrote about growing up in New York City in the thirties and forties:

> We didn't live in New York City or, or even the Bronx—we lived "in Visitation [parish]." That geographical definition lingered for years. Some time later, at the Friday Good Shepherd [another Bronx parish] dances, after my opening gambit, "Do you come here often?"—tossed off suavely with each and every partner—I'd move in with, "Where do you live?" which was invariably answered by, "in St. Brendan's," or "in St. Philip Neri's," or the like.[37]

To punctuate Grimes's tale, consider this 1965 classified ad in his family's newspaper: "Our Lady of Refuge Parish, 4 rm furn. apt. with full kitchen & bathroom, 2 or 3 Irish girls, $40 weekly, incl. gas, elec, TV and washing machine. WE3-8789."[38]

Later in his memoir, Grimes began a neighborhood anecdote by describing his subject: "Mr. Rollins was the classic example of the community pillar made of salt. An officer of the Holy Name Society, the owner of a comfortable warehouse business. . . ."[39] Membership in the Holy Name was mentioned as though it were nothing unusual—he had a job, he was married, he belonged to the Holy Name, just like everybody else. In the 1950s and 1960s, being Catholic was part of being Irish. Most Irish neighborhoods were Catholic neighborhoods.

Depending on the circumstances of the time, various waves of Irish immigrants have carried with them their generation's brand of ethnic identity and nationalism that was heavily connected to the Church. In the immediate post-famine years, "emigrants generally were more faithfully practicing Catholics than their predecessors and more likely to perceive formal religion and Irishness as synonymous."[40] In the 1880s the Land League and the tenant rights struggle in Ireland shaped Irish immigrant and Irish American nationalism across class lines. According to Eric Foner, working-class Irish who were more often than not immigrant Irish identified the land question in Ireland with workers' rights in America, comparing landlords to capitalists. Their nationalism, born in a struggle to own land in Ireland, helped to develop a radical labor movement among Irish workers in America. More conservative, middle-class Irish Americans identified with the Land League as one more step in the struggle for an independent Ireland. Their view conformed to the position of the Catholic Church, which endorsed the league's alliance with Parnell and his fight for home rule.[41] In the 1920s, the immigrant veterans of the Irish Civil War, still bearing the scars of that bitter battle, entered the country carrying an intense Irish Ireland brand of nationalism that, as Marion Casey has argued, sought to legitimize Ireland's political independence through a policy of cultural isolationism.[42] The split in the country formalized by the peace treaty separated the six predominately Protestant counties in the north from the twenty-six predominately Catholic counties in the south, reinforcing religion as a point of division between Ireland and Great Britain.

At least until the second decade of the twentieth century, the Irish identity was always forged in opposition to some British influence, whether landlordism or Protestantism. When that anti-British, anti-landlord, anti-Protestant mentality entered a capitalist society ruled by Protestant politicians and civil servants, the Irish immigrants became more firmly entrenched against the perceived enemy in their position as Irish Catholic outsiders in the New World.[43] While their experience in Ireland prepared them well to negotiate the local prejudices and social and legal orders of the nineteenth century, it also strengthened their identity as Irish Catholics. As time went on and the Irish clergy gained more power in the administration of the Church, having the physical presence of their own ethnic brothers and sisters as leaders of the Catholic institutions reinforced their pride and confidence.

Not only have the Irish typically been identified with Catholicism, but the

Church, like the police force, has typically (or stereotypically) been identified as Irish in the popular culture in America. Movie priests, personified by Bing Crosby, Barry Fitzgerald, and Pat O'Brien, were as ubiquitous as Hollywood's Officer Kelly or McNamara, the corner cop from the old country.[44] But it has been said that most stereotypes are conceived partly in truth. And in post–World War II New York, the facts were that many priests and nuns were Irish and the presence of the clergy and religious, Irish and non-Irish alike, in the daily lives of Irish Catholics was fairly constant.[45]

The head of the New York archdiocese has historically been a very visible and a very political office. Some of the Church's most charismatic leaders have held the spot.[46] In the 1950s and 1960s the post belonged to Francis Cardinal Spellman, perhaps the most powerful and political of all the men to lead from St. Patrick's pulpit. Spellman was an Irish American raised in Massachusetts who did not identify with his ethnic background. He instructed his biographer not to describe him as Irish American. Spellman spent many years in Rome, training and working at the Vatican, and developing an impressive network of contacts and friends, including Eugenio Pacelli, the future Pope Pius XII, all of which aided his rise to the top seat in New York City.[47] In the secular world, Spellman included young John Fitzgerald Kennedy among his many influential friends. At least one scholar suggests that Spellman may have been in the middle of early American involvement in Vietnam because both he and Kennedy were supporters of Ngo Dinh Diem, a Catholic, who aggressively opposed Communism.[48] And following the death of Al Smith, former New York governor and Democratic presidential candidate, it was Spellman who inaugurated the Al Smith Foundation dinners in October 1945, an event begun as a fundraiser to build a wing on to St. Vincent's Hospital in Greenwich Village.[49] The dinner became an annual affair, typically attracting both major party candidates in any election year.

Under Spellman, the Catholic Church in New York underwent an aggressive building campaign that included not only the expansion of hospitals like St. Vincent's, but orphanages and, most significantly, schools. In a twenty-year period, from the early 1940s to 1961, with most activity occurring in the 1950s, the archdiocese built 81 new elementary schools, replaced 46, and added on to 87 primary buildings, while it closed another 27. The number of high schools in the archdiocese rose to 99 from 87. In this same period the numbers of primary and secondary students in Catholic schools in the archdiocese rose from 119,429 in 1939–40 to 216,013 in 1960–61.[50] By 1968, the number of pupils enrolled in nonpublic schools grades K through 12 in New York City (which included the Diocese of Brooklyn) was 448,778.[51] The Catholic Church, like the rest of postwar New York, was enjoying a tremendous surge of growth, strength, and power.

As demonstrated in chapter 2, postwar census data indicated that the Irish lived in neighborhoods where a significant proportion of children attended parochial schools.[52] Given the population in these neighborhoods and the presence of active parish schools, it can be presumed that the children of many Irish living in New York attended Catholic schools. Supporting these census figures, studies for

1964 and 1974 showed that nationally, in families where both parents were Catholic, 44 percent of their children attended Catholic school in the first sample compared to 29 percent in the later study. This same study showed that in 1974, when Catholic school attendance nationally was dropping, 29 percent of Irish Catholics still sent their children to parochial school, placing them among the top four (out of ten) ethnic groups mostly likely to support nonpublic education.[53]

Academically, the Catholic school experience was very important in the Irish move up the socioeconomic ladder. Studies have shown that children attending parochial school are more likely than public school students to attend college. Between the World War II and Vietnam War generations the percentage of Catholics attending college rose by almost one-third.[54] Catholic colleges in the New York City metropolitan area enjoyed tremendous success in the years after World War II. In the fall of 1967, St. John's in Queens and Fordham in the Bronx were among the top five Catholic colleges in the country in terms of total enrollment. St. John's (a commuter's campus) had 11,677 students, 7,957 of whom were full-time. Fordham enrolled 10,450, 7,897 of whom were full-time.[55] Schools such as Iona, Fordham, and St. John's catered to the children of immigrants and ethnic Americans who were very often the first in their families to attend college. The growth in attendance was achieved in no small part by the availability of government loans through the GI bill program that helped to finance the education of thousands of World War II veterans.

Iona College began as a small college in the suburb of New Rochelle. The Irish Christian Brothers founded it in 1940, just before America's involvement in World War II, which ultimately interrupted the education of many of the institution's early class members. The first graduating class was awarded diplomas in 1947. The group numbered thirty-two and included nine members of the first 1940 class. Note the names of those nine graduates: Howard J. Barry, John A. Callaghan, William A. Culhane, Henry P. Dart, Joseph J. Doherty, Arthur J. Lyons, James E. O'Ryan, David J. Richards, and John C. Ryan. The Irish presence in the school was also evident by the existence of the Gaelic Society, one of the campus's first language clubs. The president of the society formed a pipe band in the 1960s which was so popular that it appeared in the 1966 St. Patrick's Day Parade on Fifth Avenue, winning a trophy for its performance. In 1971, a college history noted that the society was still active, "beginning a series of annual drives . . . to collect food, toys and clothing for the poverty-stricken people of Appalachia."[56]

In the third semester of the 1945–46 academic year, Iona's registration numbers rose steadily from 75 to 144 to 270. More than half (160) of those 270 were veterans.[57] The following September saw 800 war veterans register among 1,020 incoming students. The impact of the returning soldiers was such that a college historian noted:

> This student body was different: petty regulations designed for adolescents were out of place for those who had gone through the hell of Guadalcanal and Normandy. Faculty

members might be divided on the question of whether the veterans' college experience was to be the pursuit of knowledge for its own sake or a means of qualifying for a profession and settling down.[58]

The pursuit of a college degree for economic mobility bore fruit for the Irish after World War II. It is difficult to say if those GIs who took advantage of the government's offer of money would have gone on to postsecondary education without the financial assistance. The Irish were certainly positioned to make a move up the education ladder. They had been ahead of the national average for college achievement since World War I. Second- and third-generation Irish had established themselves economically and socially to support and encourage their children as college students through the Depression and World War II years. Like the rest of American society they profited from the postwar growth and expansion. By the 1970s Irish Catholics were the most successful white ethnic group in the country by the standards of income and education.[59]

An annual feature of a popular ethnic magazine offers proof of Irish success and the role of Catholic colleges in their ascent. The publisher of the monthly magazine *Irish America,* who also publishes the *Irish Voice,* annually identifies the "Business 100"—100 of the most successful Irish Americans in the country. A quick scan of the roster for 1994 reveals a number of New Yorkers, many of them graduates of New York City Catholic colleges and universities: John J. Dooner, Jr., CEO, McCann Erickson Worldwide, Iona College business graduate school; Margaret Duffy (emigrated in 1962), audit partner, Arthur Andersen, Fordham University; Thomas H. Ferguson, president and general manager of the *Washington Post,* St. John's; William J. Flynn,[60] chairman, Mutual of America, Fordham University; James B. Irwin, Sr., chairman, IMPAC, Fordham University; Michael J. Larkin, executive vice president and COO, A&P, Iona College; William J. McKenna, chairman, president, and CEO, Kellwood Company, Iona College; Thomas J. Moran, president and COO, Mutual of America, Manhattan College; Joseph M. Murphy, chairman, Country Bank, Iona College; John J. O'Gorman, senior executive vice president, UJB Financial, Iona College; Jeremiah F. O'Leary, senior vice president, Chemical Bank, Manhattan College; Joseph J. O'Neill, president and CEO, New York Cotton Exchange, Manhattan College; Pat Purcell, president and CEO, News America Publishing, Inc., St. John's University; Edward J. Robinson, president and COO, Avon Products, Inc., Iona College; Daniel P. Tully, chairman & CEO, Merrill Lynch & Co., Inc., St. John's University; Joseph M. Walsh, chairman and CEO, Curtis Circulation Company, Iona College; Patrick J. Ward, chairman, president, and CEO, Caltex Petroleum Corp., Fordham University; and Daniel P. Weadock, president and COO, ITT Sheraton, Fordham University.[61]

For those Catholics who attended parochial schools in the fifties and sixties, before Vatican II, the experience went beyond the academics and discipline typically associated with parish schools. Catholic school students were identified as distinct from other students.[62] Most obviously, they wore uniforms and were often told by the religious who taught them that they were special. But in the days of the Latin Mass, Catholic school education was wrapped in the same mystique of ritual and mystery as all Catholic ceremony. Major school events *were* religious events— May crownings, which honored the Mother of Jesus during "her month"; Stations of the Cross on Friday afternoons in Lent; confession every first Friday of the month. The influence and indelible markings of a Catholic school education had as much to do with education as it did with Catholicism and the power and personality of the religious in charge of the student body.

> For those of us who grew up Catholic, religion is at the heart of memory. The tremendous beauty and ritual of Catholicism: the ornate darkness of the church, the statues, the Stations of the Cross, the hushing of conversation upon entering, the sign of the cross at the holy water font, the celebration of Mass, the solo voice of the priest followed by the voices of the congregation kneeling at the communion rail to receive the Body of Christ, the songs of the choir, all instill in us a reverence for the sacred, an honoring of the mystical. Our highest most holy selves rise like angels.
>
> Whenever I smell frankincense burning I remember the church of my childhood at the top of a steep hill in upper Manhattan. I see the dark stained glass windows and I hear the choir's lilting songs. I don't know if I ever believed, but I do know I liked the feeling that entered my body as Mass began, soothing me. That feeling was something larger than just myself; it connected me to my mother, sister, and everyone else in church.
>
> I used to sneak into church during recess or after school and light all the votive candles to free the poor souls in Purgatory. I saw them ascending into Heaven, flocks of white birds.[63]

It was an era when young women fantasized about becoming nuns.[64] An Irish American writer who attended St. Patrick's grammar school in Long Island City remembered the impact made by her seventh grade teacher:

> It was during my months with Sister Rose Edmond that I decided to become a nun when I grew up. I, too, would wear a pretty habit and live in a convent full of women. I would be the teacher of adoring children and, like Sister Rose Edmond, would let my pupils distract me into telling stories instead of finishing math lessons.[65]

Some memories of religious teachers were not pleasant, but lasting nonetheless. Sister Rose Edmond eventually disappointed her enraptured student when she could not satisfactorily explain why women could not serve at the mass like the altar boys or priests.

> Sister had sided with the boys. She had betrayed us. How could I trust her after that. . . . Everytime I saw the boys at the altar in their splendid red cassocks, my prayers dissolved in a wash of anger, envy, and confusion. I went to communion with a troubled spirit, always aware that, beyond the rail, there were no girls at the altar.[66]

Pete Hamill remembered a cruel brother who taught his Park Slope eighth grade class at Holy Name:

In the seventh grade, we'd had a soft and saintly man named Brother Rembert as our teacher. We heard scary tales about Brother Jan, but nothing really prepared us for the reality of this snarling, vicious brute. On his desk, Brother Jan kept a thick eighteen-inch ruler called Elmer. He used it on someone every day.[67]

Hamill never once fantasized about entering the seminary, but he did envision himself beating Brother Jan senseless. And as the rest of Hamill's autobiography made clear, the author has been battling authority and rejecting the institution of Catholicism ever since.

Children in general are greatly influenced by the men and women in charge of their education. Most people have very strong memories of their school days, and affection or disdain for specific individuals who made a particular impact on their lives. But for those children who attended Catholic schools in the years after World War II, the presence of priests and nuns in their lives every day was bound to make a strong impression. Those religious were part of the Church. They were symbolic of the mystery and holiness of God. They dressed differently from the rest of the community. They lived differently than the rest of the community—segregated in convents and rectories with other nuns and priests. They were special, and they were part of what it was to be Catholic in postwar New York.

On the parish level, interviews with migrants and clergy themselves reveal the centrality of the Church and its ordained ministers, Irish and non-Irish, to the daily lives of Irish Americans. While Cardinal Spellman was not necessarily recognized for his ethnicity, other prominent and popular New York clerics were more closely identified with their heritage, including Archbishop Fulton J. Sheen, an Irish American who achieved wide fame as an inspirational speaker and spiritual leader of the Church, using the podiums of a nationally televised weekly program and a newspaper column in New York City's *Journal American*.[68] No centralized data exist that break down the ethnic composition of convents and seminarians in New York City. But in many of the Irish parishes of the 1950s and 1960s the records show a significant number of clergy with Irish surnames.[69] And anecdotally, it has been said that every Irish family had at least one daughter in the convent or one son in the priesthood.[70]

Personal interviews and a glance at the *Irish Echo* also suggest that church personnel and church functions were integral to the everyday life of postwar Irish. Ads for the Catskill resorts such as the Sligo Hotel in Leeds, Greene County, claimed to be "convenient to swimming and all amusements, stores and churches." The Shamrock House in East Durham featured "home-cooked meals, churches and Irish-American music."[71] A classified ad for housing positioned the property in a "Fine Irish-American Section Upper West Bronx; 9 Rms . . . Near Catholic School."[72]

One fifties emigrant said he liked "Tollantine" [St. Nicholas of Tollantine in the Bronx] because the "Irish were there."[73] Another woman remembered attending wakes with her friends in the first years after emigration because it was a good way to meet and keep in touch with relatives and acquaintances from home. She read the obituaries for the names and home towns of the Irish she knew. She and her friends traveled around the city to these wakes in an effort to make contact with other Irish.[74]

In the 1950s fraternal organizations such as the Emerald Societies of the police and fire departments, the Holy Name Society of the police department, and the Ancient Order of Hibernians organized regular communion breakfasts throughout the year, obviously reinforcing ethnic as well as religious solidarity among the members of the respective organizations. Father Sean Reid recalled that the "11 o'clock Mass was always the High Mass and before that Mass, the Hibernians assembled at Fordham Road and with the Cork Pipers band leading them they marched down the Concourse to 181st Street where they turned left in to the church. At their head in habit and white cloak marched Fr. Donald O'Callaghan."[75] The son of a migrant whose father belonged to the Holy Name Society of the fire department, a Catholic fraternal group, recalled the annual communion breakfast, held the Sunday after Easter, when Holy Name members would attend mass said by the cardinal, then march out of St. Patrick's Cathedral and down Fifth Avenue to the Commodore Hotel on 42nd Street for breakfast.[76] The symbolism and visibility of these ceremonies and parades reflected the importance and tradition the community invested in its highly integrated religion and culture.

The *Irish Echo* of the fifties and sixties was filled with stories of newly ordained priests and nuns, the sons and daughters of proud parents from the Bronx and Queens and the thirty-two counties of Ireland. Announcements of priests and nuns taking final vows or being assigned to schools and missions domestically and internationally were as popular as wedding announcements.

The paper also posted notices for benefit dances and speeches for visiting priests from Ireland who were in the United States to raise money to build churches back in Ireland or to finance missions in Africa or South America.[77] The headlines offer a glimpse of the high profile of priests and nuns in the Irish Catholic life of the postwar New Yorkers: "Brother Sean Takes First Vows," for example, and "Priests' Mission Assignments," which listed the overseas placements of forty-eight priests and two brothers, including twenty-six ordained students of St. Joseph's Missionary Society, in Mill Hill, Ireland.[78]

The commission and recruitment of priests and nuns to America from Ireland provided more than a religious presence in the parish. Like secular migrants the religious from Ireland carried the contemporary Irish culture with them. Depending on the individual or the community, the strength of the religious' allegiance to things Irish kept the Irish culture alive in their Irish American parishes and institutions.

In 1933 Father Sean Reid, a Kilkenny-born Irishman, was ordained a Carmelite priest in the chapel of St. John Lateran Seminary in Rome and assigned to the American province of the Carmelites, which at the time had five houses in New York—one on 28th Street in Manhattan, one at St. Simon Stock priory in the Bronx, another in Tarrytown, and two in Middletown.[79] After a series of assignments around the United States, he was assigned to the post of pastor at the Mt. Carmel church on 28th Street. The highlights of Father Reid's career illustrate clearly the active role of the priest in the everyday lives of the faithful.[80]

Father Reid's personal background reinforced a strong sense of Irish nationalism in the priest. He was a fluent Irish speaker (one immigrant from St. Simon Stock parish recalled the sermons delivered in Irish by Father Reid[81]) and declared that Eamon De Valera was his childhood hero.[82] His extracurricular activities throughout New York—including two terms as Gaelic Athletic Association (GAA) president, his presence at cultural events, and his appointment as grand marshal of the St. Patrick's Day Parade in 1964—all demonstrated his personal commitment to Irish culture and his passion for perpetuating the culture among the Irish and Irish Americans he served in New York.[83] But his activities also demonstrated the impact that Irish clergy and religious could have on the preservation and evolution of Irish culture and identity in the New York ethnic community.

One of Father Reid's first assignments after arriving in New York in 1933 was to judge an Irish step dancing contest at what he said was the first New York feis (a festival of Irish dancing, sports, music).[84] After World War II loosened up emigration from Ireland, Father Reid—a champion hurler in Ireland[85]—organized a hurling club for his home county, Kilkenny, drafting athletes from the thousands of young men entering New York looking for work.[86] As two-term president of the GAA in New York City, he recruited players, linesmen, and referees, as well as sponsors for the county teams he fielded. He was part of the everyday life of his parishioners and students, as were many religious of the time. And in that position he influenced more than the souls of his ministry. He could impart his passion for Irish culture and politics.

Part of the reason clergy were so prominent in Catholic life was the fact that in the 1950s there were just more of them. The archdiocese could support a large educational system because it did not have heavy faculty costs. While the Archdiocese of New York operated schools throughout the three boroughs of the Bronx, Manhattan, and Staten Island, some of the schools and parishes in the city were staffed and administered by individual communities of priests and nuns from the United States and around the world, including the Carmelites.

As pastor of a very poor community, Father Reid moved outside his parish to raise funds to sustain the Church and its programs, which included a school. In the fundraising effort he developed a wide network of friends and acquaintances throughout the city, including business people, professionals, politicians, and union leaders, some Catholic, some not; some Irish, some not. As a parish priest, it was not unusual for him to be approached by members of the community for help finding jobs and housing for relatives, often migrants from Ireland. His contacts throughout the city enabled him to offer referrals and advice to those who sought his help. On a day-to-day basis Father Reid was undoubtedly, like many priests of his day, working among blue-collar and lower-income families in the city. He functioned as job placement and real estate broker as often as he did as spiritual adviser.

In the period immediately after World War II, the priest was often better educated than his parishioners. For many sons of working-class and blue-collar families, the priesthood offered a step up socially, academically, and economically. According to a Catholic sociologist conducting a study of 133 prelates in 1957, only 5 percent of the subjects' fathers had graduated from college, while 65 percent had not even gone to high school,[87] suggesting that the priesthood offered opportunities for education, prestige, and power that otherwise might not have been available to them. In the 1950s and 1960s, the census review of the Irish neighborhoods isolated in chapter 2 showed that fewer than half of the general population had a high school diploma.[88] It is conceivable that a priest, drawn from a similar background as his parishioners but with the polish and education that seminary study provided, would in fact draw the respect and deference of the people to whom he ministered.

The more popular and involved pastors were highly visible at the social and cultural events of their parishioners. In Mary Ford's memoir of her youth in the Bronx, one of the regular players in her aunt's Friday night card games was a priest. As her aunt and family members aged, the priest continued to visit the house until the old woman died.[89] Priests and nuns were everywhere in the life of Irish Americans, even when they vacationed. A poem written for the anniversary of the local paper in Rockaway, a popular Queens beach resort, recalled summers in the 1940s:

> In the middle 1940s
> Beach 116th Street
> The penny arcade
> The movie (forgot the name)
> And Curley's Atlas Hotel.
> Hamburgers on a bun with onions made by
> a nice little old lady, Mrs. Cronin, and only a
> quarter.
> My Mom, Molly being a waitress in the dining room.
> It was mostly frequented by priests and sisters.
> I was a locker girl in the back.
> Busy place on weekends.[90]

An elderly woman waiting to visit a priest in the rectory vestibule of St. Nicholas of Tollantine parish mournfully recalled the days when the school children would proceed from the park across the street into the church for May crownings in the spring. In 1995 the park was covered with litter, and she and another elderly woman complained of the petty crime and purse snatching that dominated current street life. For her the absence of the May crowning ceremonies symbolized the much greater demographic changes that occurred in the previous thirty years and put the neighborhood she clearly loved forever in the past.

The changes in urban and suburban parish life extended beyond safety in the streets. After fifty years of upward mobility and improved quality of life, American Irish Catholics in 1995 were more affluent and sophisticated than their parents and grandparents. According to Greeley, "maybe three-quarters of adult parishioners are college graduates. Parish priests, however, are not necessarily more sophisticated than they were a generation or two ago."[91] The dynamic between priest and parishioner, at least on a socioeconomic level, had changed.

McCaffrey and Greeley also discuss the poor quality and ineffectuality of the current priesthood, who no longer command the automatic respect and acceptance of the parishioners by virtue of their calling. Religious life is no longer the only avenue for the best and brightest. As second- and third-generation ethnics moved up the socioeconomic ladder, they could provide better academic and social opportunities for their children outside the convent and the seminary. But what Catholics expect from their church leaders has risen accordingly. The clergy are challenged by the lay community to provide more stimulating and articulate sermons. However, according to Greeley, many priests, because of advanced age or inability, routinely disappoint their Sunday audiences.[92]

But the rising affluence of Irish Catholics in the postwar period was not the only factor affecting relationships between the rectory and the parish body. Changes in official doctrine and the loss of clerical staffing within the Church also diminished the absolute authority and often unquestioned power of the Church hierarchy. At the very least, the loss of vocations reduced the visibility of the clergy and religious in the daily lives of Irish and Irish American men, women, and children.

In the late twentieth century fewer priests served around the world, and the churches and schools in New York were more likely staffed by lay teachers and administrators than by religious.[93] Likewise many inner-city Catholic schools in New York now are filled with non-Catholic pupils who attend for the discipline, order, and academic stability the parochial school offers.[94] Those religious who do exist have lost their obvious visibility in the community. Nuns no longer wear the body-concealing habits that set them apart and lent them mystery. The updated uniforms, if worn at all, are conservative and nondescript, unlikely to mark the wearer as anything but fashion delinquent.

One nun who currently lives and works in Galway as a nurse and hospital director estimated that 10 percent of her graduating class in the 1950s had entered the convent.[95] Records from the Mercy Congregation in Ireland show that in the years after World War II the number of young women entering the order each year was around 100 through the 1950s and as high as 131 in 1961. New vocations dropped dramatically in the late 1960s and never rose over 30 per year after 1970. Finally, in 1993, 1994, and 1995, the congregation registered no new entrants at all.[96]

The irony of Vatican II and its subsequent changes in regulations, language, and ceremony in the Church is that the changes made it somewhat "easier" to be a Catholic. But eliminating restrictions for eating meat on Friday, easing fasting and abstinence regulations, liberalizing dress codes, and replacing Latin with native languages also made being Catholic less distinctive than it had been. There was no mystery to the service and ceremony, and no common hardship to share with other Catholics that would signal your faith to the outside world, such as no snacking after midnight on Saturday night, ordering fish on Friday, or wearing a mantilla to church on Sunday. Many of the great symbols and ceremony of being Catholic were gone. And while that may seem very superficial, when it was combined with the migration to less ethnically dense suburbs, Irish Catholics in the metropolitan area, both in the city and in outer communities in the tristate region, felt the loss of some common identity.

In Ireland, the change in the Church coincided with a social and economic awakening that replaced the spiritual with the material. Gone were the days of frugal comfort in Ireland. While Ireland remained a "Catholic" country, by the 1980s and 1990s the Church did not carry the authority and power it once had. A younger, better-educated, more urban population was just as likely to follow its own lead or rebel as to blindly fall in place behind the clergy and Church hierarchy. One priest interviewed in Ireland worried about drawing the youth of Ireland back to the Church.[97] The survey of New Irish in the 1980s showed that 45 percent attended mass as often as they did at home, while 49 percent attended less often.[98] Of course, attendance records are no indicator of devotion. They may just as likely reflect the absence of social and family pressure to go to church, especially since the New Irish were of an age when it is typical for practicing Catholics to lapse temporarily. And since the migrants did not indicate the frequency of their trips to church, the survey cannot show whether regular attendance was once a year or once a week. But a contemporary poll commissioned by the *Sunday Independent* and a television program provided further evidence of the drift away from formal religion in Ireland: "In 1974, 91 percent of respondents said they attended mass once a week, in 1989 the number was 85 percent and today [1995], it is just 64 percent."[99]

In New York, it is a little more difficult to get recent numbers on the religious behavior of Irish Catholics. A neighborhood survey of Irish Americans taken in New York around 1975 reported that 53 percent of respondents, 89.5 percent of whom said they were Catholic, attended church at least once a week, and 14.9 percent never attended.[100] (Remember that Greeley identified the low point in American church attendance as being between 1968 and 1975.)

In a study of American Catholic college graduates published in 1969, Andrew Greeley found that Catholics who attended Catholic colleges were more likely to attend church weekly than those who attended non-Catholic institutions. Three years out of college, 92 percent of graduates of Catholic colleges attended mass weekly, compared to 67 percent of graduates of non-Catholic schools. Ninety-eight percent of the former group still identified themselves as Catholics, compared to 80 percent of the latter. After seven years, 82 percent of Catholic-college alumni attended mass weekly, compared to 61 percent of non-Catholic-college alumni; 96 percent of the first group and 87 percent of the second group still considered themselves Catholic.[101] Like Greeley's 1995 numbers for American Catholics, which claimed that 85 percent of American Catholics go to church, these were not broken down by ethnic or geographic groupings. One can only assume that the Irish in New York conformed to the rest of America.

The Church's Response to Immigrants in New York

Despite diminishing numbers and a more confrontational congregation, the Church in Ireland and New York remained involved in the Irish American and immigrant communities. The level and type of involvement were representative of the changes between 1950 and 1990.

The religious health of immigrants has been a concern of Church leaders in Ireland since the diaspora of millions of Irish in the nineteenth century. Responding to mass emigration throughout the 1800s, particularly in the decades after the famine, various religious orders followed the emigrants to America to maintain the Catholic faith of Irish. Stories of migrant Irish falling away from the Church were enough to initiate a parade of nuns responding to invitations from bishops and mothers superior looking for help ministering to migrants on the West Coast, on the frontier and in cities, and particularly to teach the children of immigrants, not only reading and writing, but the catechism as well.[102]

By the 1950s the faith and religious practice of emigrants was still a concern for the Church in Ireland. In fact, the government report on emigration referred to the life of immigrants abroad in Great Britain and the opportunities for them to involve themselves in parish life as they did in Ireland, as well as the temptations that existed: "It is hardly surprising, however, that a proportion should tend to give up the practice of their religion and to fail in the matter of sexual morality."[103] Throughout the 1950s a religious group called the Legion of Mary met prospective emigrants prior to departure from Ireland to encourage them to "continue the practice of their faith." The primary impetus in this effort was fear that the Irish would lose their religion in a foreign country, particularly in England, where many Irish had no family to meet them. Often they provided emigrants with addresses of Catholic groups that could help them find jobs and housing.[104]

According to the staff of the Emigrant Advice office in Dublin, the first pre-emigration service was established "during the war [World War II] years." It was called the Emigrant Section of the Catholic Social Welfare Bureau and was set up by Archbishop John Charles McQuaid in 1942. One of the clear objectives of this body was to secure the religious faith and practice of the Irish living abroad. For those headed to England, the emigrant's proposed destination could be given to the Emigrant Section office in Dublin, which would then contact the local priest where the emigrant was going to live and that priest would contact the emigrant upon arrival.

Among the services provided by the Emigrant Section were the following:

- putting emigrants in touch with Catholics at their destination;
- making enquiries as to whether or not the proposed employment in Britain was suitable for Catholics;
- securing proper facilities for emigrants to fulfill their religious duties;
- providing for their social welfare in new and often difficult surroundings.[105]

It seems that no formal outreach existed in America to aid the immigrants specifically, beyond the help available to the Irish through regular parish channels and informal family and social networks that may have included the local priest. Migrants entering New York in the two decades after World War II moved into communities in which they relied on the references and generosity of relatives and friends from home for information about jobs and housing. The religious health of the immigrants was probably not a problem because most migrants lived with families in communities that were very involved with parish and church activities.[106] In the 1950s the Church was not experiencing a crisis of faith. Institutional intervention did not seem necessary. It may well have been that Irish officials were more focused on the Catholics leaving for England because their numbers were dramatically higher and Irish Catholics there were not as strong a community as in America.[107] Anecdotally, migrants have also said that the Irish were not as welcome in England as they were in New York. One man who spent time in both places said he was just "Paddy in England," but in New York he received more respect.[108]

Thirty years later the Church responded to what it saw as an immigrant community in need of help in America. But this time the initiative came from New York,[109] and the approach taken was not nearly as paternal or proselytizing as that taken in the 1940s and 1950s. It sprang from a concern for the social and emotional well-being of the migrant. The effort of the Church leaders on both sides of the Atlantic in the 1980s suggested that the clergy understood that the New Irish would not respond to overt religious or moral messages of outreach; rather, they saw a clear demand among the migrants for aid and assistance in acculturating to a new land.

The primary vehicle of assistance between the Church and the New Irish community in the 1980s and 1990s was Project Irish Outreach, a branch of the New York Archdiocese Catholic Charities organization, with its main office on First Avenue and 56th Street in Manhattan. The executive director, Monsignor James J. Murray, said that Project Irish Outreach was created in response to the Immigration Reform and Control Act (IRCA) of 1986. According to Monsignor Murray,[110] in February 1987, following the implementation of IRCA, he met with Adrian Flannelly, a popular Irish American radio personality, and James Hallisey, a New York attorney with close ties to Charles Haughey, a prominent politician in Ireland. They were worried about the Irish who would fall through the cracks in the new legislation—those not eligible for amnesty and those who would not receive Donnelly visas. Hallisey learned from his sources in Ireland that Haughey, preparing for a national election, wanted the Church in New York to make a statement about the Irish immigrants in the wake of the legislation. On February 12, Monsignor Murray issued a statement in New York claiming that the Church would do everything it could for those who qualified for amnesty and the new visas, as well as for those otherwise disadvantaged by their status.

Haughey's party went on to win the election, and he became prime minister. Monsignor Murray drafted a proposal for an outreach program that would cater directly to the social service needs of the New Irish, including the assignment of at least two Irish priests to live in the New Irish community. The proposal, dated August 1987, was actually completed in May and June of 1987. Public service announcements (PSAs) introducing Project Irish Outreach aired in July 1987 on *The Adrian Flannelly Show*. Murray traveled to Ireland with Hallisey in late June and early July and met with Prime Minister Haughey's representatives to see what could be done for the New Irish by the Irish government. He also met with representatives of the Irish Bishops' Episcopal Commission (also known as the Irish Episcopal

Commission for Emigrants) to discuss the possibility of assigning Irish priests to work among the New Irish in New York and the presentation of such a proposal to the annual bishops' meeting in Maynooth in November.

The monsignor returned to Ireland in September to meet once more with the bishops' commission and with Charles Haughey. Later that month, during a visit to New York, Deputy Prime Minister Brian Lenihan announced the creation of the special liaison office and Immigration Working Committee in New York. It was also in September that Project Irish Outreach officially opened its doors at the Catholic Charities headquarters on the East Side of Manhattan. It was directed by Patricia O'Callaghan, a native Irish woman and former producer for *The Adrian Flannelly Show,* and was staffed by a social worker from Ireland named Clare Barnwell and a secretary.[111] The project was primarily a counseling and referral service for the New Irish who called or visited its offices. According to Ms. O'Callaghan, 59 percent of the calls received in 1988 were related to legal problems, 18 percent to medical problems, 13 percent to employment, and 10 percent to a variety of other issues such as homelessness or day care. The calls were split pretty evenly between men and women.[112]

Monsignor Murray traveled again to Ireland in October to meet with some individual bishops and members of religious communities who might recommend candidates for chaplains, much like the mothers superior and bishops of the nineteenth century who solicited missionaries to service an earlier immigrant population. He also met again with Prime Minister Haughey. In November the bishops' commission met with Monsignor Murray in Maynooth and voted to send at least two priests to New York. In February 1988 the first chaplain arrived. Within a year three priests and one religious sister lived among the Irish in the Bronx. Both the Newark and Boston archdioceses reviewed the New York outreach program for consideration in their parishes. On March 2, Bishop Francis Mugavero of Brooklyn announced the creation of an Irish apostolate office in St. Teresa's parish, Woodside, Queens. The office was under the direction of the diocese's Catholic Migration and Refugee Office and dealt specifically with the needs of the New Irish in Brooklyn and Queens.

In the early months and years of the outreach programs the chaplains typically made contact with the New Irish where they gathered—in bars, at Gaelic Park in the Bronx, at church, in their apartments. According to one of the chaplains, the New Irish did not initiate contact. Usually it was the clergy who sought out the New Irish. For example, they visited apartment buildings in their neighborhoods and asked where the New Irish lived. Then the chaplains would wait at the buildings and greet the immigrants when they returned to their apartments at the end of the workday. The chaplains' goals were based on friendship rather than worship. They wanted to reassure the New Irish that the Church had not abandoned them. The religious interviewed said that at the very least the outreach to the New Irish consisted of the comfort provided by a voice with a familiar accent in a strange city.[113]

Two points about the New Irish must be reiterated to drive home the differences between the two immigrant communities. One is that in the 1980s the extended family and social relationships that the 1950s migrants enjoyed in New York were virtually nonexistent. The advanced age and anemia of the immigrant community into which the New Irish migrated was complicated by the second significant difference: the legal status of the new immigrants. As undocumented aliens most of the New Irish were wary of anyone who was not a member of their immediate peer group. They lived outside the mainstream and felt they could not be completely honest with anyone for fear of revealing their status. As such, the 1980s Irish immigrant experience was unlike that of any previous generation of Irish immigration to New York or anywhere else in the United States.

In Ireland, the Church continued its course of intervention, but there the outreach evolved to counseling prospective emigrants who were in the midst of making the decision to leave the country. The Emigrant Advice (EA) office in Dublin provided clients with facts about life in the United States, including how much money to bring, the availability of jobs, the legal bureaucracies they might encounter, maps of the city, and newspapers. A visitor to the EA office in the fall of 1994 saw bulletin boards posted with the business cards of American lawyers, accountants, and employment agencies; announcements for a meeting of returned émigrés to discuss readjusting to life in Ireland; racks of pamphlets on emigrating to Australia, New Zealand, Germany, and the United States; and a listing of the Irish Chaplaincy Offices in London, Munich, Paris, and New York. EA's objective was to present as realistic a picture of America as possible. In its 1989 annual report, the EA staff demonstrated its awareness of the migrant population and the problems it faced abroad, living independently for the first time in their lives. (Most of the clients who sought help from the center were between 18 and 25 years old.[114])

> Emigration for many young people in particular, means leaving home for the first time. The type of skills most required when leaving home or emigrating are not the academic kind. What is essential is that people have the "coping skills" which will enable them to make a successful transition from living at home in Ireland to living alone in another country. This means possessing the qualities/skills of confidence, communication, assertiveness, independence, budgeting, home management—cooking, laundry, etc.

On both sides of the Atlantic, the Church focused—officially anyway—on the unhealthy, potentially disastrous social and emotional dynamic created by the isolation of a community of young people, left to their own devices in a new city in a strange country and forced to live outside the mainstream of society. Instead of focusing strictly on religious salvation, the Church functioned as social worker, intervening with counseling, referral advice, and, in some cases, direct medical assistance (automatic care and service at the archdiocese's Catholic hospitals).

On February 25, 1989, a conference sponsored by the National Conference of Catholic Bishops Committee on Migration and the United States Catholic Conference Office of Migration and Refugee Services was held at Boston College in Chestnut Hill, Massachusetts. A few of the speakers attending the session identified the Church position on its responsibility to the New Irish. Two in particular, a nun from Boston and one of the Irish chaplains working in the Bronx, made it clear that the day-to-day duties of those working directly with the New Irish were survival and assimilation support. These representatives of the Church helped the New Irish find jobs, medical assistance, immigration attorneys, and housing.[115] They also recognized the dangers inherent in a group of alienated young people living on their own for the first time in a new city. But in offering help they recognized the contemporary attitudes of the New Irish to the clergy:

> Their attitude toward the priest . . . varies. On the one hand, those who would put him on a pedestal think he has the cure for all ills—think he can cure cattle, can cure people, and solve almost any problem. On the other are those who see him as the root of all evils in Ireland.[116]

The chairman of the American Bishops' Committee on Migration, Archbishop Theodore McCarrick of Newark, spoke to the session as well. His remarks were more spiritual, claiming that the Church's responsibility to the migrants was to find the "pastoral solutions" to their problems. Archbishop McCarrick advocated that "the teachings of the Church and the proclamation of the Gospel . . . be witnessed by nations everywhere" through the work of the Church among the migrant community.[117]

While clearly acting as representatives of the Catholic Church and driven by the moral and social doctrines of charity and faith that the Church espouses, the speakers made it clear that the Church's response to the New Irish was not just an effort to save their souls. Its on-the-ground action was one of social service to meet the immediate physical, medical, and psychological/emotional needs of the community, all the while keeping them within the "embrace" of the Church, if not actually creating daily communicants.

A flyer announcing the services offered by Project Irish Outreach presents a good example of the priorities set by the organization. It is a fairly innocuous-looking document with few hints that the project was a Catholic organization. No crosses or religious symbols adorned the page. The only clues were the address, which was that of Catholic Charities, and the religious titles of the executive director (Monsignor James Murray) and the chaplains. Otherwise the flyer provided an "A to Z" listing of its services, from legal advice to employment and education counseling, visa requirements, and housing and driver license questions. Another flyer, demonstrating the evolution of services and the progression of the community, boasted an illustration of the Statue of Liberty and announced information about applying for United States citizenship. On this document a simple outline of a cross bracketed the Catholic Charities signature on the bottom of the page.

Project Irish Outreach remained active through the 1990s and into 2000, even after the majority of immigrants had presumably applied for, received, or remained eligible for nonimmigrant or immigrant visas and were no longer troubled primarily by their legal status. The need for an agency remained, according to director Patricia O'Callaghan and counselor Paula O'Sullivan, because emigrants still needed assistance adjusting to a new culture and were particularly vulnerable in

New York, whose environment was perceived to be challenging and hostile. Young mothers in particular worried about raising their children in the city.[118] Ironically, according to officials of Project Irish Outreach and the Irish consulate, some of those emigrants who received visas and exercised the freedom to enter the United States and find work legally were less prepared than some of the illegal aliens who emigrated in the early and mid-1980s. The first waves of emigrants wanted to go to New York, and many were aware of the hazards of being illegal after the passage of IRCA. However, many of the Donnelly and Morrison visa recipients had applied for the documents because it was the thing to do at the time, and they were not completely committed to or prepared for the transition from Ireland to New York.

Some of the biggest adjustment problems were among young mothers, who, as R. H. observed, found life alone with small children in a strange city with no ex-tended family lonely and intimidating. The Bronx Young Irish Center, also known as Tir na n'Og ("land of the young" in Irish), was established by Project Irish Out-reach and opened in May 1991;[119] it ran four mother-toddler groups a week in 1992. At the same time, the Brooklyn-Queens center, operated by the Brooklyn diocese, also sponsored women-and-toddler group sessions on Tuesdays. Sister Bridgh, who ran the outreach programs there, concurred with the other professionals that cul-tural adjustments and loneliness were the biggest problems for young women with no extended family.[120]

In addition to the parenting groups, both organizations sponsored social and sporting events, educational and language classes, counseling, and, in the Brooklyn-Queens center, VCR-TV nights on Wednesday and Friday.[121] In 1989 (three years after the passage of IRCA and the Donnelly visa program) Project Irish Outreach responded to the changing status of the population with eight career seminars, co-sponsored by the Irish Business Organization, that included sessions on traditional "immigrant employment" like construction, hospitality, and self-employment, as well as professional fields such as accounting, health care, banking and finance, and advertising and public relations.[122]

As the outreach programs in the dioceses progressed, both the agencies and the events and counseling they offered continued to project an image that empha-sized social work. The fact that they were Catholic agencies was only very subtly suggested. The signature on the bottom of the ad for the career seminars identified Project Irish Outreach as part of Catholic Charities, offering "counseling to [the] newly arrived Irish immigrant on immigration, health, maternity, pastoral and so-cial matters." Maternity support included shelters for unwed mothers, a reminder of the church's pro-life position. And, according to the Outreach staff, a folk music mass was offered at St. Brendan's in the Bronx. The folk group that played was connected with Tir na n'Og and attendance at the folk mass was not forced, but the feeling was that the mass would help to "ground" those who did go.[123]

Another example of the not-too-distant presence of the Church in its out-reach to immigrants was the formation of an immigrant group to help the home-less. The group was founded by Catherine Sheehan and Monica Comiskey, two New Irish who were inspired by Tomás Cardinal O'Fiaich of Ireland, who spoke at

St. Brendan's in 1990. "His message was strong, direct and simple: The Irish should not think of New York as just a place of employment and income; they should try their best to give something back. 'The sermon really struck home with me,' says Monica. 'Many of us wanted to contribute to the city that has given us jobs,' adds Catherine."[124] Working through St. Brendan's and Tir na n'Og, the group traveled throughout the city one night a week delivering food, soup, and coffee to the homeless.

In the 1980s the Church in New York recognized an immigrant population in crisis and stepped in to fill the vacuum created by the absence of the extended family, social, and parish networks that supported and guided the Irish immigrants of the 1950s and 1960s. Functioning as a social service agency, it chose to target the temporal needs of that community as a priority, downplaying the religious and spiritual health of the population until it was secure and stable.

The proactive stance of the Church to meet the needs of the Irish reflected the still very strong presence of the Irish among the leadership of the Catholic Church in New York. Monsignor Murray, who piloted the plan to bring missionaries to New York, is the son of Irish immigrants; he said that his efforts on behalf of the New Irish were in part a "payback" to the Irish for what they have contributed to the country.[125] The late Cardinal O'Connor, who gave final approval to the outreach program, was himself a proud Irish American who was identified by the *Irish Echo* as an "O'Connor from Castlereagh in Co. Roscommon."[126]

In the 1980s, New York City was a city filled with immigrants, many of whom were Catholic. The demographics were such that the Brooklyn diocese demanded that before ordination its seminarians learn at least one other language from among the scores of languages spoken in the city. Yet the Project Irish Outreach program was unique. The strength and maintenance of the program can be traced to the ethnic heritage of the leadership of the Church, its ties to Church leadership in Ireland, and its ability to extract financial, personnel, and moral support from the Church and government in Ireland.[127]

The Church response to the New Irish in the 1980s also represented the evolution in the relationship between the institution of the Church, its representatives, and the lay community. In the 1950s the Church on both sides of the Atlantic enjoyed tremendous power. In Ireland the bishops controlled religious life and had a very prominent role in the public and political activity of the country. Ireland had very rigid moral and social standards that were dictated by Catholic theology.

The Church in New York was also quite powerful, but Catholicism was not the dominant social or moral voice in the country. Within the Catholic population, though, the religious practice of pre–Vatican II days demanded strict adherence to very specific standards of behavior and tradition. But in the still vital ethnic communities into which the Irish settled, the commonality, comfort, and ritual of the religion was a common bond. The Archdiocese of New York enjoyed a boom in building and population among its primary and secondary schools, as well as its city colleges. Vocations were still strong, so the Church had ample personnel to staff its schools and hospitals and parishes. Pre–Vatican II standards aside, parish vitality was in some ways reflective of the first- and second-generation immigrant population of the Irish community. The Irish neighborhoods were dominated by immigrants from the twenties and thirties whose religion was still important to them, and the Irish represented a significant proportion of the religious community of New York, which created a bond and pride that was undeniable.

By 1980, loss of vocations, Vatican II, the closing of Catholic schools, and the aging of the ethnic communities had seriously weakened the Irish Catholic communities and traditions of New York City. In Ireland changes in the Church and in the country's government and economy evolved into a less than healthy Catholicism. A disproportionately youthful population left secondary school with dim prospects for the future and very little faith in the Catholic Church. Clerical scandal and the refusal of the Church and the Irish government to change their positions on divorce and birth control created a social environment that some in the population found intolerable. The social intolerance, coupled with poor economic prospects, drove thousands of young Irish to New York, with no families and little in common with the ethnic communities into which they migrated. To its credit the Church chose to address the problems in the immigrant community symptomatically, attacking the most obvious needs first and letting the immigrants dictate the demand. The approach seemed less dogmatic and more pragmatic than the pastoral techniques of the Legion of Mary and the pre-departure agencies in Ireland of the 1950s. It had evolved over fifty years to the point in the 1980s and 1990s where the mental, financial, and employment status of the immigrants took precedence over their spiritual state as they prepared for departure abroad.

While the relationship changed, the Church remained involved in the lives and welfare of its baptized on both sides of the Atlantic. That relationship and the response to emigration from leadership in both countries are instructive and offer another dimension to the differences between the emigrant population headed to the United States in the 1940s and 1950s and the New Irish of the 1980s and 1990s. In the 1940s and 1950s the Church recognized the need to protect its people from the distractions and temptations of the New World, but relied on the strength of the Irish community in America to preserve its faith and maintain religious practice. In the 1980s and 1990s the faith of the New Irish seemed to be in jeopardy before emigration. By all accounts the Church was more stable in the United States than in Ireland, despite widespread disagreement among Americans with the Church's position on women, birth control, and other lifestyle issues.

The evolving position of the Church in Irish society helped determine how the Irish of the 1980s and 1990s defined themselves. An institution so indelibly tied to the country and its identity is not likely to fall, but it is undergoing an obvious period of transition. Symbolically, the change can be traced back to the 1970s when the special place of the Catholic Church was written out of the constitution and the government focused greater energy on the economy than on the culture of Ireland. Twenty years later the shift became apparent when the generation raised in the 1970s came of age and to power in the country. Signs of the new relationship between the Irish and their Church range from the ministry of missionaries in New

York and other major cities to the confrontation between the Irish Lesbian and Gay Organization and the Ancient Order of Hibernians. In Ireland and in America, the lay community in the Catholic Church of the 1980s and 1990s was less passive than the faithful of the 1940s and 1950s. Vatican II, improved education, socioeconomic progress, and the loss of religious vocations created a congregation that was more selective, more demanding, and less likely to defer to clerical authority. Given the historic connection between the Irish and Catholicism, the evolving dynamic between the two has significance not only for what it means to be Irish, but also for what it means to be Irish American.

6

Who Are the Irish?

Irish Americans are no more Irish than black Americans are
Africans.
        —Bob Geldof, musician, quoted in *Irish Echo*, 1987[1]

What defines the Irish? What is an Irish American? What is the difference between
the two? Since the nineteenth century, any given generation of the community in
New York included immigrants as well as first-, second-, and third-generation Irish
and Irish Americans. And within that population were immigrants who had left
the homeland at different points in Ireland's development and for vastly different
reasons.

Examples of the layers within the ethnic population exist throughout history
and have been recognized by novelists and historians alike. Peter Quinn made it
quite clear in *Banished Children of Eve* that the American-born children of Irish
immigrants considered themselves separate from their Irish-born peers. The two
groups fought each other for control of the neighborhood streets of Civil War New
York.[2] Eric Foner made distinctions in class and motivation for the immigrant and
American ethnic support that the United States Irish community gave to the Fenians and home rule in the 1870s and 1880s.[3] And writing about the early twentieth
century, Marion Casey observed that the image of what was Irish in America was
so far removed from what Irish-born Irish understood that by the 1920s Irish "culture" in the United States existed on two levels: a popular culture driven by stereotypes formed over several generations of immigration, and a subculture fed by a
Gaelic nationalism originating in Ireland and invigorated by the immigrant refugees of the Irish Civil War.

What is fascinating to the observer of these different communities is that
often to the outside world the "Irish" community appeared to be homogeneous.
And at any given moment in time the general population had a specific, singular

image of the Irish that did not reflect the diversity within the ethnic population. The conflicts within the Irish community typically occurred between new immigrants and the Irish establishment into which they entered. In the case of the post–World War II migrants to New York, this kind of misconception involved the Irish American community led by migrants of the 1950s and their reception of the New Irish in the 1980s. By 1980 the ethnic community in New York was composed primarily of immigrant and first- and second-generation Americans whose image of Ireland was shaped in the years before 1960. The urban, educated, and arguably arrogant Irish youth who entered the United States in the 1980s clashed with the older generation's image of the Irish. In the forty years following the first post–World War II wave of immigration to America, Ireland had changed radically, producing a different citizen and therefore a different migrant than the American Irish could recognize as one of their own. The older migrants' years spent in America and the romance of memory ran parallel with very real changes in the society, economy, and culture of Ireland, producing two very different populations whose only commonality was an ethnic heritage and the migration experience.

Historically Irish identity has been linked to language, nationalism, and Catholicism in Ireland[4] and to nationalism, Catholicism, and, for a time, the Democratic Party in the United States. In recent years historians have grappled with the evolution of Irish and Irish American identity in the wake of Irish political and economic independence, its membership in the European Union (EU, formerly known as the European Economic Community or EEC), Vatican II, and scandal and popular disaffection with the Church in Ireland, as well as the American diaspora to the suburbs and the dilution of ethnic community as urban parishes dispersed throughout the metropolitan area.[5] If, for example, the Church and parish life were the centerpiece of Irish identity and Irish social and cultural life in Ireland and America, what happens to the community and its collective identity if the Church is no longer the center of Irish life? Some American social historians in the 1970s claimed that the Irish were dying as an ethnic group. But advocacy groups working among older Irish immigrants and Irish Americans in the seventies argued that the Irish community was very much alive, if overlooked, in the city: "Despite the popular mistaken assumption that Irish ethnicity has ended, the ancient 'Clan Na Gael' never dies: It may rest, but it still is a basic component of the character and tradition of the Irish-American, regardless of when his people crossed the Atlantic."[6]

In Ireland, observers debated the core of Ireland's soul in the late twentieth century. In the first decades of independence, attempts at de-Anglicization and cultural preservation proved claustrophobic and stagnating. But the economic development program initiated in the early sixties opened the society to accusations of materialism. What had the Irish lost by entering international society? The weakness of the language revival and the decline in clerical authority gave the nation nothing with which to define and sharpen its identity.[7] In the postwar world the Republic of Ireland was an independent country, no longer battling with England for autonomy. "Nationalism [was] the posture provoked by imperialism."[8] What was Ireland as a "free republic"?

The shape of Ireland in the future, remains unpredictable, largely because "the people who run our affairs have taken their ideas from the bankrupt stock of our large neighbours in Europe and America."[9]

When you come right down to it, there is almost no civic sense at all; that concept is too wide for people's life experience . . . they have little sense of a nation, and none of a polis.[10]

Ireland is a nation caught in the middle of an identity crisis . . . [it has to find] a way to cast off the protective skin of nationalism and still say "we are Irish."[11]

This chapter examines the social and cultural behavior of the two major migrant groups and the ethnic community in general in the post–World War II period. It will consider how the social and cultural life of the Irish in New York in the second half of the twentieth century related to life in Ireland. In order to understand how they saw themselves, what shaped that image, and how they reacted to each other, both migrant populations are observed in terms of how they responded to their new environment, the organizations they formed, the music they enjoyed, the recreation they pursued, and their contributions to American society. When the activities Irish Americans pursued and their perception of Irish culture and ethnicity are examined, the dynamic within the community becomes even more complex. It also becomes apparent that what is Irish in Ireland is not necessarily Irish in America.

County Organizations

In comparing the two migrant populations of the postwar period, it is revealing to look at the types of organizations they created and joined. In the 1940s and 1950s the county organizations in New York City were very active social and networking clubs. Membership depended on the county of birth in Ireland. The organizations held regular meetings, sponsored dances, and organized commemorative masses and communion breakfasts on a regular basis throughout the city.[12] Many of the meetings were held at the Irish Institute, founded by Paul O'Dwyer in the early 1950s and located at 326 West 48th Street between 8th and 9th Avenues. The United Irish Counties Organization,[13] as well as several of the other county organizations, held their meetings there. One immigrant said that the gatherings were good opportunities for new migrants to meet local people from Ireland and establish friendships and networks that eased the transition to life in New York.[14] "We were just more comfortable being with our own kind,"[15] said another woman who joined soon after immigrating in 1949.

By the late 1960s and 1970s membership in the organizations dwindled as the Irish aged, families moved out to the suburbs, and immigration slowed. According to a report of the United Irish Counties Community Action Bureau, the 1970 census cited the median age of the Irish in New York City to be 61.8 years.[16] In 1995 an immigrant admitted that he and a companion looked around a recent county meeting and wondered where the club would be in ten years. All the attendees were older, and no prospects existed for younger, newer members.[17] Another immigrant, an officer in the Donegal Association, said that the group was looking for ways "to keep [the association] alive for the next generation." According to her, the younger members that the Donegal Association had attracted were Irish Americans who attended major social events, but often did not make the monthly meetings on a regular basis.[18]

Immigrants from the 1940s and 1950s tell stories of securing jobs because they came from the same county as the union leader or crew boss. Donegal men were known to be sand hogs, for example: the laborers who dug the Lincoln Tunnel. The immigrant from Donegal remembered her aunt sending her out to look for a job at Acme Fast Freight on Lafayette Street in lower Manhattan. She was told to go see the personnel director, who was also a "Donegal man," and who gave her a job.[19] The following classified, found in the "News from Boston" section of a 1957 edition of the *Echo*, demonstrates the selectivity of one Tyrone landlord: "Two Rooms for Rent—four quiet business girls, sisters or friends . . . Tyrone girls preferred."[20]

For whatever reason, the New Irish did not join the county organizations. In the survey conducted among the New Irish, only 13 percent of respondents attended "Irish or county organizations."[21] Whether they did not have any kinship with the older members of the groups or whether they did not feel the need to network or build roots with the American Irish, the New Irish avoided the county associations.

Outside the New Irish "ghettoes" of Woodside and the Bronx, Shane Doyle, owner of Sin é Cafe on the Lower East Side of Manhattan, made it clear that some of the New Irish were deliberately choosing to avoid the "safe haven" of the outer-borough Irish communities. They did not want to "tap into the fears" of the New Irish and felt the ethnic neighborhoods they favored were too restricted and inhibited about life in the city.[22] Yet Doyle and his friends were not likely to join the county groups either.

Fraternal, Ethnic, and Cultural Societies

The Irish also formed ethnic and fraternal organizations based on labor and professional alliances, such as the civil service Emerald Societies, the American Irish Teachers Association, and the Brehon Society (lawyers). These groups were not exclusive to immigrants. In fact most members were probably second-, third-, or fourth-generation Irish. As described by Tim Meagher and G. Q. of the Irish American Business Coalition, these were groups patronized by ethnics who not only liked to socialize or network with career peers, but who were trying to make some connection with their past.

On March 15, 1958, the *Echo* announced the first police officer elected to the Grand Council of Irish Societies, which encompassed all the Emerald Societies and ethnic organizations in federal, state, and city civil services. The new president, Sergeant William J. McGowan, presided over 65,000 members.[23] The size of the body illustrates not only the popularity of the ethnic societies, but the popularity of civil service occupations among the Irish.

Despite the historically high numbers of Irish in the police force, the Emerald Society of the police department was not established until 1953, when some officers decided it was time to advocate for the rights of the Irish in the police department. The society remained active through the 1990s, reaching an all-time membership high of 6,000 in 1995.[24] A detective, responding to surprise that the Irish needed a voice in the police force in New York, explained that in the early fifties, other ethnics formed societies to advocate on their behalf, including the Italians and African Americans, so the Irish organized as well.[25] Thirty years later, the society was still seeking what they considered to be fairness for its members. In a statement published in the winter 1986 newsletter of the Emerald Society *Newsletter*, Officer John McCann, Emerald Society representative to the Coalition for Merit in the Civil Service, spoke before the New York State Assembly Subcommittee on Human Rights, complaining about the discrimination inherent in the "Quota System":

> The most severe [impact] is the discrimination being done by denying promotion to our members because of their Heritage. I bring to your attention that we have been discriminated previously, prior to the Quotas, in the United States. This just sets us back temporarily in our drive to attain Equal Rights under the Law. . . . I hope the City and the Law-makers would see the sense in returning to the Merit System, which was enacted to prevent patronage and special favors and ensuring city residents of being served by the best qualified.[26]

In addition to advocating equity, the Emerald Society in the 1980s and 1990s continued to host communion breakfasts, sponsored a band that marched annually in the St. Patrick's Day Parade, offered high school and college scholarships to the children of its members, and organized membership dances, golf tournaments, and trips.[27]

A common feature of many of these ethnic organizations, including the Emerald Societies, was Catholicism. The 1987 newsletter inviting Emerald Society members to march in the St. Patrick's Day Parade asked the officers to join "in honor of our Patron Saint."[28] Anniversary masses for past members were common events, and many of the associations had a chaplain.[29] To belong to the Ancient Order of Hibernians one had to be Catholic.

"The Cathedral Club of Brooklyn [was] a Catholic lay organization founded in the diocese of Brooklyn, on March 1, 1900 . . . 'to advance Catholic interests, to promote the moral improvement of its members, to foster among them a true Catholic spirit, and by frequent social intercourse to unite them more closely in the pursuance of these ends.' "[30] The club membership was predominately Irish. In the 1950s, principal speakers at the club's annual dinner included Senator John F. Kennedy, Senator Michael Mansfield, Congressman John W. McCormack, and Senator Eugene McCarthy. In 1995 the guest of honor was William J. Flynn, chairman of Mutual of America and an active participant in Northern Ireland peace negotiations during the 1990s. The officers who welcomed Mr. Flynn were Eleanor Breslin,

Sharon Miggins, Betty Anne McConough, Michael Carr, and John P. Sullivan,[31] the majority of whom were Irish Americans.

In the immediate postwar period the feat of proving loyalty to both Irish and American ideals was focused for many Catholic Irish on support of Senator Joseph McCarthy and his position on Communism. The *Tablet*[32] (Brooklyn diocesan paper) and Francis Cardinal Spellman were both decidedly anti-Communist and pro-McCarthy. But they were not alone. In a 1954 *Echo* column, Harry Rapp proposed a write-in campaign for McCarthy, calling him the "most important Red hunter in the country," and argued that "we want 100% Americans who consider this country first."[33]

At St. Nicholas of Tollantine parish in the Bronx, the Catholic Action Committee was formed in the 1930s and remained active through the 1950s. It evolved in response to an anti-Communist speech delivered at a communion breakfast. The group supported fundraisers, toy drives, classes on parliamentary procedures, and speakers, all working toward the ultimate goal of thwarting Communism.[34]

According to one observer of the period, "the issue of communism was at once religious and political." American Catholics were tired of "having their true patriotism and true Americanism" challenged. Supporting McCarthy was a chance "to show they were both 100% Catholic and 100% American and patriotic."[35] The sentiments echoed earlier demonstrations of patriotism among the Irish Catholic community and the Church hierarchy. In the years leading up to American involvement in World War I, the Church urged its parishioners to follow the lead of American neutrality and not support any of the European Catholic powers. Leaders feared accusations of anti-American sentiment against ethnic Catholics.[36]

Some Catholic voices did criticize the anti-Red campaign. But even as Auxiliary Bishop Bernard J. Sheil of Chicago spoke out against McCarthy, the Wisconsin senator addressed 6,000 police at a communion breakfast.

The tie between religion and patriotism suggested that Catholics, many of whom were immigrants or just one or two generations away from migration, still felt insecure in the Protestant-dominated society of America.

It must be remembered that a Catholic still had not been elected president, and that during his campaign for the White House, Senator John F. Kennedy had to deflect speculation that his first allegiance was to Rome. Just weeks before the election, Dr. Norman Vincent Peale, a leading Protestant minister, expressed strong anti-Catholic prejudice. He stated that Kennedy's possible election was a "threat" to American culture. "I don't say [American culture] won't survive [Kennedy's election], but it won't be what it was."[37]

In addition to religion, the Irish rallied around their history and culture for solidarity and to celebrate what the Irish brought to America. They formed groups such as Irish language societies, the New York Irish History Roundtable, the Irish Institute, and the American Irish Historical Society (AIHS). The AIHS was actually created in Boston near the turn of the century and moved to New York in its early years. It was created to help the evolving Irish middle class establish a proud past for the Irish so that the economic security and success they had achieved could be matched by acceptance in American society, which was neither ethnic nor Catholic. Part of the early AIHS strategy to bolster Irish history and identity was to prove its loyalty to America and its ideals.[38]

Marion Casey has also written about the desire of the founders of the feis in the 1930s to perpetuate the culture of the Irish, preserve their ethnicity, and at the same time demonstrate their loyalty and patriotism to America. She argues that through the 1930s the focus in Irish American culture shifted from a nationalist one—what Irish Americans could do for Ireland—to what immigrants could bring to the United States. As an example, she quotes from the official program of the United Irish Counties Association 1941 feis:

> You must be the apostles of Irish culture who will carry these facts to your friends and to your associates. The task is a great one, but is lightened by the knowledge that wherever Irishmen have gone, they have brought with them a culture that has developed and enriched that of their adopted homeland. For they bring the ideals of Eire—faith in God, love of mankind, and unswerving patriotism.[39]

While the leaders of the feis in the 1930s tried to emphasize what the Irish could contribute to the United States, the leaders and advocates for the New Irish talked about past achievements of the Irish and the "rights" of the New Irish to partake of the American Dream. They presented the New Irish as victims twice violated, by the failure of Irish economic policy and by American immigration policy.[40] To fifties migrants, who did not enjoy the benefits of Irish economic reform, universal education, and socialized medicine, the complaints and hardships of the New Irish fell on deaf ears. They could not understand why the New Irish were not satisfied with what was offered to them.

The contributions presented by the leaders of the 1933 feis were carried again to America in the postwar period. Traditional Irish culture in New York enjoyed highs and lows in the following fifty years. Music, sports, step dancing, and language survived in New York (and across the United States) with the attention of immigrants and Irish Americans alike.

That Ireland's native tongue was spoken in America was nothing new. Kerby Miller estimated that one-third to one-quarter of the famine emigrants of the mid-nineteenth century spoke Gaelic as their primary or only language.[41] By the 1920s and 1930s Irish speakers who came to America perpetuated the language as part of a political and cultural ideal to preserve and legitimize the "Irish Ireland" that the newly independent government sought to establish.[42] By the 1940s and 1950s the ideals of Irish Ireland were still current among segments of the immigrant population. Immigrant testimony and ads in the *Echo* suggest that the Irish language in New York was still present in the home and in Gaelic societies and clubs.[43] But as Marion Casey observed in her treatment of post–Irish Civil War culture in Irish New York, it is difficult to measure how pervasive the language was among the general immigrant and Irish American population in New York.[44]

An active Irish speaker in the 1940s and 1950s, J. H. recalled that the "three very active branches of the Gaelic League [consisted] predominantly of Irish Americans with the solid backing of a hard core of Irishborn, many of whom were Irish speakers, if not native speakers." The league was formed to promote Irish language, dance, music, and art. (The Emerald Music Society ran an ad in 1949 seeking new members from among the recent arrivals from Ireland to join a "benevolent" society to aid the needy professional musicians who had played Irish music all their lives and were faced with emergencies.[45]) However, H. and his league comrades were disappointed that the resumption of immigration in the post–World War II period did not bolster membership in the league. "The majority of young Irish favored the dance halls that had a mix of Irish Ballroom, a mad version of the Siege of Ennis and modern dancing." He called the Gaelic movement in the New York area a "largely unrecognized force in those years."[46]

Music and Dance

While it is difficult to know exactly how many Irish were "culturally active" in New York, among the immigrant and second-generation Irish of the forties and fifties interviewed for this book, many had not studied Irish step dancing or language as children growing up in New York, nor did they all attend the feis. As parents not all provided formal Irish cultural training for their children either.[47] Yet other observers and members of the community note that "seisuns" (spontaneous, informal gatherings of Irish music and dance) of Irish music and dance were held in homes around the city in the forties and fifties.[48] Perhaps the lack of participation among some migrants reflected their dissatisfaction with the Irish Ireland campaign of postwar Ireland, negative associations with cultural nationalism, and dissatisfaction with De Valera's economy of "frugal comfort." Observers have noted that some Irish may have wanted to get past the peasant traditions of Ireland in the New World, others may have been too busy or too poor to provide lessons, and still others may just have wanted their children to be American in America.[49]

Forty years later traditional dancing was still practiced in New York, and in fact enjoyed a renaissance in the 1980s and 1990s, as did the Irish language. The Irish Art Center offered dance and language classes, New York University's Ireland House featured readings in Irish throughout the academic school year, Irish language classes could be found in adult school programs in suburbs across the metropolitan area, and step dancing competition for children thrived.[50] Again, the depth of participation cannot be determined, but the fact that programs existed proved that artists and speakers were at work to keep the art forms alive, and that they could attract an audience.

In the 1960s and 1970s Irish traditional music enjoyed great popularity as the great hall dances and big bands of the 1940s and 1950s disappeared and music moved into the snugger quarters of the pubs and small bars of Dublin, London, Liverpool, and Greenwich Village, New York. Balladeers and folksingers enjoyed great popularity. Groups such as the Clancy Brothers, the Chieftains, the Bothy Band, De Danaan, and Planxty gained international fame with traditional folk songs.[51]

As has been evidenced over time, the practice of Irish art and culture in the United States is subject to local adaptation. Traditional ceili and step dancing, as well as music, often changed when it traveled outside Ireland. A New York dance teacher who learned the ceili in the 1970s "with the revival of the Irish folk arts" found that the dance "differed sharply" from what he remembered his migrant parents performing at New York City house parties in the 1950s.[52]

Eileen Ivers discusses the evolution of Irish music in America in the documentary *From Shore to Shore: Irish Traditional Music in New York City.* She admits that other kinds of music influence her Irish fiddle sounds. But she defends this as a natural growth of the traditional music, in some ways proving the strength and durability of the original.[53] The adoption of Irish dance and music in America is nothing new. Irish musicians and observers note that "along the majestic Appalachian Mountain range, many fiddle tunes, songs and stories remain to the present day practically unchanged from the day they left their native Irish shores, several from as far back as the mid-1700s." Some of the original art survives more intact than others depending on its contact with other cultural influences. The steps and format of American square dancing trace their roots back to Irish and Scottish reels brought by eighteenth- and nineteenth-century settlers to the mid-Atlantic states.[54]

In November 1994, a single dance piece created to fill the intermission at a competition in Ireland debuted in London and then in Dublin in January 1995 to critical and popular acclaim. The program, called *Riverdance,* opened at Radio City Music Hall in New York City in March 1996. The original dance and the show were choreographed by Michael Flatley, an Irish American from Chicago whose mother and grandmother were champion dancers in Ireland, and was performed by Flatley and Jean Butler, an Irish American woman from Long Island. Flatley's style has been identified as progressive, with more hand touching than traditional Irish dancing, but the attention and publicity surrounding *Riverdance* raised interest in the art form "even as the 'tradition' is more and more refined."[55] The success of *Riverdance* and the exposure it provided Irish culture was made all the more intriguing by its Irish American origins. According to Flatley the Irish sometimes "dismiss[ed] Irish Americans who became imbued in Irish music or dance—a feeling that the native Irish were the only ones who could carry on the centuries old traditions."[56]

Sociologist Mary Corcoran noted that the music favored by the New Irish as well as the bands emerging from Ireland and the immigrant community were contemporary rock-and-roll bands that were quite American in spirit, but also incorporated modern Irish lyrical themes and traditional Gaelic sounds and rhythms.[57] The work of U2, the "Bronx pub band"[58] called Black 47, Sinead O'Connor, Bob Geldof, and the Boom Town Rats were decidedly in the contemporary pop and rock-and-roll category, making them nontraditional in the sense that they appealed to a wide international youth culture. However, songs such as U2's "Sunday, Bloody Sunday" and the name "Black 47," which refers to the potato famine, identify the musicians as Irish. Lyrically, some of the songs betrayed Ireland's historic links with America, as well as young Ireland's critical view of American political policy.

U2's album *Joshua Tree* was a case in point.[59] The American influence is apparent, beginning with the cover photo shot near a Joshua tree in the Mojave Desert in the southwestern United States. A popular video from the CD, "Where the Streets Have No Name," was shot from a rooftop in the streets of Los Angeles. Lyrically two songs offered examples of the American presence in Irish music. "Bullet the Blue Sky" criticized United States military policy in Central America, while "In God's Country" described the American Dream as both sad and seductive.

The music reflected the love/hate relationship that many young Irish had with America. Lured by its size, its opportunity, and its freedom, they were simultaneously repulsed by its arrogance, its aggression, its overt capitalism, its military power, and the fact that they liked it so much.

U2 was clearly not a traditional Irish band. It was a commercial rock-and-roll band that appealed to a broad audience, but it was also representative of the contemporary Irish youth culture which blended Irish themes and sounds with American and European images and trends that were carried into the country by international electronic and print media. In a very broad sense U2 was symbolic of the New Irish relationship with America: very much aware of the historic links between the two countries and energized by what America offered, yet at the same time reluctant to separate from Ireland entirely. Both were influenced by America culturally and depended on the United States and its market economically.[60] Author Roddy Doyle said, "As for the United States, I've seen the films. . . . I've read the books and I've eaten the hamburgers, I love it, I love the place . . . but I honestly can't see myself leaving Ireland."[61]

Black 47 offered a different take on the immigrant experience in New York, one that expressed anger and alienation directed at Ireland, as well as loneliness in New York and the solace found in the bar. In one track, the song's narrator left Ireland for New York, leaving his pregnant girlfriend behind:

So here I am up on Bainbridge Avenue
Still in one piece but glad I'm alive
Drinkin' dirty big glasses of porter
Playin' me jigs and me reels and me slides
Think of you, Bridie, whenever I'm sober
Which isn't too often, I have to confess
Take good care of the Morris Minor
Bad luck to your Da and give the baby a great big kiss from his Daddy in the Bronx.[62]

Ironically the fifties and eighties immigrants were similar in that the music and dance they favored in New York reflected the American pop culture of the period; where they differed was that in the 1980s some of the music originated in Ireland. The contemporary youth culture of Ireland in the 1980s and 1990s was modern and quite progressive, so they did not have to leave Ireland to hear anything fresh or new.

As far as preservation of the traditional, the fifties community seemed to have a more active core of Irish speakers, dancers, and musicians. While the traditional music culture was apparently vigorous in Ireland up through the early eighties, according to one observer, traditional bands into the 1990s "find precious little work in Ireland due to the lack of support from the Irish media who row in behind the more lucrative home markets of rock, pop and country."[63]

Pursuit of traditional culture was not dead in New York during the eighties and nineties. Traditional bands that "flourished" up to the early eighties in Ireland followed the lead of emigrants and toured outside the country. They claimed it possible to "see more familiar faces at any given venue in the [United States] than it was at an Irish venue at home."[64] But alongside the traditional, immigrants pursued their own contemporary style.[65]

Promotion of Irish Culture and History

Immigrants and Irish Americans throughout the postwar period have stepped forward to maintain and perpetuate the culture and tradition of Ireland. Paul O'Dwyer founded the Irish Institute in the early 1950s in order to preserve and encourage Irish culture and heritage in America.[66] The institute owned a building on West 48th Street between 8th and 9th Avenues that became the headquarters for the UICA and many of the county associations. It was available for meetings of the various ethnic groups throughout the city and was notable for the meeting spaces it offered as well as its accessibility by subway from various points around the city. The institute was forced to sell the building in the late 1970s due to lack of use, but dedicated the proceeds of the sale to an endowment that it draws on to contribute to individuals and organizations that share its vision for promoting Irish culture.[67] Among the projects it has supported: the Irish American Cultural Institute, the Irish Immigration Reform Movement, New York University's Ireland House, and *The New York Irish*, a collection of essays initiated by the New York Irish History Roundtable and published in 1996.

The revival of "Irish folk arts" in New York included handicrafts. Rosaleen Fitzgibbon emigrated in 1947. In the 1960s she opened the Irish Pavillion Shop to "represent the best of Irish handcrafts" including batiks, weaving, pottery, and baskets. The shop also appeared at the 1964–1965 World's Fair in Queens. Fitzgibbon eventually shut down the Irish Pavillion Shop because it became too costly and difficult to maintain an inventory from across the Atlantic.[68]

In 1972 a group of political activists with roots in the counterculture of the 1960s created the Irish Arts Center in New York City because they believed that what was left of Irish culture in America was superficial, symbolized by the "St. Patrick's Day Parade and its association with drinking, shamrocks, leprechauns, stage Irishmen and Tin Pan Alley songs." One of the center's leaders declared at the center's opening:

> There are few real Irish people in the United States. They know little about authentic Irish culture and care less. The Irish American is a victim of cultural disintegration, as much so as the Mayan Indian. We have to go back to the beginning, to learn again what it means to be Irish.[69]

The New York Irish History Roundtable was founded in 1985 by immigrant and second-generation Irish scholars and genealogists whose primary goal was to preserve and record the history of the Irish in New York, as well as to focus the energies of those Irish Americans who wish to uncover their personal family histories. The group has a relatively small membership of less than five hundred, but continues to be an active body at the turn of the new century. It publishes an annual journal and newsletters, sponsors regular lectures, and conducts tours of the city. In 1996 it published *The New York Irish*, a collection of essays that reviews the Irish impact on New York politics, culture, and immigration from the colonial period to the present. The majority of the roundtable's members are older immigrants and Irish Americans. Few New Irish joined the organization.

Professional groups such as the American Irish Teachers Association also promoted Irish culture in the period through annual seminars, speakers, and tours of Ireland.[70]

In the 1970s and 1980s scholars, academics, and university curricula reflected a trend toward serious examination of Irish culture, literature, history, and the arts. The American Conference for Irish Studies, the Irish American Cultural Institute, and Irish studies programs such as the one created at Boston College in the late 1970s and New York University's Ireland House in the 1990s introduced Irish Americans, many of them students, to the history, language, music, writing, and drama of Irish and Irish American artists and scholars for the first time. Lawrence McCaffrey argues that as Irish America shrinks in quantity, its intellectual and cultural revival thrives on quality.[71] The resurgence of interest in Irish culture in America corresponded to a national interest in European "roots" exploration in the 1970s. Some observers claimed that renewed strife in Northern Ireland accounted for the ethnic revival in America,[72] but the renaissance also coincided with the emergence of a trend in scholarship that veered away from a "consensus" view of the past which argued that the country shared a common set of values and goals regardless of ethnicity or class.[73]

Much of the new history was written by a generation of academics who were the sons and daughters of the immigrant classes. American scholars of ethnicity focused their social and historical research on the immigrant communities and experiences that shaped American society and urban life in the nineteenth and twentieth centuries. For students, the microstudies and themes offered in history, literature, and sociology courses presented opportunities to understand and appreciate their own family histories. For some older Irish Americans, studying the arts and history of Ireland and Irish America proved a rewarding way to explore their heritage and meet other ethnics with the same interest in their ancestry.[74]

The IIRM and ILGO

In the 1980s two of the more prominent organizations created by the New Irish were the Irish Immigration Reform Movement (IIRM) and the Irish Lesbian and Gay Organization (ILGO). The groups reveal a great deal about the New Irish.

The IIRM was born in frustration over the established community's slow response to the issue of immigration reform. Warned by many to keep quiet and stay out of trouble, the leaders of the IIRM went very public with their demands for visas and with the problems faced by the undocumented community. They faced both the United States government and the Irish government head-on with their agenda and successfully negotiated the institutional and ethnic networks that facilitated their goal of providing visas for all the New Irish who wanted and needed them. What the IIRM symbolized was the confidence of the population, their refusal to be content with the status quo, their knowledge of the American power structure, and the historical relationship between Ireland and the United States and their courage to exploit that relationship. In some ways their youth, confidence, and nerve in changing American immigration legislation reflected the arrogance and entitlement of a generation told they were the best the country had produced. Unlike the fifties migrants, who were active within their community in fraternal clubs and parish events and were happy among their own, the New Irish, arguably by force of circumstances, were not happy to sit back and let their elders take care of things. They confronted the system and risked exposure of their status to secure a legal place in the society.

ILGO represented many of the same qualities of confidence, outspokenness, and frustration with the status quo. They attacked a visible symbol of Catholicism and Irish ethnicity in the United States by protesting the refusal of the Ancient Order of Hibernians to allow them a spot in the St. Patrick's Day Parade. Their objective was not so much to march in the parade as to legitimize and display their lifestyle. They challenged the authority of the Church and the Irish American establishment by disrupting the most prominent symbol of ethnicity in New York. Their protests spotlighted the very real changes in the relationship between the congregation and the clergy in Ireland, as well as the emerging public posture taken by nonconformists in Irish society. The great visibility and media attention granted the parade offered a wonderful opportunity for ILGO to publicly address their desires for recognition, if not acceptance, and to protest the social and religious discrimination suffered by those practicing alternate lifestyles in Ireland.

The IIRM and the ILGO paralleled the more self-directed ambition of the New Irish as well as the more cosmopolitan view they possessed. The fifties migrants were eager for success too. The county associations were vehicles of social and fraternal support as these migrants tried to feel comfortable in the United States by not disrupting the society and by proving their worthiness as Americans. The New Irish were not seeking that kind of acceptance. They were less interested in achieving the American Dream than they were in seeking self-fulfillment, and they were not afraid to buck public opinion. They were not that different from other migrants who could not find a place for their ambition in Ireland, but not all were sure that New York was the only place to satisfy their dreams. Yet while here they demanded to be recognized in their own right and accorded the opportunities granted their predecessors.

The Irish American response to the New Irish provided a noncontroversial issue around which Irish Americans could rally. For many second- and third-generation ethnics, unwillingness to become involved with the politics of the north, Sinn Fein and the IRA, prevented them from joining some Irish American groups.[75] The New Irish demands for immigration reform and the immediate needs of the undocumented population were causes that ethnic Americans could embrace easily and thus obtain a solid, and sometimes personal, link with their Irish heritage. Immigration was an experience they could understand. So for some of the Irish Americans—such as Monsignor James Murray and G. Q., the founder of the Irish American Business Coalition, who participated in the programs and projects that emerged in response to the needs of the undocumented population—their activity was an opportunity to express their support as part of an overall desire to explore and celebrate their heritage.

Sports and Social Recreation

In terms of informal or recreational culture, activity in the postwar period was as vibrant as the prevailing immigrant population. Participation in the Gaelic Athletic Association field games seemed to rise and fall with the population of young immigrant athletes. As the experience of Father Sean Reid, discussed in an earlier chapter, demonstrated, county affiliation had significance for the Irish immigrant in the 1940s and 1950s beyond the county organizations. Just after World War II, Father Reid and a friend, Dick Quinn, formed the Kilkenny Hurling Club, recruiting players from among immigrants and the rosters of other county teams already formed. It was not uncommon for athletes in Ireland to be lured to an American team with the promise of a job.[76] In the early 1980s, when emigration resumed after two decades of decline, talented players were also offered union cards and Social Security numbers to play for certain teams until the general increase in the immigrant population made recruiting unnecessary.[77] (In both decades, these opportunities existed only for men.) By the end of the eighties the bleachers and team rosters at Gaelic Park swelled once more as the number leaving Ireland rose.

According to some New Irish, one of the hardest parts about life in New York was the absence of Irish spectator sports. The young Irish sports fans could not go to a park to watch their favorite professional football game (soccer in America). Reacting to that demand, bar owners in the ethnic neighborhoods installed satellite dishes for their establishments to pick up the playoff and championship games live from Ireland during the sports season. With the time difference, fans assembled in the borough bars early in the morning to watch and cheer. The popularity of Irish sports was evidenced by their coverage both in the *Irish Echo* over the fifty-year period and in the *Irish Voice* in the 1980s and 1990s.

In the 1950s big band dances were the most popular form of entertainment among young immigrants and Irish Americans. While all the county associations sponsored dances at least once a year, City Center Ballroom on 55th Street on the West Side and the Jaeger House on 85th Street and Lexington Avenue on the Upper East Side opened every weekend, and were two of the biggest attractions at the time. The dances featured such bands as Brendan Ward's, which played City Center on Friday, Saturday, and Sunday nights for ten years. Born in County Mayo, Brendan Ward migrated to New York in 1955 to form a dance orchestra for the ballroom, which was owned by Kerryman Bill Fuller. Fuller had owned ballrooms in Dublin and London. As Ward explained, "[Fuller] followed the young crowd to New York."[78] Fuller was married to Carmel Quinn, a featured singer and performer at City Center and other venues throughout the city in the fifties and sixties.

The dances featured big band music made popular during World War II by Glenn Miller, Tommy and Jimmy Dorsey, and Woody Herman. The music was familiar to the Irish, who had listened to the radio broadcasts from the BBC, and, as one historian suggested, represented the modern, contemporary culture and an escape from the poverty and "peasant" culture of Irish Ireland.[79] At City Center, Ward played for forty minutes, then smaller Irish bands would play traditional ceili music and/or Irish waltzes and ballads for twenty minutes, and the music would alternate between the two groups all night.[80] According to immigrant interviews, the ballroom dances drew immigrants and Irish Americans alike. City Center attracted up to two thousand dancers on a Saturday night, some coming from out of state to enjoy the music and the "Irish scene."[81] The ballroom's location made it easily accessible by subway from the Bronx, Queens, and Brooklyn, and according to Rebecca Miller, its midtown, Broadway location lent the spot the glamour of "New York City nightlife and culture."[82] *Irish Echo* editions through the 1950s and into the 1960s displayed prominent ads for City Center in particular, as well as Jaeger House.

By the seventies and eighties the big bands were gone, and although they did not favor the county association meetings or dances, the New Irish were not unlike the fifties migrants in that social and recreational networks were the lifeline to employment and housing in New York. But for the New Irish, particularly those who settled in the Bronx and Queens, their networks focused on the bars and pubs found in those traditionally ethnic neighborhoods.[83] Sixty-five percent of those responding to the New Irish survey spent their leisure time in a bar. While some of the men obtained jobs and friendships through the Gaelic Athletic Association (GAA), most of the New Irish contacted for this study found that the bar was the place where they could find friends and relatives from home, news about immigration reform, and information about jobs and apartments. The popularity of the bar scene was evidenced in the *Irish Voice* by the weekly two-page photo spread of young Irish smiling in their favorite locals throughout the city.

While bars were certainly present in all the Irish neighborhoods of the immediate postwar period—and according to at least one immigrant account, different bars in the neighborhood were designated for different groups within the community, such as working men, older people, or single young men and women—they did not seem to be the singular social outlet that the bar became for the New Irish.[84] According to New Irish surveys, some in the community would have preferred alternatives such as dances or nightclubs, but these did not materialize.[85] As other interviews suggested, parish and church groups did arise, offering socializing and recreational opportunities, including some sports. But for the most part the bar was the primary gathering place for the New Irish, and unlike the dances of the fifties and sixties they were fairly exclusive to the New Irish. No great effort was made in the New Irish community to mix with Irish Americans or anyone outside their own group.

Drinking was apparently a serious problem among the New Irish. Letters to the *Irish Voice,* survey results, and interviews from other community studies expressed concern about alcohol abuse. One woman responding to the survey worried that "the young Irish spend too much time in pubs, drinking their money and congregating with their own."[86]

An ethnographic study of the community in Queens attributed excessive consumption to a newfound freedom among the population. Bar hours were longer, no parents were present to monitor behavior, and because the New Irish often cashed their checks at the bars they felt obligated to spend money there. With "cash in hand" they had the power to buy drinks in an "otherwise powerless existence" outside the New Irish community.[87] It was a curious dynamic created by their status and life away from family social restrictions.[88] It could also be argued that they were seeking refuge in New York from what they considered a hostile environment by virtue of their status.[89] Most likely, though, the New Irish were simply exercising freedom from more personal and parochial bonds, rejecting the social, moral, and cultural restrictions they experienced in Ireland.

Typically young Irish in Ireland lived at home, even if they had a job. They did not live independently, as was common among young adults out of school in New York. Since most New Irish worked "under the table," they paid no taxes, shared living expenses with roommates, ate in the restaurants and homes where they worked, or were live-in nannies with little or no room and board to pay. The lifestyle in America was new to them, and they were experimenting with their freedom.

Just as the fifties migrants "tended to stay amongst themselves," the New Irish were quite clannish. But they removed themselves not only from their American peers, but from the Irish American community as well. The New Irish survey found that 83 percent of the respondents claimed their friends were Irish, while only 21 percent admitted to having Irish American friends. Part of their reticence was their legal status: they feared detection and deportation. But when the survey results were broken down by documented and undocumented respondents, the same number, 83 percent, identified their friends as Irish, while 20 percent of undocumented had Irish American friends, compared to 18 percent of the documented. Frankly, if the INS had chosen to round up the illegal Irish in New York, they could have easily found them by checking the *Irish Voice* for its spread of New Irish, which always identified where they were photographed.

The self-imposed isolation in the 1980s demonstrated an ambivalence toward assimilation and commitment to life in America. Many of the Irish viewed their time in America as temporary, as a lark or as a time to earn money until they returned to Ireland.[90] When asked if they planned to spend the next five years in

New York, 43 percent of the documented and 39 percent of the undocumented Irish responded that they were unsure. Of course that uncertainty could reflect ambivalence about New York, but considered in conjunction with other New Irish behavior and interviews, the eighties migrants were less sure about their future in America than their counterparts of the 1950s had been. It may be that the New Irish did not foresee themselves as Irish Americans. They certainly did not relate to or identify with the existing Irish American community.[91]

The global economy, as well as the communication and transportation technology of the late twentieth century, offered the contemporary migrant more alternatives than those of forty years prior.

> Increasingly, we [the Irish] are no longer the product of the cultural tradition of any one nation in the way that generations who went before us were. More and more of us have lived our lives in more than one place.[92]

For most of the migrants who left Ireland in the 1950s, the initial trip to America was considered a permanent one; families and villages held wakes on the eve of their departure. The immigrants "came to stay."[93] In the 1980s a young man could get a call from America on a Friday night in Cavan and be on a job in New Jersey on Monday. International travel and communication were far more frequent and convenient in the late twentieth century than in the 1940s and 1950s, particularly in Ireland. Despite the strictures of their legal status, the New Irish felt far more freedom and flexibility about emigration than their predecessors, even if they could not always exercise it.

Film, Literature, Drama

The international recognition of Irish rock musicians and singers coincided with the emergence on the world stage of other art forms from modern Ireland, including film, literature, and drama. The new art of Ireland embraced contemporary themes of urban life—alienation, dysfunctional families, substance abuse, etc.—and was quite successful, earning international acclaim and popularity. The images of and from Ireland through these two decades differed from any that had preceded them. They proved that Ireland harbored a vital, creative artistic community, and they revealed the warts of modern Irish society.

Locally, the Irish who were the subject of some of the new art rejected the unflattering portrayals of the population. The characterization of a Dublin housing project family in Roddy Doyle's television drama *Family* met with severe complaint from Irish citizens who claimed not to recognize the characters, the worst of whom was Charlo, an alcoholic and abusive father and husband. But, as a social worker who worked in a similar community observed, they feared negative "stereotyping again," particularly the Charlo character.[94]

The music of U2 and other Irish rock bands, as well as the literature and drama of writers like Roddy Doyle, Neil Jordan, and Patrick McCabe, was the product of an urban, modern, Western twentieth-century sensibility. They represented the awakening of Irish society from the censorship and claustrophobia of an inward-looking, insecure past. They dealt with Irish relationships to the Church, to alcohol, to nationalism, to the United States and emigration, and to the changes in Irish society and family generally. But the freedom of expression exercised by these artists raises real questions about the soul of Irish culture. How does a culture maintain its core in an international environment that influences not only the conception of the art but its distribution as well? Or does that core change with society, technology, and international relations? Could it be that the urban, industrial landscape is a universal canvas that blots out all individual nationalities in a world so closely linked by computers and commerce? Did the opening of the society lead to the corruption of the culture, as "experts" warned in the 1950s? Are the lines among all cultures blurring toward a point when it will be hard to distinguish one from another? While it may not be possible to answer these questions, they need to be considered in terms of the New Irish because of their transience and because they are the first generation of "modern" Ireland.

In New York, the New Irish brought contemporary Irish film and drama with them. Mary Doran led the Irish Film Association that screened modern and historic Irish films monthly at the Anthology Film Archives cinema on the Lower East Side of Manhattan. The effort began in 1992 as an attempt to correct the image of the Irish in America. "Originally, it had as much to do with the image of Irish people that was presented here as anything else," Doran said. "We thought that the images of Irish people in film were often negative, and didn't coincide with those we had of ourselves, so we wanted to bring real Irish films here."[95] The film group also helped to distribute and screen the original productions of New Irish artists.

In addition to film groups, drama and theater groups featuring New Irish writers, actors, and directors staged old and new works, such as John M. Synge's *Playboy of the Western World* and Janet Noble's *Away Alone,* a contemporary piece about the New Irish experience in New York. The Irish Repertory Theater, formed in 1988; the Irish Bronx Theater Company, organized in the early 1990s; and the Irish Arts Center were among the groups actively producing Irish drama in New York.[96]

The popularity of Irish contemporary music, writing, and film in America contributed to the ethnic renaissance that accelerated in the United States with the emigration of New Irish in the early 1980s. The renaissance provoked interest in the Irish American heritage that was fed by a series of scholarly and commercial works, including a historical documentary and book on Irish immigration to America called *Out of Ireland;* a documentary on music, *From Shore to Shore: Irish Traditional Music in New York City;* and the revival of Brian Friel's *Philadelphia Here I Come,* which charts the plight of an immigrant in the late 1950s.

Throughout 1995, the story of Irish immigration received considerable academic, political, and media attention as part of the 150th anniversary commemoration of the first year of the Great Famine in Ireland and the mass migration that followed, including a major academic conference at New York University in May that drew scholars from the United States and Ireland. The attention paid to things Irish no doubt created popular interest in traditional forms of Irish culture throughout the metropolitan area such as step dancing, the Irish language, and Gaelic sports. Just as the ballroom dances of the 1950s switched between swing and reels, the traditional and contemporary coexist at the end of the century.

In the music world in 1995, the traditional Irish band, the Chieftains, which had achieved commercial, critical, and popular success performing Irish music with traditional "Irish" instruments, released *The Long Black Veil,* a CD with twelve selections featuring guest singers drawn from rock-and-roll, pop, and folk backgrounds. The guest list included Sting, Mick Jagger and the Rolling Stones, Sinead O'Connor, Mark Knopfler, Ry Cooder, Irish star Van Morrison, and Welsh pop star Tom Jones. The CD combined the traditional with the contemporary—the instruments included the uilleann pipe, tin whistle, bodhran, harp, and fiddle—and the Irish with the American: Sting sang "Mo Ghile Mear" a cappella and in Irish, and Tom Jones sang the "Tennessee Waltz/Tennessee Mazurka." The CD demonstrates how the traditional can influence the contemporary, particularly the haunting vocal style of Sinead O'Connor and the use of the fiddle in contemporary arrangements. While the Chieftains had been enjoying popular success for decades, the joint venture with pop superstars exposed more mainstream listeners to the sounds of traditional music.[97]

"Traditional" Irish culture in Ireland and America has been influenced and modified in varying degrees by American and international exposure. While the merger of styles and sources disturbed certain purists, the exposure also offered a potentially broader audience for the culture, which could ultimately generate interest and prolong the life of Irish tradition, as Eileen Ivers and Michael Flatley proved.

As a medium that can represent the Irish character and culture of the Irish to America, no other art form is as powerful or pervasive as film. Popular movies produced prior to 1980 and advertising did little to update American images of Ireland. They offered simplistic images of Ireland as a romantic rural idyll untouched by modern society or a dark, violent, suspicious place wracked by sectarian struggles. But up until 1980 most films about Ireland or Irish themes screened for general American audiences were produced by American or British filmmakers. According to John Hill, an Irish film historian, the perspective of these filmmakers probably reflected their respective country's own relationship with Ireland. In other words, because of America's immigrant history U.S. films such as *The Quiet Man* (1952), directed by John Ford, focused nostalgically on the old country, while the English viewed Ireland as dark and dangerous because of its colonial past and nationalist activities. The bleak and claustrophobic *Odd Man Out* (1947), directed by Carol Reed, is a case in point. But Ireland was guilty of projecting ambiguous images as well. Tourist Board television commercials in the 1990s described the country as the "Ancient birthplace of good times," with scenes of uniformed schoolgirls running through lush green fields and old men in caps and wool overcoats grinning into the camera.[98] It was a place to escape reality and the pressures of contemporary life. Even the "sellers" of Ireland, the Industrial Development Authority (IDA), wrestled for decades with how to package their product. IDA executives in 1994 admitted that for offshore executives interested in Ireland they deliberately presented a twofold opportunity: a modern, sophisticated, literate workforce, with an investment-friendly government eager to accommodate international business *and* an urbane lifestyle that featured the Irish countryside along with the charm and wit of the Irish people.[99]

It was not until the 1980s that Irish-made films and American productions supervised by Irish-born artists featuring Irish actors introduced a more realistic, urban Irish Republic that disrupted past stereotypes. The language in Roddy Doyle's *The Commitments* (1991) disturbed some elderly immigrants, who claimed that profanity was not common in the Ireland they remembered. Like Doyle's *Family,* the modern images were hard to accept for many in Ireland and America.

Films dominated by the romantic landscape of the Irish countryside were replaced by films that focused on Irish society's more urban reality. Such films as *The Snapper* (1993) and *My Left Foot* (1989) were set in housing projects or suburban developments and featured families whose mothers were worn and tired from raising large families. They were not as glamorous as Maureen O'Hara and the husbands were certainly not John Wayne. The contrast was striking. Even in fantasy films like *Into the West* (1993), the "Traveler" family characterized depended on government welfare, and the Gypsy father betrayed his past by leaving life on the road for the city. The films not only reflected contemporary Ireland, but presented characters struggling with the changes in modern Irish society.

Irish-made productions focusing on the "troubles" reflected the complexity of the issues facing Northern Ireland and the people who live there. Films such as *In the Name of the Father* (1993), *Some Mother's Son* (1996), and *The Boxer* (1997) suggest that neither side of the conflict is completely guiltless or victimless. They offer a view from inside the controversy in a way that American and British filmmakers cannot.

In 1995 a small vacuum in the Irish American film culture was filled with the introduction of a movie called *The Brothers McMullen* (1995). Written by Ed Burns, an Irish American who also starred in, directed, and produced the film, it is a contemporary account of three Irish American brothers from Long Island.[100] The young men are in their early to late twenties, facing adulthood and romantic commitment after their father dies and their mother returns to Ireland to marry her long-lost love. The film is refreshing because it deals with the Irish American experience in the suburbs. The McMullen brothers are the kids who left Queens for Long Island with their parents in the 1970s. They are the product of the disapora. The film, which won top prize at the Sundance Film Festival in Utah, offers a contemporary alternative to stories about the Westies, IRA conspiracies, and explosions that recent films have exploited.[101]

While it does not avoid stereotypes altogether, particularly the guilt-wracked, Catholic conscience of one brother and madonna-whore gender conceptions, *The Brothers McMullen* offers subtle and familiar, if superficial, symbols of an American Irish Catholic upbringing in the sixties, seventies, and eighties.[102]

Burns admitted to overdoing the stereotype, but claimed to be having "fun" with it.[103] One of the real strengths of the movie from this perspective was that the brothers considered themselves obviously Irish Catholic, but the script did not suggest any overt cultural traditions such as Irish dancing, language, or feis. The only real "Irish" cultural symbol employed was the gift of a claddagh ring by the Ed Burns character to his girlfriend. (The claddagh symbol of a heart between two hands, topped with a crown, glorifies love and friendship. The ring is a traditional Irish wedding band.)

The McMullens were just ordinary Irish Americans dealing with relationships, growing up, and leaving home. While the Irish American characters were not running guns for the Irish Republican Army (IRA), they also were not police officers and they were not priests. But they were recognizable as Irish Americans to any New Yorker who grew up in an ethnic community in the seventies and eighties. More room exists for treatment of the "ordinary" suburban Irish American experience on film.

In late-twentieth-century Ireland and America, filmmakers and writers were moving away from the Irish and Irish American world that incorporated Ireland before 1960 and the American urban ghetto of the mid-twentieth century. "Baby boomers" on both sides of the Atlantic were sharing their reality of Ireland and Irish America as both moved into the twenty-first century.

In the print world, Niall O'Dowd, immigrant publisher of the *Irish Voice*, introduced a monthly magazine called *Irish America* in the 1980s, which celebrates the accomplishments and achievements of the Irish, past and present. Every year O'Dowd publishes two lists (among others) of Irish Americans—one that recognizes the top 100 Irish Americans in the country and another that identifies the top Irish American business people. While both lists create great publicity and advertising opportunities for O'Dowd's publications, they also spotlight successful and talented Irish ethnics. However, the Top 100 list, in particular, focuses quite heavily on politicians, celebrities, and show business figures—Ed Burns made the 1995 list—and could be a more inclusive representation of Irish American achievement. In 1995 *Irish America* did select historian Robert Scally, New York University's Ireland House director, and in 1999 the list included Robert Durkin, principal of Washington Irving High School in Manhattan; John Fahey, president and chief executive officer of the National Geographic Society; Kathy and William Magee, Operation Smile; and Gerald Lynch, president of John Jay College of Criminal Justice in New York City.[104]

Among the prominent politicians featured on O'Dowd's lists were Representative Brian Donnelly of Massachusetts, Ambassador Jean Kennedy Smith, and her brother Senator Edward Kennedy. For more than one hundred years the American Irish have been closely linked with politics, first with urban ward politics and then with national office, from the president to the Speaker of the House. Irish nationalist politics as well have shaped the Irish and Irish American character for centuries.

Politics and Nationalism

Any description of who the Irish are has to include politics, both New York City politics and the politics of the north and south in Ireland. By the early 1950s Irish political power in the city was on the wane. Irish voting numbers had dwindled and their public leaders were forced to negotiate coalitions with the emerging interest groups of the postwar period. The last major Irish victory was William O'Dwyer's election as mayor in 1945. "All five of the city's Democratic county leaders were Irish in 1945, as were four of the eight incoming members of the Board of Estimate, including the mayor-elect. It was an impressive performance at a time when only one New Yorker in fourteen was of identifiably Irish stock, but it was deceptive." [105] The "Irish" had won thanks to the Jewish vote. [106] And in the decades to follow ethnic tensions in the Democratic Party and in city politics generally would shake Irish dominance permanently. So, in the context of this study, politics was significant not for what it was, but for what it was not. This period represented the twilight of Irish dominance in city government. It symbolized the shrinking significance of the Irish as a major force in city politics and prefaced the eventual exit of the Irish to the suburbs.

By 1961 Tammany Hall was dead, and the Irish faced the "bitter reality that they were being displaced." [107] Not only were they outnumbered by other immigrant groups and voting blocs, they were losing control of the Democratic Party leadership. The soul of the party in the twentieth century was divided between conservative Catholics led by the Irish who ran the party machine and socially liberal Jews who supplied a reliable voting base. As the voting power of the Irish declined, second- and third-generation Jews began to take control of the party leadership and philosophy. [108] The Irish era in politics was over; the Irish would never dominate City Hall or the party mechanics of elections again. Throughout the city, American Irish officials such as 1995 council members Walter McCaffrey and Joan Griffin McCabe continued to hold office, [109] but they no longer controlled politics in New York.

In terms of nationalist politics in Ireland, the "troubles" in Northern Ireland and the debate concerning reunification of the six counties in the north with the Republic in the south existed in both migrant generations. For the postwar immigrants, the division of north and south was the result of a bloody civil war that directly involved them, their fathers, mothers, grandfathers, uncles and aunts, and cousins. The agreement separating the thirty-two counties divided families and friends, even religious communities. [110] The Civil War was a fresh wound that was slow to heal. For the migrants of the forties and fifties the emergence of the new nation of Ireland had direct impact on them personally, economically, politically, and culturally. It shaped their lives, just as the Depression ingrained habits of thrift and economic caution among those raised with the constant threat of unemployment and the memory of breadlines.

In America the debate surrounding the separation of the thirty-two counties and activities aimed at unifying the north and the south was covered weekly by the *Irish Echo*. Many in the New York Irish community in the 1950s were veterans of the Civil War and members of the Irish Republican Army, a volunteer group of nationalists who advocated the use of force to reunify the country. Its political arm was Sinn Fein, which translated to "Ourselves Alone" in Irish. [111]

Support for the IRA has been a fact of Irish American life for decades. According to one expert, the strongest and best organized of the advocacy groups was Clan na Gael, which was founded in 1867 to heighten awareness and raise funds to secure an independent Ireland. "It was the Clann under John Devoy that funded the 1916 uprising."[112] The group was suspended between 1939 and 1945 because of the war and "FBI [Federal Bureau of Investigation] surveillance," but reorganized in 1946.[113] Its chief function was to raise money to finance the IRA in Ireland. In the 1950s New York was one of the Clan's more active satellites.[114] But the Clan was not the only group organized in sympathy for the "troubles" in the north.

Advocates organized themselves or split off from other groups throughout the postwar period. In the years immediately following the war, Tim Pat Coogan estimated that Irish Americans donated up to $3,000 a month to the IRA and related causes.[115] American interest in the north reached its peak between 1956 and 1962 during the so-called border campaign when the IRA staged a series of incidents along the border between the north and south to disrupt the British government and bring attention to the division. In November 1958, one Bronx supporter was arrested for gun running when police found crates full of guns and ammunition in his cellar.[116] The "incidents" totaled "one million pounds in outright damage and approximately 10 million in increased police and military patrols. Six young Royal Ulster Constabulary men and 11 Republicans were killed." In addition they were said to have caused the fall of the Dublin government in 1957 and discouraged foreign investment in Ireland.[117]

The border campaign ended on February 26, 1962, when the Irish Republican Publicity Bureau announced that the IRA was putting down its guns and all "full-time service volunteers have been withdrawn."[118] But between 1969 and 1972, the cause was reborn following Catholic civil rights campaigns in Ulster and the British killing of thirteen unarmed Catholic civilians in Derry on "Bloody Sunday," January 30, 1972. Overt IRA hostilities resumed, led by the "Provisional" IRA, a splinter group which broke off from the official group in a dispute over recognition of the parliamentary governments in the Republic and Ulster, and the IRA's participation in them. Over time the "Provos" became the major force in the republican movement.[119]

In New York, Northern Ireland civil rights sympathizers and IRA activists reorganized in the late sixties and early seventies in a variety of groups around the city. These included Northern Aid or NorAid, which backed the Provos; Republican Clubs, which supported the Official IRA; the American Congress for Irish Freedom; the Northern Ireland Civil Rights Association; and others concerned with the discrimination against Catholics in Northern Ireland.[120] Fundraisers were held throughout the city at the Irish Institute, Jaeger House, the Tower View Ballroom in Queens, and other dance halls. Supporters included former IRA members, immigrants and young second-, third-, and fourth-generation Irish American men and women. Mario Biaggi, a New York City congressman, formed an ad hoc committee on Northern Ireland which "claimed the support of over 130 senators and congressmen" in Washington, D.C. Biaggi reportedly had close ties with Michael Flannery, leader of NorAid and the Irish Caucus, an "umbrella committee of Irish-American organizations."[121]

According to one magazine report, NorAid raised between $150,000 and $300,000 between 1970 and 1972. IRA support groups met with controversy and criticism in the United States and Dublin primarily because they were supplying money to a known "terrorist" organization responsible for death and property damage in Northern Ireland and Great Britain. But aside from the violence, some in the New York Irish community opposed the socialist policies of the IRA, even if they supported the reunion of north and south.[122] The division was particularly apparent in 1969 following the formation of "People's Democracy, a militant leftist group within the Northern Ireland civil rights movement." It exploded during the American speaking tour of Bernadette Devlin, whose socialist philosophy and empathy with the African American civil rights movement "enraged" Irish American groups and caused deep rifts among the different U.S. support groups for Northern Ireland.[123]

Increased awareness of the Northern Ireland situation was apparent in the very public and very ethnic forum of the New York St. Patrick's Day Parade. According to a historian of the parade, the 1970 event was "the first time in many years the eyes of most Irish Americans were focussed on events taking place in Northern Ireland. . . . Groups interested in Northern Ireland sprung up all over the metropolitan area and some of them wanted to use the parade as a sounding board for the propaganda."[124] In the years that followed, demonstrators and marchers declared their sympathy for the Republican cause on the parade route and on the sidelines.[125] In 1978, Governor Hugh Carey, "a Brooklyn Irishman," suffered the consequences of a "series of unpopular speeches on Northern Ireland." The *New York Times* reported:

> Worse was in store for Governor Carey. On parade with half a dozen of his red-haired children, he quickly left the stand at the Arsenal—perhaps to have lunch, perhaps to avoid being there when the Irish Northern Aid Committee came by.
>
> The committee representatives—all civilians and many young—chanted: "Carey Out! Carey Out! Carey Out!"[126]

But the most controversial parade of all, as far as the north-south conflict was concerned, was the 1983 event, when the Ancient Order of Hibernians chose Michael Flannery, leader of NorAid and a Civil War veteran, to be grand marshal. Prominent politicians boycotted the parade, and several marching bands, including all army units, withdrew.[127] A parade historian observed that media criticism of the grand marshal choice was

> a campaign tinged with anti-Irish propaganda which resembled the worst of times in the 19th century. Even the long forgotten caricatures of Irish people with ape-like countenances were featured by cartoonists for the largest selling New York daily—not just on one occasion, but on several.[128]

Reportedly, the parade drew a large crowd despite the controversy, and was "more orderly" than it had been in previous years.[129]

For the rest of the decade the Irish spotlight in New York was shared if not overwhelmed by the immigration of young illegal aliens from Ireland. For the generation raised in the 1960s and 1970s Ireland was a land of prosperity, opportunity, and new beginnings. They were going to be the first graduates into an economy that could actually support them and provide meaningful work and a prosperous life in Ireland. That the economy failed and they felt forced to emigrate, just as generations before them had, came as a great disillusion to many. Upon meeting in America the two generations of Irish immigrants possessed very different views of Ireland and very different expectations of what life and a future in America would be.

Among the issues that crystallized the difference between the two populations was the debate on Northern Ireland. Between 1980 and 1986 events in Northern Ireland dominated the headlines of the *Irish Echo*, the major ethnic newspaper at the time. In 1987, with the birth of the *Irish Voice*, the *Echo*, the medium for the established Irish community, faced competition for its headlines for the first time in years. The *Voice*, the self-proclaimed advocate of the New Irish,[130] put the issues of emigration, the undocumented Irish, and immigration reform on the front page. The *Echo* was forced to refocus its editorial thrust and consider the issues that mattered to a new reading audience of immigrants.

In the 1980s the New Irish did not seem to be as concerned with events in Northern Ireland as many in the Irish American community were.[131] Their primary interest was the Irish economy and their ability to get well-paying jobs. Father Martin Keveny, an Irish priest living in the Bronx as part of Project Irish Outreach, said people in Ireland were more preoccupied by the economy than by "the troubles." When Cardinal O'Connor was greeted and praised in the Republic of Ireland for his "mission of peace" trip in July 1988, according to Father Keveny, the Irish people honored the cardinal for his concern and efforts on behalf of the young Irish immigrants living in New York. Irish Americans praised the trip for the attention it brought to the problems in Northern Ireland.[132]

Consider this exchange of letters in the *Irish Voice* in the wake of a February 1989 visit to New York by Diana, Princess of Wales, and the absence of New Irish at a staged protest:

> Are [the New Irish] so selfish and uncaring as to not be concerned about British oppression and terror in the six counties? . . . The young Irish of today are complacent and apathetic, both in Ireland and when they emigrate here. Why should I, an American, be concerned about their plight and their status, when they will not take a few hours of their time to demonstrate in support of their brothers and sisters in the six counties? Why should I care about them and about Ireland, when they seem not to care themselves?[133]

> The majority of young immigrants came here to work, not to become political activists. We were forced to emigrate because the Irish government failed to provide jobs. Stone [the first letter writer] might think it some golden rule that once [in the United States] we are all obliged to turn into raving Provos [supporters of the Provisional Irish Republican Army].[134]

While the economic and immigrant status of the New Irish distracted many Irish Americans from the problems of the North, interest in the issue did not die, nor did U.S. involvement. One of the more notorious cases of the 1980s was the arrest, internment, and battle to extradite Joe Doherty. Doherty was an IRA man and accused murderer who fled Northern Ireland following a jailbreak. The FBI arrested him in 1984 in New York City, where he was tending bar. Doherty was kept in an American prison for eight years as a court battle raged regarding his status as political prisoner or illegal alien. He was eventually deported on the latter charge to Belfast, where he was again jailed to serve a life sentence for murder.[135]

The Doherty case drew major media attention in New York and the rest of the United States, and his situation earned sympathy among the local Irish American community. How deep the support was for the IRA generally is difficult to determine. Black 47 sang in support of resistance:

> So hold on to your rifles, boys, and don't give up your dream —
> Of a Republic for the workin' class and economic liberty.[136]

And one historian observed, "so long as there is trouble in Northern Ireland, some Irish-Americans will support the Provisionals . . . and energetic, intelligent pro-IRA activists are constantly emigrating to the [United States]" to keep attention focused on the north.[137]

While the New Irish population may not be as active as the previous generation in republican activities, one of their own, Niall O'Dowd, publisher of the *Irish Voice,* led a party of Irish American business leaders and politicians to negotiate a peace settlement in Northern Ireland in the late summer of 1994. In the course of the following six years, unionists and republicans in Northern Ireland moved cautiously toward an agreement that was ultimately finalized with the intervention of President Bill Clinton's designated facilitator, former Senator George Mitchell, on Good Friday, April 10, 1998.[138] The Good Friday Peace Accord, as it became known, was a multifaceted agreement that brought together the Republic of Ireland, Northern Ireland, and the United Kingdom with the approval of all the Irish people and their respective governments. Most significantly, it restored local governing power to Northern Ireland, and established a north-south council to deal with a variety of cross-border issues. The accord broke down in February 2000 over the timing of Irish Republican Army disarmament. The British government reimposed direct rule over Northern Ireland, leaving the political future of the north in doubt once again.[139]

The perceived apathy of the New Irish for the Northern Ireland issue represented just one of the many misunderstandings between the two populations, misunderstanding that stemmed from ignorance on the part of Irish Americans about what modern Irish society had become and the priorities of the new immigrants, and unwillingness and impatience among the New Irish to defer to the age and perspective of the Irish Americans.

Complaints from the New Irish community about the established community suggested that the New Irish resented feeling as if they "owed" the Irish American community for all the help it could or might provide for them. In the 1980s and 1990s the Irish no longer looked to America for assistance. America's Irish cousins were considerably more comfortable and better cared for at home than was true in the first decade after World War II. Thanks to social welfare programs and mass consumerism, remittances from America, including packages of used clothing and goods from relatives in Queens and the Bronx, did not have the financial and emotional impact that they did in the forties and fifties. Indeed, among the New Irish surveyed, 51 percent sent money back to Ireland, "either to family or a bank account." [140] More often than not these deposits went to a personal account accumulating in anticipation of the immigrant's return to permanent settlement in Ireland. An observer of the Irish community wrote in 1985 that Irish Americans who visited relatives in Ireland were sometimes met with resentment because they were seen as "relatively prosperous returned Yanks assuming a condemnatory attitude toward the alleged backwardness of siblings or cousins who had been the recipient of their emigrant remittances." He noted that "the young of Ireland are hardly impressed, as their elders had been, by visiting American relatives simply because they are Americans." [141]

This resentment stemmed from ignorance on the part of some Irish Americans about what modern Irish society had become, and unwillingness among some Irish to recognize that their "wealthy" American cousins were probably average working-class or middle-class citizens who had saved for years to return to the land of their ancestors. Neither really understood or appreciated the situation of the other.

Ironically, as the New Irish awoke the Irish American population to their immigrant past, they were unrecognizable as Irish to the generation of migrants who preceded them. For that matter, the Ireland of the 1980s and 1990s was often unrecognizable to anyone who had left forty years previously. [142] The historical identity markers of nationalism and Catholicism were no longer valid. The Irish emerged from the restrictions of a colonial, church-centered society and explored the freedom of a secular, international marketplace.

As the new Ireland evolved, the New Irish seemed less eager to assimilate in New York than their predecessors. At least they indicated less desire to prove their allegiance and loyalty to America. Granted, the fifties had their share of immigrants who ridiculed the "narrowbacks" and lamented the separation from their homeland. [143] But many New Irish did not view immigration as a one-time or final venture. They were products of the late twentieth century and truly citizens of the world. They were more transient and mobile than immigrants of the past. Their attitude probably said as much about the technology of the age as it did about their character or nationalism.

What of the relationship between Ireland and the United States and the definition of ethnic identity? The ties between the two countries are too strong and Ireland is too small to sever the link. Not only are families joined by the past, but economically, Ireland depends on the United States to build its future. IDA and Irish business and government leaders nurtured the bonds between the two very carefully. Just as remittances once contributed to Ireland's gross national product, the jobs, profits, and business that American companies can send to Ireland are vital to its survival. Much of Ireland's current economic success is due to American corporate and financial presence. Ireland and Irish American business leaders recognize the ties between the two, and among the *Irish America* "Business 100" are corporate leaders who have participated in alliances with Ireland through the Irish-U.S. Council for Commerce and Industry, the Irish prime minister's Ireland American Economic Advisory Board, and Ireland Chamber of Commerce, U.S.A., as well as the American Ireland Fund and direct investment in Ireland.[144] Ireland is not afraid to exploit those historic and often emotional ties.

But how will "Irish" be defined in the future? And how will that definition affect Irish American identity? It is clear from the past that the identity must be cultivated—either by the practice of traditional customs and culture or by a less definable, less articulate recognition or acceptance of the identity. As in previous generations, immigration sparked interest in ethnicity. But in the past it was the tight-knit urban communities centered around church and fraternal groups that provided a center and an energy for the culture.

In the seventies and eighties Irish identity persevered, but under less secure conditions in the more diverse and diluted environment of the American metropolitan suburb. In the eighties and nineties the New Irish rejuvenated ethnic neighborhoods in New York, but gave no indication that they would build the urban pockets of ethnicity that their predecessors did. More problematic is the change in Irish identity that they represented. As the New Irish move away from the past, they create a new culture that will affect Irish identity in the United States. But what will define the character and culture of the Irish in the next century? Will the traditions that have defined the Irish in the past be preserved, and by whom? The answers reverberate across the Atlantic to Irish America where the immigrant generation traditionally carries Irish identity into the ethnic community. But if the New Irish choose not to build a life in America, the familiar means of transmitting Irish identity is suspended. Clearly the connections between Ireland and America remain, particularly in New York City. But Irish America in the twenty-first century is a work in progress.

Conclusion

In the 1940s and 1950s Irish migrants were just as likely to live in Irish neighborhoods, work for Irish bosses, and socialize in Irish pubs as the New Irish in the 1980s and 1990s. But real differences existed between the mind-sets of the two groups. The majority of New Irish lived among themselves and avoided interaction with Irish Americans and the previous generation of immigrants; they did not join the ethnic clubs and county organizations in the numbers that their predecessors did. Many New Irish resented the relatively menial work available to them. The first postwar generation of Irish left their country desperate for work and security and the opportunity to build a future. They felt lucky to find work and were willing to fill the positions offered them by friends and family. These immigrants also entered the country legally and did not face the same risks as the undocumented aliens of the eighties.

For the most part, the earlier generation also left Ireland with the intention of staying in the United States permanently. Their "waked" departure, the expense and length of traveling between countries, and the stagnant aura that pervaded Ireland in the fifties offered no incentive to return. On the other hand, the New Irish were not prepared to leave Ireland as they went through school. Their expectations were focused on a future in Ireland. While emigration was not unknown to most Irish families, it was not supposed to be the road to success for the generation raised during Ireland's years of economic expansion. When that expansion stopped and school graduates were once again looking abroad to find a future, many met the reality with resentment. Others saw emigration as a temporary hiatus until better opportunities presented themselves back home.

While the New Irish were anxious to build a future, they were not experiencing "mere survival" at home. They were not threatened by material deprivation or cultural boredom as were their counterparts in the fifties. The latter's past and future expectations in Ireland were gray; America presented them with a rainbow of opportunity that they pursued willingly, but often with a great amount of personal pain. Contact with home in the 1950s was primarily achieved by letter, which could take at least a week to cross the Atlantic. For most migrants, visits home were out of the question because of the expense and inconvenience. When an emigrant left for America in the years after World War II, the departure was considered permanent. That perspective of "no going back" necessarily affected immigrant attitudes about living and working in New York, as did the hopelessness that pervaded Irish society and economy in the fifties. It made it easier to break away from home and overcome the inevitable homesickness, because there was little other choice. They were more likely to integrate with the established Irish community in the United States, and to build relationships that would enable them to succeed in a strange city, albeit within a tight ethnic network.

On the other hand, technological advances in overseas communication and transatlantic travel gave the New Irish such superior access to home that they did not have to make a clean break with their past. Coupled with their ambivalence about being in America, the New Irish always seemed to have one foot in America and one foot in Ireland, never committing to either.

Irish migrants historically have sent wages earned in America back home to support farms and supplement family income. The *Emigration Report* recognized the importance of these remittances to the more equitable distribution of wealth in the country. The New Irish survey and interviews showed that the New Irish continued to send money to Ireland in the 1980s, but they deposited their cash in personal accounts, presumably in anticipation of their return.

The New Irish were often accused by the Irish American community in New York of arrogance, apathy, and disregard for those who came before them and for a lack of appreciation for the country that offered them work and opportunity. The perception was as much a generational clash as a cultural one. The New Irish were not coming "right off the farm" with the inexperience and ignorance of their predecessors. While they may have encountered culture shock arriving in New York, their adjustment was that of moving from small towns to a large, complex urban environment. They were generally well informed about American pop culture, politics, and society through a secondary education and media exposure to the outside world that immediate postwar emigrants had lacked. The latter were arguably more humble because of the cultural and social isolation that dominated Ireland in the 1950s. The New Irish expected more and settled for less. And in the eyes of many in the established Irish American community the New Irish were not grateful enough or considerate enough of their elders.

But the New Irish did not have the same goals as their predecessors, and could not relate to them on many levels. Even though both were children of Ireland, their concept of Ireland and their experience in Ireland were completely different. And as emigrants they shared little common ground other than the act of leaving. Their reasons for leaving, their expectations and perception of America, and their general immigrant experience and reception in New York were quite different.

In the early to mid-eighties the majority of the New Irish population was undocumented and chose to live in the New Irish communities of the Bronx and Queens; other groups of New Irish chose to live outside the New Irish ghettos, but they were just as removed from contact with Irish Americans. Included among them were other undocumented aliens, as well as young professional university graduates granted work visas following their recruitment by American corporations, engineering firms, brokerage houses, and law offices. Regardless of status, lifestyle, or address, the fact remained that conflicts between old and new immigrants arose from their perception of what Ireland was, as well as their attitude about emigration, America, and their own future. The emigrants of the 1940s and 1950s and the migrants of the 1980s came out of two very different Irelands.

What does their clash mean to the evolution of Irish American identity in New York? At the same time that the New Irish began their migration to New York, the ethnic community in the metropolitan area, which extended beyond the first- and second-generation urban population to suburban ethnics, embarked on a renaissance of Irish culture that celebrated not only traditional Irish art forms, but the heritage of the Irish in America and New York.

Ironically, artists within the new immigrant community were also expressing themselves, but their culture was a deliberate move away from the traditional. The New Irish were exploring the social, economic, and cultural changes that Ireland had experienced since the 1960s. These various groups converged in the 1980s in New York, all seeking to express or understand their heritage, nationality, and ethnicity—all going in different directions and all calling themselves Irish.

These young people were building on the broken symbols of their past: Catholicism and nationalism. The writing, film, and music of late-twentieth-century Ireland dealt with the breakdown of the old, traditional Irish ways. Roddy Doyle, Patrick McCabe, Black 47, and other Irish and Irish American artists wrote and sang of modern Ireland—exposing an urban society with broken families, empty churches, disgraced priests, and abused children that clashed with familiar images of a quaint countryside and laughing children.

What does this portend for the future of the Irish in New York? It is impossible to say how or which of the traditions will survive or which of the groups will emerge to define the Irish. What the behavior does show is the strength and persistence of the need to be identified with a group: to belong to and understand one's past and one's legacy. How the different players within that arena will come to agree on or merge their vision of "Irish" has yet to be played out.

The stage for this development is much broader than it has been for past generations. Ireland is no longer an isolated island or a colony struggling to shape itself in opposition to Great Britain, and Irish New York is no longer an urban village, creating a cocoon to protect and nurture Irish American culture. The diaspora of the Irish in the late twentieth century continues on a much larger scale and from many different starting points, so that the core of what is Irish does not emerge from a single source. In New York and in Ireland Irish identity has been exposed to a variety of influences from the intrusion of electronic media into Irish and Irish American homes and to the transience of the Irish people themselves. Mary Robinson, former president of Ireland, said that Ireland disperses her people around the world, and that they carry the best of Ireland with them. In an address to the Houses of the Oireachtas (Irish Parliament) she described the "contribution and adaptation" involved in emigration as "one of the great treasures of [Irish] society."[1] But the cultural exchange flows both ways, and the Irish cannot help but be influenced by their exposure to the rest of the world.

Ireland has had a long history of emigration, and the descendants of its people can be found around the world. What changed in the 1980s dispersal of Irish people and culture was that the mainstays of Irish culture—Catholicism and nationalism—collapsed as markers of Irish identity. As the Irish once again sent their young people out into the world in the 1980s, they were struggling with their own identity in the absence of traditional symbols. In New York, where renewed immigration and an ethnic renaissance sparked hope that the Irish could rejuvenate the cultural and social vitality of past decades, the resistance of the New Irish to the traditions of Irish America was met with resentment and disappointment.

The Irish postwar migration to New York was not unlike that of previous generations in that Irish citizens, reacting to a complex mix of push/pull factors, left for New York in pursuit of what they could not achieve or attain at home. The numbers were smaller, but such was the legacy of the Irish in New York, and America, that the migrants could rely on ethnic neighborhoods and church, business, and political leaders to ease their transition to life in the new city. And as in previous decades, the new migrants entered "layered" ethnic communities that comprised several generations of Irish and Irish Americans at various levels of economic and educational achievement. What made the late-twentieth-century migration different from past movements was the changes that had taken place in Ireland in the 1960s and 1970s, when the flow of migrants to America virtually stopped. In that twenty-year period Ireland became a "modern" society and lost its dependence on the Church and the cultural nationalism that had defined the country in the past. When the New Irish entered the ethnic community of New York in the 1980s they, like generations before them, carried Ireland with them. But it was an Ireland in transition. As the New Irish struggled with their own identity, Irish Americans looked to the migrants for clues to their own past and often did not recognize what they saw.

The position of the Catholic Church in Ireland had seriously weakened in the 1960s and 1970s. In the wake of Vatican II, vocations declined precipitously in Ireland and the United States, so there were fewer clergy and religious in both countries ministering to the faithful. In Ireland the status of the Church and its bishops was furthered compromised by an increasingly secular society. In the 1980s the New Irish came of age in the midst of fierce debates in Ireland over abortion, divorce, and contraceptive rights. Surveys showed that attendance at mass declined in Ireland, and among the New Irish surveyed by the author, 49 percent said they attended less often in New York than at home.

The issue of nationalism is more complex. While the debate about the political status of the north progressed under the glare of international attention in the 1980s and 1990s, the nationalist passion of the Civil War veterans who migrated in the 1920s and the generation who left in the 1950s did not have its counterpart in the 1980s. The New Irish have no memory of the Easter Rebellion, the Civil War, or any of the heroes of the new Republic. Eamon De Valera died in 1975. The modern generation's memory of the Irish Republic is rooted in the present, not the past.

Despite these changes, the good news is that the ethnic community in New York—both Irish Americans and immigrants—is alive and vibrant. Tim Pat Coogan said that the sign of an authentic Irish Republican organization is the splits within the group; so too for the Irish in New York. It is doubtful that the Irish in New York will ever again have the nurturing core of urban neighborhoods with their overlapping reinforcements of church, school, jobs, and families to perpetuate the culture. But the will to maintain identity persists, even as it is defined variously by different groups within the community.

Beyond the "splits," it remains to be seen how the culture survives the transience of the immigrant population. While the economic, political, personal, and cultural connections between the two countries remain certain, will Irish people continue to migrate and settle in New York? In the past the constant influx of migrants kept the ethnic community alive in New York. But in the late twentieth century, with the ease of travel and communication, the migrant cannot be depended on to perpetuate the urban villages of the past. The questions then arise: What role will the migrant play in the maintenance of a vital ethnic culture, absent the old neighborhood communities? How will the Irish culture be sustained and carried from Ireland to New York to future generations? These questions cannot be answered. The Irish American community in New York will certainly carry on through the twenty-first century. The connections between the United States and Ireland are too strong for it to break apart. It may not be the neighborhood/parish-centered culture of the past 150 years, but whatever form it takes, it will reflect Ireland and Irish America just as it has for generations.

Epilogue

As this book goes to press in the twenty-first century, the number of people leaving Ireland runs at more than 18,000 a year.[1] Between 1990 and 1998 the number of people entering Ireland each year ran between 30,000 and 44,000. Recent census data from Ireland reports that net in-migration (the immigration figure after adjusting for births and deaths in Ireland) to the country in 1998 was 22,800, up from 15,000 in 1997. That number resulted from a record number of Irish-born migrants returning to Ireland and an increasing number of foreign-born immigrants and refugees seeking asylum in Ireland.[2] In 1996 and 1997 the Irish government reported that 6,600 documented and 6,000 undocumented Irish immigrants returned to Ireland.[3] The influx, widely reported in the media on both sides of the Atlantic, hid the fact that young Irish emigrants continued to leave Ireland for the United States. The actual numbers of emigrants for 1998 and 1999 were 21,200 and 18,500 respectively, down from a peak of 61,100 in 1988. In terms of destinations, the numbers traveling to Great Britain have dropped, while the percentage of Irish leaving for Europe, the United States, and other parts of the world have dominated the movement since 1993. In 1998, the United States accounted for almost one-quarter of the total migration, up from about 10 or 15 percent in the 1980s.[4]

One of the reasons offered for the remarkable jump in migration *to* Ireland in the last few years is the extraordinary economic prosperity that Ireland enjoyed at the end of the twentieth century. Ireland had the fastest growing economy in the European Union (EU). The unemployment rate for January 2000 was 4.9 percent, down from 5 percent the previous month and lower than the 5.6 percent annual rate for 1999. An inflation rate of 4.4 percent in January 2000 was higher than the

3.9 annual rate posted in December 1999, and the January rate was the highest posted for the European Union (EU).[5] But the figures are significantly lower than the double-digit numbers posted for inflation and unemployment in the 1980s that initiated the exodus of New Irish. The upturn has attracted white-collar and blue-collar workers back to the Republic.[6]

Despite the strong economy in Ireland and the various visa programs inaugurated since 1986, migration to the United States persists, and many of the migrants still enter on visa waivers as visitors and overstay their visit. While the migrants have not yet reached the numbers estimated to have entered in the mid- and late eighties, emigrant advocates in the United States and in Ireland claim that the current wave of immigrants is at greater risk than the population who arrived ten or fifteen years ago. The most recent migrants are younger, less equipped for the transition to the United States, less skilled, and with less prospect of obtaining a green card. Without proper work authorization, they live outside the mainstream of the American economy, are unable to secure a driver's license, and work without insurance coverage or medical benefits. According to immigrant advocates, they will probably never be able to change their status. Recent legislation enforces a very unwelcoming environment for undocumented aliens in New York City and across the country.

About one-quarter of the Irish who enter the United States settle in New York City.[7] Advocates at the Catholic Charities office in Manhattan, the Emerald Isle Immigration Center (EIIC) in Woodside, Queens, and the Aisling Irish Center in Yonkers, New York, describe most recent migrants as under 25, with about half younger than 21. They have few skills and the equivalent of a high school education, though some have a university degree; most are without work authorization, immigrant visas, or permanent resident status. In a change from the previous decade, the advocates are seeing many more emigrants from Northern Ireland as well. A recent report puts the annual outflow at 12,000.[8] Sister Edna MacNicholl of the Aisling Center, Patricia O'Callaghan of Catholic Charities, and Carolyn Ryan, executive director of Emerald Isle Immigration Center, all agree that the Celtic Tiger—Ireland's economic boom—roared past these emigrants. They have been unable to participate in the surging economy that marks Ireland as the fastest-growing member of the Common Market. These young men and women set out for the United States quite soon after leaving secondary school, lured by the stories of predecessors earning high salaries and the romance of adventure and independence that surrounds emigration. New York has been a traditional destination for generations of young Irish, so it is often the first stop on the emigrant's journey.

While the age and skill level of the current crop of migrants may be slightly lower than that of the eighties population, what distinguishes the American experience of this group from that of its predecessors is the current state of immigration law in the United States. The variety of visa programs and regulations passed during the 1990s has complicated the process for illegal immigrants to become "documented" and pushed many into a state of legal limbo. New fines and penalties for employers hiring illegal aliens also reduce labor opportunities for the undocumented. It is more difficult now than it has ever been for an undocumented alien to secure a green card from the available visa programs. In addition, those who violate visa law are subject to harsher penalties, which drives them further underground than their pre-1986 predecessors. Legislation passed in the 1990s also prevents immigrants who enter the United States after August 1996 from collecting welfare and Medicaid benefits until they have paid Social Security taxes for ten years or become U.S. citizens, except for emergency Medicaid. But probably the harshest penalties are the three- and ten-year bars on admissibility.[9]

The three- and ten-year bars restrict the admissibility of aliens who are illegally present in the United States for a period of time, leave the country, and then attempt to re-enter. If a person has been illegal for more than six months but less than one year after April 1, 1997, then departs and tries to re-enter, he or she will be banned from the United States for three years. If an illegal alien who has been undocumented for one year or more after April 1, 1997, leaves and tries to re-enter, he or she is barred from the United States for ten years. What further complicates the restriction are status variables surrounding "adjustment" and whether or not an alien is required to leave the country to complete the appropriate paperwork and meet consular regulations or if the transition to documented alien can be accomplished in the United States. Ironically, situations exist where an illegal alien receives an opportunity to obtain a visa but must leave the country to complete the adjustment, then by doing so triggers the three- or ten-year ban on admissibility. As a result many immigrants decide to remain in undocumented or overstay status, risk detection, and take a chance that the three- and ten-year bars will be rescinded or that new legislation will be passed, changing their status. Advocates in the community are also hoping that Congress will grant amnesty to illegal aliens much as it did with the 1986 Immigration Reform and Control Act.[10]

The unrestricted visa programs of the late 1980s, including the Donnelly and Morrison Programs, are exhausted. The remaining special visa opportunities include the diversity program and the Walsh visa. The diversity visa is an oversubscribed program that attracts more than six million applications from around the world every year. The Irish secured 652 of the 55,000 visas available in the 1998–99 program year.[11] The Irish Peace Process Cultural and Training Program Act of 1998, also known as the Walsh visa for its sponsor, Representative James Walsh, is a special program created in response to the peace accord between Northern Ireland and the Republic of Ireland. This act was signed into law on October 27, 1998, and grants 12,000 temporary visas over a three-year period to natives of Northern Ireland and the border counties. Four thousand visas a year will be distributed to "young adults (18–35 years old) and long-term unemployed from disadvantaged areas" in Northern Ireland and Louth, Monaghan, Cavan, Leitrim, Sligo, and Donegal Counties in the Republic to live and work in the United States. These are temporary non-immigrant visas designed to upgrade the recipient's labor skills. Nine categories of employment are targeted for the visa holders: hospitality and tourism; customer services; information and communication technology; pharmaceuticals; engineering; sales, marketing, and promotion; agriculture/horticulture diversification; food processing; and furniture. The first group of seventy-nine participants arrived in Washington, D.C., on March 31, 2000; the remaining visa holders continued to arrive through the year, assigned to jobs with firms designated as program participants.[12] Beyond these two programs the Irish wishing to immigrate legally to the United States can apply for visas under the family reunification and unskilled labor preferences of the general immigration schedule, but the waiting list for these is too long for most emigrants to tolerate. As a result emigrants anxious to leave Ireland disregard the immigration and visa restrictions in the United States and take their chances as undocumented aliens.

Among the many problems facing the new immigrants is their immaturity. Young people away from home for the first time are ill-prepared and underfunded for life in a big city. Their experience echoes that of earlier migrants, with some variations. Sister Edna of the Aisling Center in Yonkers finds more young couples migrating, in a departure from a decade or so earlier when most of the migrants traveled solo, or at least as unattached singles. The scenario that often unfolds is that the young man finds work quickly in construction or the building trades and the young woman does not secure a job. She is left at home, isolated, homesick, and dependent on the man for financial and social support. Meanwhile the young man is earning money and making friends on the job and may find his partner's neediness suffocating. The dynamic leaves the young woman subject to psychological and physical abuse as the financial and social difficulties of life in New York City strain the relationship. Advocates agree that while this scenario is not commonplace, it occurs often enough to warrant concern.[13]

According to the agencies and services who work with the Irish in New York, the publicity surrounding the Celtic Tiger has rendered invisible the current situation of illegal Irish immigrants. As in the 1980s the advice agencies provide direction and information to all who seek their services. As in the past, the majority of those in need of help today are undocumented. At Project Irish Outreach, immigrants call to determine what their visa options are; they want to know how to apply for the diversity visa or how to become a U.S. citizen. Many have questions about health insurance and whether or not they can use an emergency room for medical care. They have questions about marriage and how it will affect their status.[14] They tend to need help negotiating the legal and bureaucratic networks they face as new immigrants and/or undocumented aliens.

The Aisling Center focuses on community outreach. Sister Edna MacNicholl and Father Tom Flynn are part of the program initiated by Cardinal O'Connor and the Bishops' Episcopal Commission in Ireland during the 1980s to minister to the needs of young Irish abroad. In 1997 Father Tim O'Sullivan was appointed national director of the program in the United States, overseeing chaplains in Philadelphia, Chicago, San Francisco, New York, and Boston, as well as part-time outreach efforts in Atlanta and a summer outreach program for students in Ocean City, Maryland. He has plans to expand the outreach in southern California as well, specifically in San Diego and Los Angeles.[15]

In New York Sister Edna and Father Tom view their service as pastoral and provide many of the same services offered in the previous decade. This includes mother and child sessions to bring together young women in the community who are alone or isolated at home with young children, as well as confidential counseling and referrals.[16] At the very least Aisling is a community networking station with its bulletin board advertising local housing and job opportunities. The storefront center on McLean Avenue faces St. Barnabas Church in the Bronx, a traditionally Irish parish whose weekly bulletin carries shamrock-dotted ads for Liffey Van Lines, Eileen's Country Kitchen, and the Bodhran Pub.[17]

The Emerald Isle Immigration Center also sits in the heart of an immigrant community in Queens, one block away from St. Sebastian Church in Woodside. It services walk-in clients, conducts education and career placement seminars, and publishes a newsletter with updates on immigration legislation, visa opportunities and deadlines, and seminar schedules for immigrants to advance their skills and employment options. The January 2000 newsletter announced the re-opening of a computer clinic at the EIIC office, inviting experienced and novice users to work at a computer or with a tutor. The EIIC also hosts a website featuring immigration and legislation news, visa deadlines and adjustment schedules, links to other immigration-related sites, and other pertinent information that new immigrants as well as undocumented and documented aliens need to know.

The good news is that despite the popular misconception that the Irish illegal problem in America disappeared with the hard work of reform advocates in the 1980s and economic prosperity in Ireland, the agencies that served the undocumented population fifteen years ago remain in place today. Unfortunately, the fate of the present generation of Irish illegal aliens is not promising. The legislative climate for immigrants in the United States is unfriendly at best. Congress appears to be reversing the more liberal and lenient policies of the past thirty years in order to control an enormous surge in immigration during the last decades of the twentieth century.

Many of the latest wave of Irish immigrants are trapped by legislation that restricts their access to full participation in American society. Ironically, the more things change, the more they stay the same. In the 1980s activists had apparently solved the problem of the Irish and visa status documentation. The question that concerned observers following the victories of immigration reform was whether migration from Ireland would continue at all and if so in what form. Well, the Irish continue to migrate to the United States and legal status remains a problem for most immigrants. Unfortunately the voice of this new generation is muted by the success of its predecessors and the strength of the economy in Ireland. The future unfolds apace.

Notes

INTRODUCTION

1. Susan Sachs, "From a Babel of Tongues, a Neighborhood," *New York Times*, December 26, 1999, pp. 1, 25. New York City Department of City Planning, *The Newest New Yorkers, 1990–1994*, December 1996, table 4-1, p. 52.

2. Rosenwaike, Ira, *Population History of New York City* (Syracuse, N.Y.: Syracuse University Press, 1972), p. 42, and *The Newest New Yorkers 1990–1994*, p. 52.

3. *New York and the Irish Famine: A Symbolic Meal and Keynote Address on the Occasion of the Tenth Anniversary of the New York Irish History Roundtable*, St. Paul the Apostle Undercroft, New York City, October 28, 1994 (New York: Irish History Roundtable, 1994).

4. Steven P. Erie, *Rainbow's End: Irish Americans and the Dilemmas of Urban Machine Politics, 1840–1985* (Berkeley: University of California Press, 1988), p. 2.

5. Jay Dolan, *The Immigrant Church: New York's Irish and German Catholics, 1815–1985*, 2nd ed. (Notre Dame, Ind.: University of Notre Dame Press, 1983), p. 167.

6. Immigration and Naturalization Service, *1992 Statistical Yearbook of the Immigration and Naturalization Service*, U.S. Department of Justice, October 1993, table 2. Immigration by Region and Selected Country of Last Residence Fiscal Years 1820–1992, pp. 27–28.

7. *Emigration USA*, RTE television (Ireland), March 11, 1987, Archive account number: BN307/87L.

8. *1992 Statistical Yearbook of the Immigration and Naturalization Service*, table 2, pp. 26–29.

9. Leonard Dinnerstein and David Reimers, *Ethnic Americans: A History of Immigration*, 3rd ed. (New York: Harper and Row, 1988), p. 93.

10. *1992 Statistical Yearbook of the Immigration and Naturalization Service*, appendix 1, p. A.1-6.

11. *1992 Statistical Yearbook of the Immigration and Naturalization Service*, appendix 1, pp. A.1-9–A.1-13; Dinnerstein and Reimers, pp. 85–90.

12. David Reimers, *Still the Golden Door* (New York: Columbia University Press, 1985), pp. 39–62.

13. Dinnerstein and Reimers, pp. 85–89.

14. *1992 Statistical Yearbook of the Immigration and Naturalization Service*, table 2, p. 27.

15. John Fitzgerald Kennedy was obviously the first Catholic president of the United States and an Irish American as well. However, he was not the first chief executive with Irish ancestry. Several presidents, beginning with Andrew Jackson, were of Irish Protestant or Scotch-Irish ancestry. See William D. Griffin, *The Book of Irish Americans* (New York: Times Books, 1990), p. 250

16. Reimers, p. 17.

17. Reimers, p. 63, and Elliott Robert Barkan, *And Still They Come: Immigrants and American Society, 1920 to the 1990s* (Wheeling, Ill.: Harlan Davidson, 1996), pp. 116–118.

18. New York City Department of City Planning, pp. 7–9.

19. New York City Department of City Planning, p. 9.

20. New York City Department of City Planning, p. 13.

1. THE BACKGROUND

1. This quote was offered to me by Martin McGovern, a 1980s Irish emigrant, who in the mid-1990s was the assistant to Father Bartley MacPhaidin, president of Stonehill College in Easton, Massachusetts, and a post–World War II migrant himself. It probably refers to the IRA. Tim Pat Coogan makes a similar observation about the Fenian Brotherhood, referring to their "tendency to disunity and splits." In *The Origins of the IRA: A History* (Niwot, Colo.: Roberts Rinehart Publishers, 1994), p. 11.

2. Immigration and Naturalization Service, *1982 Statistical Yearbook of the Immigration and Naturalization Service* (Washington, D.C.: Government Printing Office, 1983), table IMM1.2, p. 2. See Kerby A. Miller, *Emigrants and Exiles: Ireland and the Irish Exodus to North America* (New York: Oxford University Press, 1985), pp. 297 and 350, regarding the religion of the immigrants.

3. Ira Rosenwaike, *Population History of New York* (Syracuse, N.Y.: Syracuse University Press, 1972), table 23, Birthplace of the Population of New York City, 1865–1890, p. 67, and table 26, Country of Origin of the Total Population of Foreign or Mixed Parentage, New York City, 1880, and of the White Population, 1980, p. 73.

4. Rosenwaike, table 23, Birthplace of the Population of New York City, 1865–1890, p. 67.

5. See Eric Foner, "Class, Ethnicity, and Radicalism in the Gilded Age: The Land League and Irish America," *Marxist Perspectives* (Summer 1978): 6–7, and John Bodnar, *The Transplanted* (Bloomington: Indiana University Press, 1985).

6. Hasia Diner, *Erin's Daughters in America* (Baltimore: Johns Hopkins University Press, 1983), p. 91.

7. Nathan Glazer and Daniel P. Moynihan, *Beyond the Melting Pot* (Cambridge: MIT Press and Harvard University Press, 1963), p. 217.

8. Chris McNickle, *To Be Mayor of New York* (New York: Columbia University Press, 1993), pp. 5–9. Joseph Lee, *The Modernisation of Irish Society, 1848–1918* (Dublin: Gill and Macmillan, 1973), pp. 54–59.

9. McNickle, p. 8.

10. Glazer and Moynihan, p. 219.

11. McNickle, pp. 8–9.

12. Ibid., pp. 8–9.

13. Ibid., pp. 1–148.

14. Rosenwaike, tables C-3 and 64, pp. 133 and 205.

15. Steven P. Erie, *Rainbow's End* (Berkeley: University of California Press, 1988). See chapter 4, "The Crisis of the 1930s: The Depression, the New Deal, and Changing Machine Fortunes, 1928–1950," pp. 107–140.

16. McNickle, p. 322.

17. See Miller, pp. 297 and 350, for figures on religion of famine and post-famine migrants.

18. Miller, pp. 196–197, and Kieran McShane, "A Study of Two New York Irish-American Newspapers in the Early Nineteenth Century," *New York Irish History Journal* 8 (1993–94): 19.

19. Jay Dolan, in *The Immigrant Church,* pp. 45–46, points out that after 1850 and the first national church council in Thurles (1850), Catholic life in Ireland became more parish-oriented and that Catholicism was reinvigorated by building and a more involved and focused clergy. Immigrants brought that style of parish/church-centered religion and community life with them. For changes in Ireland see Emmett Larkin, "The Devotional Revolution in Ireland, 1850–1875," *American Historical Review* 77, no. 3 (1972): 625–652. For religion of immigrants see Miller, *Emigrants and Exiles,* p. 350.

20. Miller, p. 526.

21. Glazer and Moynihan, p. 240. Regarding relations between Protestant and Catholic Irish, Kerby Miller is in the midst of new research exploring the identity of the Scotch-Irish. Also, a study of the editorial content of Irish American newspapers in New York dates the change in Irish nationalism from one that emphasized "Irishness" as anti-British to one that focused on Irishness as synonymous with Catholicism as early as the 1830s and Daniel O'Connell's emancipation movement. See McShane, pp. 19–21. Gearoid O'Tuathaigh, *Ireland before the Famine 1798–1848*, the Gill History of Ireland (Dublin: Gill and Macmillan, 1972), p. 77.

22. Dolan, p. 165.

23. Ibid., p. 15.

24. Ibid., pp. 166–168.

25. Ibid., pp. 166–168.

26. Bernadette McCauley, "Taking Care of Their Own: Irish Catholics, Health Care, and Saint Vincent's Hospital, 1850–1900," *New York Irish History Journal* (1993–1994): 51.

27. Hugh E. O'Rourke, "The Arrival of the Fenian Exiles to New York," *New York Irish History Journal* (1993–1994): 46–51. O'Rourke describes the visit of Fenian exiles, led by O'Donovan Rossa, and the attempts by the Fenians as well as New York City and national political leaders to exploit the visit to curry favor with the Irish American population and to garner money and votes for their respective causes.

28. Janet Nolan, *Ourselves Alone* (Lexington: University Press of Kentucky, 1989), p. 20.

29. Miller, p. 430.

30. Lee, p. 3.

31. Lee, p. 5; Miller, p. 434; Diner; and Nolan.

32. Lee, pp. 5–6; Nolan, p. 36; Miller, pp. 288–291; and Larkin.

33. Nolan, pp. 21–23.

34. Miller, pp. 296–297 and 350–351. Kerby Miller estimates that about one-third of famine emigrants had Irish as their primary, if not exclusive, language. And while the majority of post-famine emigrants spoke English, he estimates that about one-quarter to one-third of these migrants were Irish-speakers as well, although usually bilingual.

35. Nolan, p. 34–35, and Pauline Jackson, "Women in 19th Century Irish Migration," *International Migration Review* 18, no. 4 (1984): 1014–1015. In her discussion of nuns, Ms. Jackson notes that although young women could achieve an education, social status, and a profession in the convent, and the population of nuns grew through the end of the nineteenth century, a woman's status in the convent depended on the size of the dowry she brought with her. Women with no money could spend their lives performing domestic duties in the convent.

36. Nolan, pp. 21–22.

37. Nolan, pp. 38–42.

38. Nolan, pp. 39–40.

39. Lee, p. 13.

40. Lee claims that letter distribution by the post office in Ireland rose from five million in 1851 to twenty million in 1914, p. 13. For examples of letters from the period, see Kerby A. Miller and Paul Wagner, *Out of Ireland: The Story of Irish Emigration to America* (Washington, D.C.: Elliott and Clark Publishing, 1994).

41. Lee wrote that the number of periodicals and newspapers in Ireland rose from 109 in 1853 to 230 in 1913, p. 13.

42. R. F. Foster, *Modern Ireland 1600–1972* (London: Allen Lane, The Penguin Press, 1988), p. 402.

43. Lee, pp. 85–86.

44. Foner, p. 21.

45. Foner, p. 11.

46. Foner, p. 12.
47. Lee, p. 93.
48. Foner, p. 11.
49. Foner, p. 21.
50. Foner, p. 11.
51. Foner, p. 20.
52. Lawrence J. McCaffrey, "Irish America," *Wilson Quarterly* (Spring 1985): 79–80. Diner, p. 72. Eric Foner in "Class, Ethnicity, and Radicalism in the Gilded Age: The Land League and Irish America" suggests that the Land League movement in the United States marked a turning point in the relationship between nativist reformers and Irish Catholics, dispelling the image of the latter as intractably conservative, anti-intellectual, and anti-reform; see pp. 30–38.
53. Glazer and Moynihan, p. 237.
54. Kevin Kenny, *Making Sense of the Molly Maguires* (New York: Oxford University Press, 1998), pp. 6–12.
55. Herbert J. Gans, "Comment: Ethnic Invention and Acculturation—A Bumpy-Line Approach," *Journal of American Ethnic History* 12, no. 1 (1992): 43.
56. Kathleen Neils Conzen, David A. Gerber, Ewa Morawska, George E. Pozzetta, and Rudolph J. Vecoli, "The Invention of Ethnicity: A Perspective from the USA," *Journal of American Ethnic History* 12, no. 1 (1992): 5.
57. Kenneth Moynihan, "History as a Weapon for Social Advancement: Group History as Told by the American Irish Historical Society, 1896–1930," *New York Irish History Roundtable Journal* (1993–1994): 34f.
58. Kenneth J. Moynihan, "History as a Weapon for Social Advancement: Group History as Told by Jewish, Irish, and Black Americans, 1892–1950," Ph.D. dissertation, Clark University, 1973, pp. 17–21.
59. Thomas J. Rowland, "Irish-American Catholics and the Quest for Respectability in the Coming of the Great War, 1900–1917," *Journal of American Ethnic History* 15, no. 2 (1996): 3–31.
60. Conzen et al., p. 13. The authors describe the coming of age of second-generation ethnics and their challenge of parental authority for leadership of the community as the "critical moment" in every immigrant group.
61. Timothy Meagher, "Irish All the Time: Ethnic Consciousness among the Irish in Worcester, Massachusetts, 1880–1905," *Journal of Social History* (Winter 1985): pp. 273–290.
62. Rebecca Miller, "Irish Traditional and Popular Music in New York City: Identity and Social Change, 1935–1975," in *The New York Irish*, ed. Ronald H. Bayor and Timothy Meagher (Baltimore: Johns Hopkins University Press, 1996), pp. 491–494.
63. Miller, pp. 485, 491–494.
64. Marion R. Casey, "Redefining 'Irish': The Impact of New Immigration on the New York Irish Community 1900–1950," Ph.D. dissertation proposal, New York University, February 10, 1992; and "Redefining 'Irish' Culture and Subculture in New York City 1900–1940," Organization of American Historians, Atlanta meeting, April 14, 1994.
65. Foner, p. 8.
66. See Glazer and Moynihan, pp. 250–262.
67. See Gans and Conzen et al.

2. THE 1950S

1. Kevin Morrissey interview, February 9, 1995.
2. Fergal Tobin, *The Best of Decades: Ireland in the Nineteen Sixties* (Dublin: Gill and Macmillan, 1984), p. 4.
3. Kerby A. Miller and Paul Wagner, *Out of Ireland: The Story of Irish Emigration to America* (Washington, D.C.: Elliott and Clark Publishing, 1994), p. 116.

4. Central Statistics Office, *Ireland Census 91, Vol. 1, Population Classified by Area* (Dublin: Stationery Office, June 1993), p. 24.

5. National Economic and Social Council (NESC), *The Economic and Social Implications of Emigration* (Dublin: National Economic and Social Council, March 1991), p. 74.

6. Immigration and Naturalization Service (INS), *1992 Yearbook of the Immigration and Naturalization Service* (Washington, D.C.: Government Printing Office, October 1993), table 2, "Immigration by Region and Selected Country of Last Residence, Fiscal Years 1820–1992," p. 27.

7. In 1958, 36 percent of all Irish-born immigrants went to New York City, and 51 percent of those Irish-born admitted to cities with populations of greater than 100,000 entered New York. In 1959, it was 37 percent for all immigrants and 53 percent for those admitted to large cities; for 1960 and 1961, the statistics were 36 percent/54 percent and 34 percent/51 percent, respectively. See INS *Annual Reports* for 1958 (p. 41), 1959 (p. 38), 1960 (p. 38), and 1961 (p. 38), table 12B.

8. In the period 1943 to 1951 the age distribution table of Irish recipients of travel permits listed in the Commission on Emigration and Other Population Problems, *Commission on Emigration and Other Population Problems 1948–1954 Reports*, Pr. 2541 (Dublin: Stationery Office, 1956), showed that two-thirds of males receiving permits were between 16 and 29 years of age, while 84 percent of the females were between 16 and 29 years of age. See p. 129, paragraph 276, table 97.

INS *Annual Reports* for the following years showed a high percentage of Irish immigrants between the ages of 10 and 29, according to table 9 of each report:

	Male	Female
1955	62.3%	70.4%
1956	61.6%	69.5%
1958	61.6%	67.1%
1959	62.3%	68.2%
1960	63.9%	69.2%

9. Kevin Morrissey interview.

10. Mary Daly, "The Economic Ideals of Irish Nationalism: Frugal Comfort or Lavish Austerity?" *Eire-Ireland*, Winter 1994, pp. 86–89.

11. Daly, p. 85.

12. Commission on Emigration and Other Population Problems, pp. 135–136, paragraphs 295 to 298, and p. 172, paragraph 432.

13. Ibid., p. 172, paragraph 432.

14. Ibid., p. 136, paragraph 295.

15. In an interview with the *Irish Press* in 1969, Sean Lemass claimed that contemporary emerging nations had many more resources, models, and advisers at their disposal than he did in the thirties. Little statistical or academic information existed about Ireland at the time he and his staff were developing policy positions and programs for industry. J. J. [Joseph] Lee, *Ireland 1912–1985: Politics and Society*, 6th ed. (Cambridge: Cambridge University Press, 1993), p. 191. See also pp. 191–194.

16. NESC, pp. 67–68. Lee writes that between 1945 and 1961 Ireland had the highest rate of female emigration of any country in Europe. See p. 335.

17. INS *Annual Reports* for 1955, 1956, 1958, 1959, and 1960, table 9.

18. Department of Commerce, *1960 Census of Population: Final Report, Subject Reports, Nativity and Parentage, Social and Economic Characteristics of the Foreign Stock by Country of Origin*, PC(2)-1A (Washington, D.C.: Government Printing Office, 1964), table 16.

19. Lee, p. 360.

20. INS *Annual Reports* 1955, 1956, 1958, 1959, and 1960, table 9.

21. NESC, pp. 67–68.

22. Tobin, pp. 4–5. Lee, pp. 341–362. John A. Murphy, *Ireland in the Twentieth Century*,

2nd ed., The Gill History of Ireland, ed. James Lydon and Margaret MacCurtain (Dublin: Gill and Macmillan, 1977), p. 142.

23. Ireland's population in 1946 was 2,955,107, less than half what it was just before the famine in 1841. Twenty years after its declaration as a free state Ireland demonstrated negative population growth (dropping from 2,971,992 in 1926)—damaging both its pride as a nation and its ability as a productive player in the world market. Central Statistics Office, *Ireland Census 91*, p. 30.

24. In the 1980s the New Irish, primarily undocumented Irish who formed the second great migration from Ireland in the late twentieth century, complained that the Irish government abandoned them and their needs abroad once they left the country. The implication was that by leaving, the migrants removed the evidence of the government's failure to provide employment and a place in society for its youth. This suggests that not much had changed in thirty years.

25. Commission on Emigration and Other Population Problems, p. 141, paragraph 320.

26. Ibid., pp. 203–206.

27. Thomas Murphy, *A Crucial Week in the Life of a Grocer's Assistant* (Dublin: Gallery Press, 1978), scene 2, p. 21.

28. Murphy, scene 11, p. 80.

29. Other plays which deal with emigration include Brian Friel's *Philadelphia Here I Come* and *Wonderful Tennessee*.

30. In the 1980s government refusal to send aid to emigrants in America or deal in any significant way with the emigration crisis in the early years of the exodus was criticized by leaders of the emigrant lobby groups in the United States. The New Irish complained that the government was glad to be rid of the emigrants because they reduced already burgeoning unemployment rates and quieted the loudest voices of protest against the Irish economic situation and the government's failure to provide jobs for the skilled and educated population it had produced through the sixties and seventies.

31. Daly, pp. 97–98. Daly argues that the report marked a major government turning point, a recognition that the population desired an improved lifestyle rather than sacrifice, and that a better quality of life would halt depopulation and emigration.

32. Commission on Emigration and Other Population Problems, p. 139, paragraph 310.

33. Ibid., p. 140, paragraph 313.

34. Ibid., p. 140, paragraph 314.

35. Ibid., p. 140. paragraphs 315 and 316.

36. Commission on Emigration and Other Population Problems, p. 139, paragraphs 301 and 302. The commission's report recognizes the historical pattern of chain migration to destinations with established and developing communities of Irish. It also hints that exaggerated descriptions of life abroad in the letters and communication with relatives and friends lure migrants away from Ireland with fantasies of a better life.

37. See Miller and Wagner, pp. 85–86, for letters recounting nineteenth-century American wakes, and Kerby A. Miller, *Emigrants and Exiles: Ireland and the Irish Exodus to North America* (New York: Oxford University Press, 1985), pp. 556–568, for good background on the origin of wakes, songs, ritual, and mythology of custom. See Robert James Scally, *The End of Hidden Ireland: Rebellion, Famine, and Emigration* (New York: Oxford University Press, 1995), pp. 218–221, for the rigor of the cross-Atlantic passage, particularly in the famine and post-famine years.

38. In *New York and the Irish Famine*, the program for the tenth anniversary of the New York Irish History Roundtable and the 150th anniversary of the Great Famine, October 28, 1994, a table entitled "Famine Facts from Ireland and America" offered the following information: a ticket to sail to New York during the famine cost $7.50 to $12.50, equivalent to a cottier's annual salary, and it could take six weeks to three months to complete the trip at sea.

According to Robert Scally, low rates of passage in 1847 were 3 pounds, 10 shillings, or

$17.50, which was about half of an agricultural laborer's annual wage. The voyage lasted 30 to 70 days by sail. Steam travel was introduced in the 1860s, reducing the voyage to 9–12 days by 1880 and 5–6 days by the 1920s. Notes, April 1996, in possession of author.

39. Janet Nolan, *Ourselves Alone* (Lexington: University Press of Kentucky, 1989), pp. 71 and 114–115.

40. Miller and Wagner, p. 125.

41. Commission on Emigration and Other Population Problems, p. 115, paragraph 250.

42. Rosaleen Fitzgibbon interview, December 1, 1993.

43. Jerry Brennan interview, October 11, 1994.

44. Taken from "The Track of the Macs," a personal memoir written by Joseph (Joe) McLaughlin and donated to the author by his son, Joseph P. McLaughlin; see p. 31. The senior McLaughlin emigrated in October 1929.

45. "An Oral History of Irish Immigrants" compiled by Robert H. Derham, December 4, 1976, University of California (Berkeley), lent to the author by Kerby Miller, p. 4.

46. Commission on Emigration and Other Population Problems, p. 135, paragraph 255.

47. Ibid., p. 137, paragraph 297.

48. Statistics quoted from *Water Wisdom*, film produced and directed for the Department of Local Government in Ireland in 1962 by Colm O'Laoghaire. Screened at "A Tribute to Colm O'Laoghaire," at the Irish Film Centre, Dublin, October 18, 1994.

49. Robert Joseph Savage Jr., "Irish Television: The Political and Social Genesis," Ph.D. dissertation, Boston College, May 1993. This thesis reviews the many parties involved in the 1950s debate on whether Ireland should institute a public television service.

50. Savage, p. 80.

51. Ibid., pp. 80–81.

52. Savage, p. 19, for the establishment of radio; read Savage also for debates over the creation of Irish national television.

53. Ibid., p. 25.

54. Ibid., pp. 23–25.

55. Martin McDonough's play *The Cripple of Inishmaan* is a fictional account of the impact that Robert Flaherty's filming of *Man of Aran* had on Ireland in the 1930s. The citizens of a western Ireland village reassure each other that if outsiders want to visit their community it must be okay to live there.

56. Letter to Linda Dowling Almeida from T. Q., June 30, 1994.

57. Letter to T. Q. from Eamon De Valera, president of Ireland, Dublin, September 2, 1961. Copy of original in possession of author, courtesy T. Q.

58. Central Statistics Office, *Ireland Census 91*, p. 10.

59. Lee, p. 360.

60. Central Statistics Office, *Ireland Census 91*, p. 30, table 6.

61. County Tipperary is divided into two sections in *Ireland Census 91*, Tipperary SR and Tipperary NR. According to the Consul General of Ireland's office in New York, SR and NR refer to South Riding and North Riding, which are geographical divisions of the county. Based on phone call to the consulate on April 26, 1996.

62. Central Statistics Office, *Ireland Census 91*, p. 17, table M.

63. Dublin County and Dublin County Borough was the only area to show a net increase in population (4 percent) between 1951 and 1961, which suggests, among other factors, that migrants leaving the rural areas of the rest of the country were heading toward Dublin, Ireland's largest city. Central Statistics Office, *Ireland Census 91*, p. 31, table 6.

Commission on Emigration and Other Population Problems, in its *1948–1954 Reports*, pp. 201–202, showed that between 1946 and 1951, Dublin City and County were the only city and county enjoying net immigration; the total in-migration was 18,000. The rest of the twenty-five counties suffered net emigration of 138,000, with a country-wide net emigration of 120,000 for the five-year period. The report concluded that the movement was primarily rural to urban.

64. Commission on Emigration and Other Population Problems, p. 177, paragraph 447. John Kelleher, in his article "Ireland . . . And Where Does She Stand?" *Foreign Affairs* 35, no. 3 (1957), wrote: "Today, three out of four Irish children still do not go beyond the sixth grade; and the education they receive is half-ruined by concentration on a language they will never speak again, anywhere. As emigrants they simply cannot compete on equal terms with Englishmen or Americans of the same class, who have had a better and longer education" (p. 495).

65. Lee, pp. 361–363.

66. Commission on Emigration and Other Population Problems, p. 177, paragraph 448. In paragraph 452, p. 178, the report recommended that "in rural areas it is especially desirable to avoid fostering an urban mentality."

67. Department of Commerce, *1960 Census of Population: Final Report, Subject Reports, Nativity and Parentage, Social and Economic Characteristics of the Foreign Stock by Country of Origin,* PC(2)-1A (henceforth *1960 Nativity and Parentage Report*), table 10, "Years of School Completed by the Foreign Stock 14 Years and Over, by Nativity, Parentage, Selected Country of Origin and Sex for United States, by Regions: 1960," p. 34. The median number of years completed for Irish natives born of foreign or mixed parentage in the United States was 11.5, with almost 30 percent having completed four years of high school.

68. The median number of years that Irish-born males 25–34 years old in the United States completed was 11; females of the same age completed 11.2 years of school. Irish-born males 35–44 completed 10.7 years of school, and Irish-born females in that age bracket completed 11.1 years of school. *1960 Nativity and Parentage Report,* table 12, p. 52.

69. The median number of school years completed in the United States in 1960 was 10.6; in New York it was 10.7. Of course this is not a strict comparison with the figures given for the Irish, because the United States and New York figures incorporate an older population, which presumably would drive down the total figure, if we assume that older generations did not attend school as long as students born later in the twentieth century. Department of Commerce, *1960 Census of Population: Characteristics of the Population, U.S. Summary,* vol. 1, pt. 1 (Washington, D.C.: Government Printing Office, 1961), table 115, p. 1-260; table 76, p. 1-207. *1960 Nativity and Parentage Report,* table 12, p. 52.

70. *1960 Nativity and Parentage Report,* table 12, p. 52.

71. Different sources put the number of Irish students going on to university study at about 50 percent of the secondary school graduates. Eileen M. Trauth, "Women in Ireland's Information Industry: Voices from Inside," *Eire-Ireland,* Fall 1995, p. 135. Industrial Development Authority (IDA), *Ireland: The Skills Center of Europe for the Electonics Industry* (Dublin: IDA, 1993), a market brochure revised September 1993; the inside front cover reports that "Half of all high school graduates enter third level education."

72. In the 1980s observers commented that although most emigrants headed for Great Britain, the more mature, better prepared, and stable individuals left for the United States because the longer trip required more planning and more savings than the trip to Great Britain. Perhaps the relatively higher level of education exhibited among the Irish in America in 1960 reflects a similar segregation between the migrants of the 1950s, the majority of whom also made Great Britain their preferred destination.

The 1950 census shows that for the New York–Northeastern New Jersey Standard Metropolitan Area (SMA), the median number of school years completed for 18- to 24-year-olds, which would include some of the 25- to 44-year-olds of the 1960 census, was 9.4 for males and 9.7 for females. The census also shows that 24 percent of all 18- to 24-year-old Irish-born in that SMA completed four years of high school, which is consistent with the observation that the younger emigrants were staying in school longer than assumed. Department of Commerce, *1950 Census Special Reports: Nativity and Parentage,* P-E 3A (Washington, D.C.: Government Printing Office, 1954), table 22, p. 3A-280.

73. Return emigrant (RE94) survey #5. The return emigrant (RE) surveys were dis-

tributed among several immigrants who returned to Ireland after living in New York for a time. Most had originally left for America in the 1940s and 1950s.

74. Marion A. Truslow, "Peasants into Patriots: The New York Irish Brigade Recruits and Their Families in the Civil War Era, 1850–1890," Ph.D. dissertation, New York University, 1994.

75. President Eisenhower approved Public Law 86 on June 20, 1953, granting naturalization to veterans who served during those years, with the following stipulations: must serve for ninety days; must be lawfully admitted to the United States, if admitted for other than permanent residence; must reside in the United States for one year before military service; standard requirements of age or length of residence waived. Immigration and Naturalization Service, *The I&N Reporter* 11, no. 4 (Washington, D.C.: Department of Justice, April 1954), p. 51.

76. Kevin Morrissey interview.

77. See Immigration and Naturalization Service (INS), *Annual Reports* for 1954, 1955, 1956, 1958, 1959, 1960, and 1961, table 8.

78. Since the *Commission on Emigration and Other Population Problems 1948–1954 Reports* published by the Irish government indicated that many adults were leaving as early as age 16, particularly the young women, I have chosen to isolate just the younger children from the no occupation category. See table 9 in the INS *Annual Reports* for designated years for age breakdowns. See table 40 in the INS *Annual Reports* for designated years for skill levels.

79. Kevin Morrissey interview.

80. RE94 survey #12.

81. RE94 survey #13.

82. Sister M. M. interview, Dublin, October 20, 1994.

83. Miller and Wagner, p. 116.

84. *New York and the Irish Famine: A Symbolic Meal and Keynote Address on the Occasion of the Tenth Anniversary of the New York Irish History Roundtable*, St. Paul the Apostle Undercroft, New York City, October 28, 1994 (New York: Irish History Roundtable, 1994), p. 10.

85. Miller, p. 510. In *Out of Ireland*, p. 69, Miller and Wagner write: "According to historian Arnold Schrier's calculations, during the late 19th century the Irish in America sent to Ireland over $260 million."

86. Commission on Emigration and Other Population Problems, p. 140, paragraph 313.

87. Ibid., p. 137, paragraph 302. The authors claimed that some emigrant letters proclaiming the good life in America were exaggerated and rarely "paint the other side" of the picture. Kevin Morrissey interview. Morrissey describes a relative from America who always wore very fancy clothes, leading him and his siblings to assume she was quite well-to-do.

88. Letter from immigrant X to couple in Dublin, January 31, 1957. Transcript of immigrant X letters, p. 7, Kerby Miller collection. Courtesy Kerby Miller. At Miller's request, all immigrants' names remain anonymous.

89. Letter from Peggy Hegarty, New York, N.Y., to Mom [D. Hegarty] and Den [brother], Co. Kerry, Ireland, March 14, 1957. Courtesy Peggy Hegarty Tanner.

90. David Halberstam, *The Fifties* (New York: Villard Books, 1993), p. 586.

91. Commission on Emigration and Other Population Problems, p. 17, table 8, "Percentage Distribution of Total Population by Age-Groups, 1841–1951," and paragraph 37. The average age in Ireland in 1951 was 32.5, almost 8 years older than a century before. ". . . our population is an aging one; in our present population of 3 millions there are 117,000 more people aged 65 and over than in 1841 when our population was 6½ millions."

For marriage rates, see Lee, pp. 360 and 381. Marriage rates hit a "trough" of 5.1 in 1957, rising to above 7 in 1970, the highest in Irish recorded history. Mean age at marriage fell from 30.6 for men in 1961 to 27.2 in 1973, and 26.9 to 24.8 for women in the same period. Lee also cited Alexis Fitzgerald's "reservation" to the majority in the *Commission on Emigration and Other Population Problems 1948–1954 Reports*, in which he claims that low marriage rates, not high emigration, were the true weakness in "our demographic experience." The report also noted in paragraph 303, p. 138, that women often left Ireland to pursue better marriage prospects abroad.

92. Immigration and Naturalization Service, 1957 *Annual Report,* table 9.

93. According to the 1950 census, 66.8 percent of all men and 67 percent of all urban males in New York State over the age of 14 were married; 62.9 percent of all women and 62.1 percent of all urban females over the age of 14 were married. These figures suggest that marriage opportunities were better in New York than in Ireland. Department of Commerce, *1950 Census of Population: Characteristics of Population, New York,* vol. 2, pt. 32, table 21 (Washington, D.C.: Government Printing Office, 1952), pp. 32–63.

94. Most of the female immigrants who were interviewed for this book were married to Irish-born men, but most met and married their husbands in New York City after leaving Ireland.

95. Department of Commerce, *1950 Census of Population: Census Tract Statistics New York, N.Y.: Selected Population and Housing Characteristics,* P-D37, vol. 3, chap. 37 (Washington, D.C.: Government Printing Office, 1952). See "Selected Population and Housing Characteristics," New York City, table 1 for each borough.

96. Department of Commerce, *1960 Census of Population: Final Report, New York, N.Y., Standard Metropolitan Statistical Area, part 1, New York City.* PHC (1)-104, pt. 1 (Washington, D.C.: Government Printing Office, 1961), p. 3.

97. Nathan Glazer and Daniel P. Moynihan, *Beyond the Melting Pot: The Negroes, Puerto Ricans, Irish, Jews, and Italians of New York City* (Cambridge: MIT Press and Harvard University Press, 1963), p. 219.

98. Department of Commerce, *1950 Census Special Report: Nativity and Parentage,* P-E 3A. See table 16, "Age of the Foreign White Stock, by Nativity, Parentage, and Selected Country of Origin for Standard Metropolitan Areas with 500,000 or More Foreign White Stock: 1950," p. 3A-122.

99. Tim Pat Coogan, *Eamon De Valera: The Man Who Was Ireland* (New York: HarperCollins Publishers, 1993), p. ix.

100. Rebecca Miller, "Irish Traditional and Popular Music in New York City: Identity and Social Change, 1935–1975," in *The New York Irish,* ed. Ronald H. Bayor and Timothy Meagher (Baltimore: Johns Hopkins University Press, 1996), pp. 484–485.

101. Coogan, p. ix.

102. All the anecdotes about Father Reid can be found in his unpublished memoirs, "Recollections of Some Sixty Years," in possession of Linda Almeida.

103. WPA Historical Records Survey, Federal Writers Project, Box 3579, "Irish in New York," folder 5, "Occupations and Location," A. Fitzpatrick, "The Irish Race in Various Industries, Professions, Etc." 1938.

104. Robert Snyder, "The Neighborhood Changed: The Irish of Washington Heights and Inwood since 1945," in *The New York Irish,* ed. Ronald H. Bayor and Timothy Meagher (Baltimore: Johns Hopkins University Press, 1996), p. 442.

105. Department of Commerce, *1960 Census of Population: Final Report, Subject Reports, Nativity and Parentage, Social and Economic Characteristics of the Foreign Stock by Country of Origin,* PC(2)-1A, table 16, p. 110, for New York State.

106. Ira Rosenwaike offered numbers that show second-generation Irish foreign stock outnumbered immigrants two to one in 1960. These numbers include Northern Ireland. Ira Rosenwaike, *Population History of New York City* (Syracuse, N.Y.: Syracuse University Press, 1972), table C-3, p. 205.

107. According to the *1960 Nativity and Parentage Report,* PC(2)-1A, table 16, the total number of foreign-born and native Irish of foreign or mixed parentage (foreign stock) for New York State was 492,041. The total foreign stock for New York City was 311,638, or 63 percent of the state's Irish foreign-stock population. The latter population figure can be

found in the Department of Commerce's *1960 U.S. Census of Population and Housing: Final Reports. Series PHC. By Census Tracts. New York, N.Y.,* pt. 1, New York City, PHC(1)-104 (Washington, D.C.: Government Printing Office, 1962). See table P-1, p. 23.

108. Letter from Peggy Hegarty, Tuesday, November 24, 1953, to Mom and Den, p. 4. Courtesy Peggy Hegarty Tanner.

109. *1950 Census of Population: Census Tract Statistics, New York, N.Y.*. See table 1 for each borough, pp. 9ff.

110. See tracts 303, 295, 293, 291, and 285 for Inwood and tracts 239, 245, 251, 253, 261,263, 269, 271, 277, and 279 for Washington Heights. *1950 Census Tract Statistics, New York,* table 1, pp. 9ff.

111. Snyder, p. 444.

112. Ira Katznelson, *City Trenches: Urban Politics and the Patterning of Class in the United States* (Philadelphia: Temple University Press, 1981), p. 82, and Snyder, p. 442.

113. Letter from J. J. S. to Linda Dowling Almeida, February 6, 1995, in response to a letter to the editor placed in *Catholic News,* the weekly paper for the Archdiocese of New York, requesting information from Irish immigrants and Irish Americans living in New York from 1945 to the present.

114. Family history of H. L. G., sent to Linda Dowling Almeida, December 12, 1994.

115. H. L. G., p. 10.

116. H. L. G., p. 2.

117. For the early recollections of H. L. G.'s life see family history, pp. 1–6.

118. *1950 Census Tract Statistics, New York.* See table 1, pp. 9ff., for the Bronx.

119. *1950 Census Tract Statistics, New York.* See table 1, pp. 34ff., for Brooklyn.

120. Pete Hamill, *A Drinking Life: A Memoir* (New York: Little, Brown and Company, 1994).

121. The addresses for Catholic schools and churches are taken from *The Official Catholic Directory, AD 1995* (New Providence, N.J.: P. J. Kennedy and Sons, in association with R. R. Bowker, 1995), pp. 692–698.

122. *1950 Census Tract Statistics, New York.* See table 1, pp. 101f., for Queens.

123. *1960 Nativity and Parentage Report,* PC(2)-1A, See table 5, table 16, p. 110.

124. INS, *1992 Statistical Yearbook of the Immigration and Naturalization Service* (Washington, D.C.: Government Printing Office, October 1993), table 2, p. 27.

125. For all borough studies, refer to *1960 Census Tract Report, New York,* PHC(1)-104. Tract data for each borough is taken from table P-1.

126. *1960 Census Tract Report, New York,* PHC(1)-104. See table P-1, pp. 145–146 and p. 23, and Halberstam, p. 587.

127. Kevin Morrissey interview.

128. Snyder, p. 20.

129. See *1960 Census Tract Report, New York,* PHC(1)-104, Manhattan census tracts 253, 261, and 269.

130. See Katznelson, *City Trenches,* and Ronald H. Bayor, *Neighbors in Conflict: The Irish, Germans, Jews, and Italians of New York City, 1929–1941,* 2nd ed. (Urbana: University of Illinois Press, 1987).

131. *1960 Census Tract Report, New York,* PHC(1)-104. See table P-1 for Manhattan, p. 132.

132. *1960 Census Tract Report, New York,* PHC(1)-104, table P-1 for Manhattan, tracts 291, 293, and 295, p. 132.

133. Ira Berkow, "Just Another Down-to-Earth Guy," *New York Times,* February 8, 1995, p. B11.

134. *1960 Census Tract Report, New York,* PHC(1)-104. See table P-1 for Manhattan, tracts 291 and 293, p. 132.

135. Snyder, p. 443.

136. Bayor, pp. 24–29.

137. Conversation with Detective J. M., president of New York City Police Emerald Society, March 1995.

138. Chris McNickle, *To Be Mayor of New York* (New York: Columbia University Press, 1993), pp. 55 and 322.

139. The following tract information was taken from the *1960 Census Tract Report, New York*, PHC(1)-104, table P-1 for each borough.

140. See census tracts 138, 146, 154, and 158 for Manhattan.

141. See census tracts 210, 216, and 218 for the Bronx.

142. See census tracts 383, 399, 405, and 407 for the Bronx.

143. See Bronx tracts 383, 399, 405, and 407.

144. This information was collected from surveys RE94 #4 and RE94 #13 and cross-referenced with listings in *The Official Catholic Directory AD 1995*.

145. RE94 survey #4.

146. RE94 survey #13.

147. Sean S. Reid, O. Carm. "Recollections of Some Sixty Years," ca. 1985. Father Reid wrote about his contacts and his efforts to secure jobs for relatives and friends of friends during his years as a parish priest in New York City, from the 1930s to the 1960s.

148. See Brooklyn tracts 171, 169, 149, 151, 153, 155, 157, 159, 139, 161, 163, 207, 215, 217, 223, and 219.

149. Tracts 130, 134, and 136 had a combined population of 14,125; 10.6 percent or 1,505 of those people were identified as Irish. Italians numbered 1,165. See *1960 Census Tract Report, New York*, PHC(1)-104, table P-1, p. 62.

150. See Brooklyn tracts 830, 832, 834, 836, and 838.

3. THE 1970S

1. Pete Hamill, "Notes on the New Irish: A Guide for the Goyim," *New York Magazine*, March 15, 1972, p. 33.

2. Fergal Tobin, *The Best of Decades: Ireland in the Nineteen Sixties* (Dublin: Gill and Macmillan, 1984). Taken from the title of his book, the quote refers to the 1960s.

3. Department of Commerce, *1970 Census of Population and Housing: Census Tracts, New York, N.Y., Standard Metropolitan Statistical Area (SMSA)*, PHC(1)-145, pt. 1 (Washington, D.C.: Government Printing Office, 1972); see table P-2, "Social Characteristics of the Population." *1960 Census of Population and Housing. Final Reports. Series PHC. By Census Tracts. New York, N.Y.*, PHC(1)-104, pt. 1, New York City (Washington, D.C.: Government Printing Office, 1962); see table P-1, p. 23.

4. *1970 Census Tracts*, PHC(1)-145, pt. 1, table P-2, "Social Characteristics of the Population," for New York County tracts 291, 293, 295, 303, 307, and 309, pp. P-316 and P-317; for the Bronx County tracts 239, 245, 251, 253, 255, 263, and 265, pp. P-216 and P-217; for Kings County (Brooklyn) tracts 157, 165, 167, 169, and 171, pp. P-236 and P-237; for Queens County tracts 249, 251, 253, 261, 263, pp. P-329–P-330.

5. *1970 Census Tracts*, PHC(1)-145, pt. 1, table P-2, "Social Characteristics of the Population," for New York County, p. P-300. See tracts 291, 293, 295, 303, and 307.

6. See Robert Snyder, "The Neighborhood Changed: The Irish of Washington Heights and Inwood since 1945," *The New York Irish*, ed. Ronald H. Bayor and Timothy Meagher (Baltimore: Johns Hopkins University Press, 1996), pp. 450–451. Throughout his paper Snyder tracks the Irish migration north and eventually out of Manhattan as blacks and Dominicans pushed up from neighborhoods to the south in search of better housing and recreation for their families. He quotes Irish residents who view the encroachment as a siege by unwanted "aliens": "There was a sense that the circle was starting to form and encircle the area" (p. 453).

7. Snyder, p. 453.

8. See Department of Commerce, *1960 Census Tract Report: New York*, PHC(1)-104,

table P-1 for Manhattan Borough, tracts 291, 293, 295, 303, 307, and 309, p. 132, and *1970 Census Tracts*, PHC(1)-145, pt. 1, table P-2, "Social Characteristics of the Population," for New York County, tracts 291, 293, 295, 303, 307, and 309, pp. P-316 and P-317.

9. See Department of Commerce, *1960 Census Tract Report: New York*, PHC(1)-104, table P-1 for Manhattan Borough, tracts 291, 293, 295, 303, 307, and 309, p. 132 and *1970 Census Tracts*, PHC(1)-145, pt. 1, table P-2, "Social Characteristics of Population," for New York County, tracts 291, 293, 303, 307, and 309, pp. P-316–317.

10. Information Center on Education, University of the State of New York, *Nonpublic School Enrollment and Staff, New York State 1973–74*, (Albany, N.Y.: State Department of Education, April 1975), p. 6. "Controlled and supported primarily by a local, State or Federal agency" is from Department of Commerce, *1960 Census Tract Report*, PHC(1)-104, p. 4.

See Andrew M. Greeley, William C. McCready, and Kathleen McCourt, *Catholic Schools in a Declining Church* (Kansas City, Mo.: Sheed and Ward, 1976), p. 10, regarding demographics of parochial schools.

11. *1970 Census Tracts*, PHC(1)-145, pt. 1, table P-2, "Social Characteristics of the Population," for New York County, tracts 291, 293, and 295, pp. P-316 and P-317.

12. See Department of Commerce *1970 Census of Population and Housing, Census Tracts, New York, N.Y. Standard Metropolitan Statistical Area*, PHC(1)-145, pt. 2 (Washington, D.C.: Government Printing Office, 1972), table P-4, "Income Characteristics of the Population," p. P-716.

13. Snyder, p. 451.

14. Snyder, pp. 450–460.

15. Snyder, p. 455.

16. See *1970 Census Tracts*, PHC(1)-145, table P-2, "Social Characteristics of the Population," p. P-201–P-202, and *1960 Census Tract Report: New York*, PHC(1)-104, table P-1, p. 23.

17. Letter to Linda Dowling Almeida from Gerald Ryan, St. Luke's Church, 623 East 138th Street, Bronx, NY 10454, March 24, 1995. Letter in possession of author.

18. The baptismal records for 1953–1959 and 1977–1985 were examined in the rectory at St. Nicholas of Tollantine Church, 2345 University Avenue, in the Bronx, courtesy of Father John Dellarusso and Father Brian Frawley.

19. Letter to Linda Dowling Almeida, July 21, 1995, from F. D. Letter in possession of author. See p. 7.

20. Ibid., p. 7.

21. Ibid., p. 8.

22. Ibid., p. 4. In a November 5, 1993, speech entitled " 'From the East Side to the Seaside': Irish Americans on the Move in New York City, 1900–1960," Marion Casey observed that improved housing and transportation links opened up "the outer boroughs for the Irish in the early twentieth century." Minutes of Columbia University Seminar on Irish Studies, #535, Laura O'Connor, rapporteur, November 8, 1993.

23. See *1970 Census Tracts*, PHC(1)-145, pt. 1, table P-2, "Social Characteristics of the Population," p. P-201, and *1960 Census Tract Report: New York*, PHC(1)-104, table P-1, p. 23.

24. See survey form RE94, numbers 1, 4, 5, and 13, in possession of author. Also interview with Mr. and Mrs. W. of Dublin, October 19, 1994. This couple emigrated in the 1950s, met and married in New York, and returned to Dublin with their children. He collects a pension from his U.S. job.

25. NESC, *The Economic and Social Implications of Emigration* (Dublin: National Economic and Social Council, March 1991), pp. 59 and 254.

26. J. J. [Joseph] Lee, *Ireland 1912–1985: Politics and Society*, 6th ed. (Cambridge: Cambridge University Press, 1993); see chapter 5, "Expansion: 1958–1969," pp. 329–411.

27. *Irish Echo*, Saturday, September 25, 1965.

28. *Irish Echo*, May 15, 1965; September 25, 1965; March 20, 1965.

29. Barbara O'Connor and Michael Cronin, eds., *Tourism in Ireland: A Critical Analysis* (Cork, Ireland: Cork University Press, 1993); see introduction, p. 1. Editor O'Connor says in

her own article, "Myths and Mirrors: Tourist Images and National Identity," p. 73, that another factor in the growing number of tourists to Ireland after 1960 was the development of "roots" tourism as successful Irish Americans used their holiday to trace their heritage and visit the homes of relatives and ancestors.

30. *Irish Echo*, September 25, 1965, p. 1.

31. *Irish Echo*, July 31, 1965, p. 3. The Grimes family, which owned the travel agency, was related to the Grimes family that published and continues to publish the *Echo*. Another prominent travel agent of the period, who recently sold his business, was Brendan Ward. Mr. Ward made a name for himself in the Irish community as the leader of a big band orchestra that entertained Irish audiences and dancers through the 1950s at City Center Ballroom in Manhattan.

32. RE94 surveys, numbers 1, 4, 5, and 13. In possession of author. Kevin Morrissey, interviewed February 9, 1995, admitted that he and his family went to Ireland after the birth of each of his children in the 1960s.

33. INS, *Annual Report of the U.S. Immigration and Naturalization Service, 1954* (Washington, D.C.: Department of Justice, 1954), table 32.

34. INS, *Annual Report of the Immigration and Naturalization Service, 1961* (Washington, D.C.: Department of Justice, 1961), table 32, p. 70.

35. *1954 INS Annual Report*, table 32.

36. INS, *1961 Annual Report*, table 32, p. 70, and *1954 Annual Report*, table 32.

37. Andrew Greeley has argued that by the 1970s the Irish had among the highest incomes of white ethnic Catholics in the United States and "They were now the most successful gentile group in American society. . . ." See Andrew M. Greeley, William C. McCready, and Kathleen McCourt, *Catholic Schools in a Declining Church* (Kansas City, Mo.: Sheed and Ward, 1976), pp. 73 and 55. See INS *Annual Reports* for 1954, table 32, and for 1961, p. 70, table 32, as well as tables 39 (p. 80) and 44 (p. 89), which show that 41,796 Irish were naturalized between 1952 and 1961, that the peak years of naturalization were between 1954 and 1956, and that the majority of Irish naturalized in 1961 entered the United States in 1954 and 1955.

38. *Irish Echo*, July 31, 1965, p. 6. Taken from letters to "Educational Notes," column by Frank O'Connor, B.A., LL.B.

39. P. M. to M. M., May 14, 1952. Kerby A. Miller Collection. Courtesy Kerby A. Miller.

40. P. M. to M. M., August 8, 1953(?). Kerby A. Miller collection. Courtesy Kerby A. Miller.

41. RE94 survey #4, in possession of author.

42. RE94 survey #13, in possession of author.

43. RE94 survey #1, in possession of author.

44. RE94 survey #5, in possession of author.

45. Letter to Linda Dowling Almeida, June 1, 1995, from Barbara A. Lingg, acting leader, Division of RSDI Research Statistics, Office of Research and Statistics, Social Security Administration, Department of Health and Human Services.

46. Social Security Administration, *Social Security Bulletin* 57, no. 1 (Washington, D.C.: Government Printing Office, Spring 1994): 39.

47. Social Security Administration, excerpts from *Annual Statistical Supplement to the Social Security Bulletin*, 1955, p. 42, table 61; 1956, p. 52, table 68; 1957, p. 57, table 77; 1958, p. 55, table 79; 1959, p. 59, table 84; 1960, p. 74, table 93; 1961, p. 87, table 102; 1962, p. 81, table 97; 1964, p. 93, table 102; 1965, p. 100, table 105; 1966, p. 111, table 111; 1967, p. 122, table 126; 1968, p. 130, table 129; 1969, p. 129, table 131; 1970, p. 128, table 129; 1971, p. 136, table 135; 1972, p. 134, table 122; 1973, p. 143, table 122; 1974, p. 147, table 120; 1976, p.170, table 127; 1977, p. 194, table 128; 1979, p. 190, table 127; 1980, p. 201, table 129; 1982, p. 189, table 115; 1983, p. 190, table 115; 1984, p.195, table 125; 1985, p. 221, table 134; 1986, p. 225, table 139; 1987, p. 240, table 5.J11; 1988, p. 242, table 5.J11; 1989, p. 222, table 5.J11; 1990, p. 216, table 5.J11; 1991, p. 233, table 5.J11; 1992, p. 247, table 5.J11; 1993, p. 247, table 5.J11; 1994, p. 1, table 5.J11. Figures courtesy of

Barbara A. Lingg, acting leader, Division of RSDI Research Statistics, Office of Research and Statistics, Social Security Administration.

48. Central Statistics Office, *Population and Labour Force Projections, 1991–2021* (Dublin: Stationery Office, April 1988), table B, p. 7.

49. *Social Security Bulletin* 57, no. 1 (1994): 39.

50. INS, *1992 Statistical Yearbook of the Immigration and Naturalization Service,* table 2, p. 27.

51. W. family interview, October 1994.

52. John P. McCarthy, *Dissent from Irish America* (New York: University Press of America, 1993), pp. 221–222.

53. Thomas Murphy, *A Crucial Week in the Life of a Grocer's Assistant* (Dublin: Gallery Books, 1978).

54. Patrick McCabe, *The Butcher Boy* (New York: Delta, 1994), pp. 28–40.

55. Even in the 1980s, small towns in Ireland were intolerant of returning migrants. A conversation with two young immigrants from a rural community in Cavan revealed that going back to live in their home town would not be easy because "they [the townspeople] would say that you couldn't make it in America."

56. Lee, p. 646. For full examination of the begrudger characters in Irish society, read pp. 643–658.

57. Ibid., p. 647.

58. Ibid., pp. 342–359.

59. Fergal Tobin, *The Best of Decades* (Dublin: Gill and Macmillan, 1984).

60. Lee, p. 465.

61. Ibid., pp. 530–536.

62. Letter to Linda Almeida from Dermot O'Sullivan, chairman, EBU Statistics Group, Radio Telefis Eireann, Dublin 4, Ireland, November 1, 1994. Note that Ulster is split into the six counties that make up Northern Ireland and three counties that remain part of the Republic of Ireland. The figures O'Sullivan cites for Ulster probably refer to the three counties in the Republic.

63. *Into the West,* directed by Mike Newell, written by Jim Sheridan (Touchstone Home Video and Miramax Films, 1993).

64. John A. Murphy, *Ireland in the Twentieth Century,* 2nd ed., The Gill History of Ireland, ed. James Lydon and Margaret MacCurtain (Dublin: Gill and Macmillan, 1977), p. 146.

65. Robert Joseph Savage, Jr., "Irish Television: The Political and Social Genesis," Ph.D. dissertation, Boston College, 1993, chapter 8 and pp. 492–494.

66. Tim Pat Coogan, *Eamon De Valera: The Man Who Was Ireland* (New York: Harper-Collins Publishers, 1993), p. 659.

67. Letter to Linda Dowling Almeida from Dermot O'Sullivan, chairman, EBU Statistics Group, RTE, November 29, 1994. Data prior to 1972 is "less available," according to Mr. O'Sullivan.

68. See *RTV Guide* [Ireland], vol. 1, no. 4 (January 28, 1977), p. 16, for January 30, 1977; vol. 6, no. 6 (February 5, 1982), p. 20, for February 6, 1982; and vol. 6, no. 10 (March 5, 1982), for March 12.

69. INS, *1992 Statistical Yearbook of the Immigration and Naturalization Service* (Washington, D.C.: Government Printing Office, October 1993), table 2, "Immigration by Region and Selected Country of Last Residence Fiscal Years 1820–1992," p. 27.

70. McCarthy, p. 91, from "Disparity of Perceptions."

71. "Focus: Brendan Ward," *Irish Voice,* October 19–25, 1994, p. 18. Brendan Ward is profiled.

72. John T. Ridge, *The St. Patrick's Day Parade in New York* (New York: St. Patrick's Day Parade Committee, 1988), p. 168.

73. Mary Ford, "To Monahan's!" *Culturefront* 4, no. 7 (Spring 1995): 23.

74. Ford, p. 24.

75. Hamill, "Notes on the New Irish," p. 34.

76. Ford, p. 24.

77. Letter to Linda Dowling Almeida, August 16, 1994, from J. H. Phone conversation with J. H., September 1994. "Cuimhni Cinn" (Remembrance), in J. H., *An Teanga Mhartha-nach* [Living Language], ca. Spring 1993, p. 24, courtesy J. H.

78. Jim Carroll, *The Basketball Diaries* (New York: Penguin Books, 1995), p. 17.

79. Barbara O'Connor, "Myths and Mirrors: Tourist Images and National Identity," in *Tourism in Ireland: A Critical Analysis,* ed. Barbara O'Connor and Michael Cronin (Cork, Ireland: Cork University Press, 1993), p. 70.

80. Luke Gibbons, "Alien Eye: Photography and Ireland," *Circa* 12, no. 10 (1986); this passage is quoted in O'Connor, "Myths and Mirrors," p. 69.

81. O'Connor, pp. 69–70.

4. THE 1980S

1. Berna Brennan interview, October 16, 1994. Mrs. Brennan lives in Ireland and at the time of the interview had two sons in America. The Irish phrase translates to "by helping one another we survive." As a mother Mrs. Brennan fears that emigration and the adoption of American values will destroy the Irish sense of community in the young emigrants.

2. Central Statistics Office, *Ireland Census 91, Vol. 1, Population Classified by Area* (Dublin: Stationery Office, June 1993), tables K and L, p. 16, and table 2, p. 25. See also J. J. [Joseph] Lee, *Ireland 1912–1985: Politics and Society,* 6th ed. (Cambridge: Cambridge University Press, 1993), pp. 360 and 381, for marriage rates and ages.

3. Central Statistics Office, *Ireland Census 91,* p. 16, table K. The estimated annual emigration between 1946 and 1951 was 24,498; between 1986 and 1991 it was 26,834. See also National Economic and Social Council (NESC), *The Economic and Social Implications of Emigration* (Dublin: National Economic and Social Council, March 1991), p. 59.

4. Data from Dermot O'Sullivan, director, corporate planning, RTE, Dublin, letters to Linda Almeida, October 25, 1994, and November 1, 1994.

5. Central Statistics Office, *Ireland Census 86, Summary Population Report* (Dublin: Stationery Office, November 1987), p. vii. In 1981, 47.8 percent of the population was under 25; five years later the figure had dropped to 46.4 percent.

6. Sean Minihane, phone interview, December 27, 1988.

7. According to a report published by the Higher Education Authority (HEA) in Ireland and reported in the *Irish Voice,* December 24–31, 1988, p. 4, 70 percent of graduates who emigrate go to Britain, 10.1 percent to North America, and 9.8 percent to the European continent. See also Damien Courtney, "Summary of Recent Trends in Emigration from Ireland," Development Studies Association Annual Conference, Queen's University of Belfast, September 1989. The author states that most Irish migrants leave for English-speaking countries, "with as many as 70 percent" going to Britain. See also NESC, *Economic and Social Implications of Immigration,* pp. 60–61. The NESC reports that in the early 1980s, about 60 percent of emigrants went to Great Britain, 14 percent to the United States, and the rest to other countries.

8. Congressional Research Office, "U.S. Immigration Law and Policy, 1952–1986," December 1987, pp. 55–7, and Anne Barrington, press and information officer for the consul general of Ireland, "Emigration from Ireland: Why and How Many?" New York, May 1991, pp. 7–8. Courtesy consul general's office, New York.

9. Immigration and Naturalization Service (INS), *1987 Statistical Yearbook of the Immigration and Naturalization Service* (Washington, D.C.: Government Printing Office, 1988), p. 68.

10. *U.S. News and World Report,* March 2, 1987, p. 15. The requests were received in January 1987, and the volume of inquiries may have been attributable to the amendment attached to the Immigration Reform and Control Act (IRCA) of 1986 (known as the Don-

nelly Bill after the Massachusetts congressman, Brian Donnelly, who wrote the amendment), which provided for 10,000 nonpreference visas for thirty-six nations considered adversely affected by the 1965 Immigration Act. Of the 10,000 visas distributed by lottery, the Irish won 4,161. See *Irish Echo*, January 10, 1987, and *Irish Voice*, November 5, 1988, p. 26.

11. The consul general of Ireland and the U.S. Catholic Conference argued for the lower figure. See Barrington, pp. 5–6; Migration and Refugee Services Staff, U.S. Catholic Conference unpublished report, "Undocumented Irish in the U.S.," March 1988 (in possession of author); and Lorcan O'Riada, *Boston Irish News*, April 1989, p. 1. The Irish Immigration Reform Movement (IIRM), the *Irish Voice*, and the Bishops' Episcopal Commission in Ireland advocated for the higher numbers. See the *Irish Voice*, December 5, 1987, and the IIRM press kit for releases citing population figures. For references to the bishops' report, see Mary Corcoran, "Ethnic Boundaries and Legal Barriers: The Labor Market Experience of Undocumented Irish Workers in New York City," unpublished paper presented at Columbia University, New York, April 1988.

12. INS, *1992 Statistical Yearbook of the Immigration and Naturalization Service* (Washington, D.C.: Government Printing Office, October 1993), table 3, p. 30.

13. Central Statistics Office, *Ireland Census 91*, p. 16.

14. NESC, p. 59.

15. INS, *1992 Statistical Yearbook*, p. 30.

16. Ibid., p. 30.

17. Barrington, pp. 8–10.

18. Kerry Emigrant Support Group, *Emigration Awareness*, ed. Sister Anne McNamara, PBVM (Tralee, Ireland: Kerry Emigrant Support Group, n.d., but includes 1993 data), pp. 62–63.

19. Immigration and Naturalization Service, *1997 Statistical Yearbook of the Immigration and Naturalization Service* (Washington, D.C.: Government Printing Office, October 1999), table 3: Immigrants Admitted by Region and Country of Birth, Fiscal Years 1987–1997, and table 2: Immigrants by Region and Selected Country of Last Residence, Fiscal Years 1820–1997, pp. 26 and 28.

20. Department of Commerce, *1980 Census of Population: Vol. 1, Sec. 2, Characteristics of Population: Chapter C, General Social and Economic Characteristics.* pt. 34, New York, PC80-1-C34 (Washington, D.C.: Government Printing Office, July 1983), table 172, pp. 931–935.

21. Department of Commerce, *1980 Census, Population Characteristics, New York State*, pt. 34, PC80-1-D34 (Washington, D.C.: Government Printing Office, November 1983), table 193.

22. See Department of Commerce, *1980 Census, by Census Tracts, New York Selected Areas*, PHC80-2-34, pt. 34 (Washington, D.C.: Government Printing Office, August 1983), p. B-6, for definition of "ancestry."

23. Department of Commerce, *1980 Census, by Census Tracts, New York Selected Areas*, PHC80-2-34, p. B-6.

24. See Department of Commerce, *1990 Census of Population and Housing, Population and Housing Characteristics for Census Tracts and Block Numbering Areas, New York, Northern New Jersey, Long Island, NY-NJ-CT CMSA (Part) New York, N.Y. PMSA*, 1990 CPH-3-245H (Washington, D.C.: Government Printing Office, July 1993), section 6, p. B-2, for "Definitions of Subject Characteristics."

25. Department of Commerce, *1980 Census, General Social and Economic Characteristics*, PC80-1-C34, table 60, p. 133.

26. Department of Commerce, *1980 Census, Ancestry of Persons, New York by Census Tracts, NY-NJ SMSA*, PHC80-2260 (Washington, D.C.: Government Printing Office, August 1983), table P-8, p. P-558.

27. Department of Commerce, *1990 Census of Population and Housing, Summary Tape File 3A on CD for New York State*, courtesy New York University Computer Center.

28. Ibid.

29. Department of Commerce, *1980 Census, Ancestry of Persons*, PHC80-2260, and *1990 Census of Population and Housing*, Summary Tape File 3A on CD.

30. The NESC report is extremely informative and filled with demographic data that are quite useful in characterizing the migrating population in general, and the push/pull forces behind the outflow of people. However, in characterizing the migrants who came to the United States, we must be mindful that only 10 to 15 percent of all migrants came to the United States, so the data do not translate exactly.

31. In the fall of 1990 the author and the Emerald Isle Immigration Center (EIIC) conducted a survey among the New Irish population using the center's mailing list of more than a thousand names, as well as distributing the survey locally with the assistance of the immigrant chaplains living in New Irish neighborhoods, friendly bartenders, and at EIIC meeting venues. In all, we put out between 1,500 and 2,000 surveys. We received 247 completed forms. The results of the survey were printed in the March 16, 1991, issue of the *Irish Voice* and were analyzed by the author in a paper published in volume 1 (1992) of *The Irish World Wide*, edited by Patrick O'Sullivan (Leicester, England: University of Leicester Press, and New York: St. Martin's Press, 1992), under the chapter title "'And They Still Haven't Found What They're Looking For': A Survey of the New Irish in New York City."

32. The NESC report contends that "the great majority of emigrants possess at best Second Level qualifications, and a significant number have no formal educational qualifications at all." NESC, p. 88.

33. The NESC report indicates that data show "migratory outflow" in the 1980s to be "broadly representative of the structure of Irish society." And as we showed for the 1950s, the migrants were "surprisingly" underrepresented by farmers. See p. 84.

34. NESC, p. 77.

35. Ibid., p. 67.

36. Immigration and Naturalization Service, *1992 Statistical Yearbook*, table 13, p. 54.

37. NESC, p.70.

38. Ibid., p. 73.

39. Kerry Emigrant Support Group, p. 4.

40. Timing was critical in conducting this survey. The transience and anonymity of the population determined that a survey was the best medium to reach as many migrants as possible in as short a time as possible. The window of opportunity for access to such a large segment of the population was closing in the months (fall 1990) surrounding final immigration legislation negotiations. We were afraid that once visas became available for the majority of the population, a real possibility existed that the New Irish would disperse, reducing easy access to a solid block of New Irish.

41. Definitions come from the Irish consul's office in New York City, April 26, 1996.

42. See NESC, chapter 6, particularly pp. 88, 123, 144–45, 159.

43. Different sources put the number of Irish students going on to university study at about 50 percent of the secondary-school graduates. Eileen M. Trauth, "Women in Ireland's Information Industry: Voices from Inside," *Eire-Ireland*, Fall 1995, p. 135. Industrial Development Authority (IDA), *Ireland: The Skills Center of Europe for the Electronics Industry* (a marketing brochure revised September 1993); its inside front cover reports that "Half of all high school graduates enter third level education." Kerry Emigrant Support Group, p. 4.

44. The figures for the 1950 migrants are based on 1960 United States census data for foreign-born Irish 25 to 44 years old. Department of Commerce, *1960 Census of Population: Final Report, Subject Reports, Nativity and Parentage, Social and Economic Characteristics of the Foreign Stock by Country of Origin*, PC(2)-1A (Washington, D.C.: Government Printing Office, 1964), table 12, p. 52.

45. NESC, p. 133.

46. Ibid., p. 133.

47. Ibid., pp. 138–139.

48. *Irish Times* [Dublin], November 8, 1988, p. 8.

49. *Irish Voice,* December 5, 1987, p. 1.

50. NESC, p. 74.

51. Central Statistics Office, *Ireland Census 91,* p. 16.

52. NESC, chapter 6, particularly p. 159.

53. NESC, p. 84.

54. See Mary Corcoran, "A Not So Distant Shore: Recent Irish Immigrants in New York City," in *The New York Irish,* ed. Ronald H. Bayor and Timothy Meagher (Baltimore: Johns Hopkins University Press, 1996), pp. 461–480. Also, *Irish Independent,* July 9, 1988, James Morrissey, cited in Corcoran, p. 690, n. 12.

55. See Joe Jackson, "Is That It?" *Irish Times* (Fall 1992?—undated photocopy), courtesy Marion Casey, and Orla Healy, "No More Blarney: The New Irish March to a Different Drummer," *New York Live: Daily News Color Supplement,* March 15, 1992, pp. 4–7, for profiles of New Irish living outside the outer-borough "ghettoes."

56. The chaplaincy program began with three priests and one nun who were assigned to parishes throughout the archdiocese (which includes Manhattan, the Bronx, and Staten Island) which were known to include large populations of New Irish. The Diocese of Brooklyn (which includes Brooklyn and Queens) began its own chaplaincy program later in the decade.

57. *Irish Voice,* December 5, 1987, p. 4.

58. *Irish Echo,* January 13, 1981, p. 25.

59. *Irish Echo,* December 18, 1982.

60. *Irish Echo,* October 12, 1985.

61. *Irish Echo,* November 2, 1985, pp. 42–46.

62. It should be noted that through the eighties the *Irish Echo* became the paper of choice for those seeking live-in or live-out care providers or jobs. One couple placed a help wanted ad in the *Echo* in 1986 and received more than a hundred responses, including one from the Jamaican woman whom they eventually hired. As the paper's reputation grew, we can assume that its classifieds were reaching beyond the Irish community.

63. New York Bell rates found in *Irish Echo,* November 6, 1982; AT&T rates based on call to international operator information, March 1989 and call volume data found in *Irish Voice,* January 7, 1989, p. 1. These calls do not include connections made on other international carriers such as Sprint and MCI.

64. The EIIC is the social services and outreach arm of the IIRM, located in Woodside, Queens.

65. *Irish Voice,* October 15, 1988, p. 17.

66. Monsignor James J. Murray interview, January 27, 1989.

67. Murray interview.

68. G. Q. interview, February 8, 1989.

69. G. Q. interview.

70. Jailed members of the IRA in Northern Ireland went on hunger strikes in protest of the problems in Northern Ireland. Several of the strikers died, the most famous being Bobby Sands.

71. Andrew J. Wilson, *Irish America and the Ulster Conflict, 1968–1995* (Washington, D.C.: The Catholic University of America Press, 1995), pp. 268–277.

72. Interview with Joe Jamison, February 1, 1989. It should also be noted that the TWU was a strongly Irish union going back to the 1930s when it was led by the well-known labor organizer Mike Quill.

73. At the 1984 national convention of the AOH, Thomas Murray, national chairman of the immigration committee, urged all Americans to support Simpson-Mazzoli, an early version of IRCA. The AOH voted unanimously in support of the bill. *Irish Echo,* August 4, 1984, p. 1.

74. Nick Murphy interview, January 29, 1989.

75. This history is taken from interviews with Pat Hurley, October 15, 1988, and Sean Minihane, December 27, 1988, and from the press materials distributed by the IIRM. See also *Irish America Magazine*, December 1988, pp. 20–23, 36–37. The cover story was about the "illegal aliens" and featured the IIRM.

76. The offshore Irish had no absentee ballot, so they had no voting leverage with elected officials at home. In the 1990s the Irish Emigrant Vote Campaign (IEVC) was formed, a committee which sought to establish absentee ballots so emigrants could participate politically in Ireland while they lived abroad. The co-coordinator of the IEVC in Ireland in 1991 was Sean Minihane, who had returned to live and work in Dublin in 1990. See *Irish Voice*, October 1, 1991, p. 4, for story on IEVC. Also, the October 29, 1991, *Irish Voice* editorial on p. 10 called on the New Irish to fight for the emigrant vote, since the Morrison visa effort was over "for now." See *Irish Voice*, October 22, 1991, p. 7, for story on Minihane and also the interview with Minihane, October 20, 1994, Dublin.

77. Written testimony of Donald Martin on behalf of the IIRM before House Subcommittee on Immigration, Refugees, and International Law Committee, September 16, 1988. Courtesy Donald Martin.

78. This interpretation based on discussions with members of the IIRM, IABC, Mary Corcoran, and others in the Irish community. See also *Irish Voice*, January 3, 1988, p. 9, and December 24–31, 1988, pp. 40–41, and *Irish America Magazine*, December 1988, pp. 20–23 and 36–37.

79. *Irish Voice*, December 24–31, 1988, pp. 40–41.

80. *Irish America Magazine*, December 1988, pp. 20–23, 36–37; *Newsweek*, October 5, 1987, p. 35; *The New York Times Magazine*, November 20, 1988, pp. 28, 30–34. Grant information based on discussions with Sean Benson of the IIRM the week of December 5 and 12, 1989. Pat Hurley's presentation at the AOH convention was discussed in the October 15, 1988, interview. The testimony and activity in Washington, D.C., during the September 1988 hearings were reviewed and discussed with various members of the Irish community, including Don Martin and IIRM members.

81. The IIRM was created to effect legislative change in the immigration policy of the United States. Sean Minihane, founder, stated that once the law was changed there would be no need for the IIRM. Essentially it was his goal to eliminate the need for the group. However, it became quickly apparent from the public response that the IIRM served a great social service to the community that would still be in demand after the legislative battles had been won. The Emerald Isle Immigration Center was formally established in July 1988 to conduct the outreach services the IIRM recognized were needed among the New Irish. It continues to operate in Queens.

82. See *EIIC News*, "The Newsletter of the Emerald Isle Immigration Center—New York's 'Irish Organization of the Year,'" December 1994, and the Emerald Isle Immigration Center *Newsletter*, October 1992, both in possession of the author.

83. An officer of the AOH complained to the author that many members of the fraternal organization did not understand why the New Irish could not "pull themselves up by the bootstraps" and make it like they did.

84. RE94 survey #13, from a County Clare woman born in 1941, who emigrated in 1961 and returned to live in Ireland in 1976. Survey in possession of author.

85. Mary, a documented alien, Bronx, New York. Letter. *Irish America Magazine*, September 1987, p. 7.

86. Mary L. Price, Mt. Horeb, Wisconsin. Letter. *Irish America Magazine*, November 1987, p. 9.

87. Interview with Teresa, November 1988.

88. An invitation ran as an ad in the March 11, 1989, edition of the *Irish Voice*. Despite the publication date, the notice did not appear after the event; the paper is on the newsstands the week before its publication date.

89. Based on discussions with Sean Benson, at the time the new full-time staff person

at the IIRM; he eventually became executive director of the EIIC. Weeks of December 5 and 12, 1989.

90. Mary Corcoran, "Emigrants, 'Eirepreneurs,' and Opportunists: A Social Profile of Recent Irish Immigration in New York City," in *The New York Irish*, ed. Ronald H. Bayor and Timothy Meagher (Baltimore: Johns Hopkins University Press, 1996), p. 472.

91. Mary Corcoran, "Ethnic Boundaries and Legal Barriers: The Labor Market Experience of Undocumented Irish Workers in New York City," unpublished paper presented at Columbia University, New York, April 1988, p. 11.

92. James Farrell interview, September 28, 1988.

93. Unless a prospective immigrant qualified for a visa with a special skill or employment category, the visas most likely available to him or her were part of the family reunification system sanctioned by the 1965 Immigration Act, or the migrant could apply as an unskilled worker. The latter was the most sought-after visa and the one with the longest waiting period; it was also the most likely category for which the majority of New Irish immigrants could apply. But because of the long waiting period, few chose to pursue it.

94. Margaret Curley interview, October 19, 1994.

95. Almeida, "'And They Still Haven't Found What They're Looking For,'" p. 206, survey results, question 36.

96. James McIntyre interview, April 6, 1995.

97. Kerry Emigrant Support Group, p. 62.

98. Ibid., p. 62.

99. Such is the opinion of the new immigrant liaison officer. McIntyre interview.

100. On August 26, 1993, Sean Benson, executive director, EIIC, was interviewed on RTE Radio 1 and urged those who did not intend to use the visas to decline their offers so that undocumented applicants already living in the United States had a better chance at receiving the visa. See Corcoran, "Emigrants, 'Eirepreneurs,' and Opportunists: A Social Profile of Recent Irish Immigration in New York City," p. 468.

Margaret Curley complained in her interview about Irish who claimed a visa only to use it on regular visits to the United States. The action angered Margaret because someone who wanted and needed the visa could have used it.

101. New Irish survey questionnaire #30, in possession of author.

102. Almeida, "'And They Still Haven't Found What They're Looking For,'" p. 205, survey results, question 37.

103. New Irish survey questionnaire #24, in possession of the author.

104. New Irish survey questionnaire #46, in possession of the author.

105. New Irish survey questionnaire #36, in possession of the author.

106. The pace of life in general in New York required an adjustment for many New Irish. Several respondents to the New Irish survey commented on the hectic lifestyle and emphasis on work and long hours in the city. It was a way of life to which they were not accustomed. Sean Minihane said in the September 1994 interview that when he first went back to work in Dublin after so much time in New York, he had to adjust to the more relaxed pace of the day.

107. In a book about a vastly different time and place and about two different peoples, Ramon Gutierrez describes how the initial contact between two cultures is like a dialogue between two people where neither quite understands the other and the potential exists for misunderstanding, misinterpretation, and exploitation. See *When Jesus Came, the Corn Mothers Went Away: Marriage, Sexuality, and Power in New Mexico, 1500–1846* (Stanford, Calif.: Stanford University Press, 1991).

108. *Irish Voice*, March 16, 1991, pp. 34–35, published results of a survey conducted by Linda Dowling Almeida and EIIC. See also *Irish Voice*, December 5, 1987, p. 1, for the results of a survey it conducted among 200 New Irish for its premier issue.

109. Undocumented aliens could not open a checking or savings account without a Social Security number. So few New Irish could go to a bank to cash checks. However, in the

February 1, 1989, IIRM newsletter, it was reported that a "full range of checking/savings services are available" through Emigrant Savings Bank branches located throughout New York City and Nassau, Suffolk, and Westchester Counties. The services listed were said to be available to "*all* Irish immigrants."

110. Maeve, in Maeve and Margaret interview, December 1, 1988.

111. Anecdotally, families also related the burden of responsibility and tension they felt living with a 19- or 20-year-old who in most cases was away from the restrictions and supervision of home for the first time and was free to socialize in the virtually unregulated environment of the New Irish neighborhoods in New York. "I don't want to be the one to have to call this girl's mother and tell her something horrible has happened to her daughter. I feel responsible for her." But as her employer, not her parent, she could not dictate the young woman's after-hours behavior.

112. Maura interview, October 26, 1988.

113. R. H. interview, December 4, 1992. Notes in possession of author. The following details about the group were gathered in this interview.

114. Interviews with Patricia O'Callaghan, director of Project Irish Outreach, December 2, 1992; Sister Edna McNicholas, Tir na n'Og, Bronx, December 1992; Sister Bridgh, Brooklyn Queens Center, December 9, 1992. Notes in possession of author.

115. Patricia O'Callaghan interview, January 31, 1989.

116. Office of the Health and Hospital Corporation and Legal Services Staff, Community Action for Legal Services, Inc., *If You Can't Pay Your Hospital Bill—Medicaid or HHC's Fee Settlement Program May Be Able to Help You Out*, December 1987. Murray interview, January 27, 1989.

117. Edward I. Koch, "City Policy on Undocumented Aliens," October 15, 1985. Courtesy City Hall.

118. Almeida, "'And They Still Haven't Found What They're Looking For,'" survey results question #11, p. 211.

119. New Irish survey questionnaire #143, in possession of author.

120. New Irish survey questionnaire #33, in possession of author.

121. New Irish survey questionnaire #201, in possession of author.

122. Kate Kelly and Trionna Nic Giolla Choille, *Emigration Matters for Women* (Dublin: Attic Press, 1990), p. 16. See Ide O'Carroll, *Models for Movers: Irish Women's Emigration to America* (Dublin: Attic Press, 1990), pp. 99–100, for other evidence of what O'Carroll describes as the "misogynist message of Irish society."

123. Francis Morrone, "The New Irish," *City Journal*, Summer 1993, pp. 102–103.

124. Bishop Eamon Casey, a pioneer in counseling and ministering to emigrants in England, created headlines in the early 1990s when his long-silent lover went public with the information that the bishop had fathered her son. In the fall of 1994, Ireland was rocked with the news that an Irish priest had been accused of several accounts of child abuse and that his behavior was known to the Church hierarchy, which had transferred him to parishes around the country without punishment or treatment and had not warned parishioners of his past problems. Public reaction was so strong as to call for the resignation of the bishop who authorized the perceived "cover-up."

125. *Irish Voice*, June 22, 1991, p. 7.

126. Niall O'Dowd, "Periscope: ILGO Insights," *Irish Voice*, January 17–23, 1996, p. 10.

127. Lee, p. 468.

128. Andrew Greeley, "Why Do Catholics Stay in the Church: Because of the Stories," *New York Times Magazine*, July 19, 1994, pp. 38–41.

5 . THE CATHOLIC CHURCH

1. Oliver Wendell Holmes as quoted in *The Poet at the Breakfast Table* and cited in Charles B. Keely, "The Effects of International Migration on U.S. Foreign Policy," in *Threatened Peoples, Threatened Borders: World Migration and U.S. Policy*, ed. Michael S. Teitelbaum and Myron Weiner (New York: W. W. Norton and Company, 1995).

2. Niall Williams and Christine Breen, *The Luck of the Irish: Our Life in County Clare* (New York: Soho Press, 1995), pp. 106–107. Williams was born in 1958 and his wife in 1954. This is the fourth book they have written describing their experiences leaving professional careers in New York City for life in a small village in the west of Ireland. The others are *O Come Ye Back to Ireland, When Summer's in the Meadow*, and *The Pipes Are Calling.*

3. Pete Hamill, *A Drinking Life* (New York: Little, Brown and Company, 1994), pp. 110 and 111.

4. J. J. [Joseph] Lee, *Ireland 1912–1985: Politics and Society*, 6th ed. (Cambridge: Cambridge University Press, 1993), pp. 313–321, and Tim Pat Coogan, *Eamon De Valera: The Man Who Was Ireland* (London: HarperCollins, 1993), pp. 647–649.

5. Lee, p. 468.

6. Coogan, *Eamon De Valera*; chapter 31, "When Bishops Were Bishops," begins on p. 648. Quote can be found on p. 648.

7. Quotes taken from "Irishwomen, Eurocitizens, and Redefining Abortion," a paper presented by Laurie Oaks at the New England Regional Conference of the American Conference for Irish Studies, October 16, 1993; courtesy Ms. Oaks. See J. H. Whyte, *Church and State in Modern Ireland: 1923–1979*, 2nd ed. (Dublin: Gill and Macmillan, 1980), p. 36; Basil Chubb, *The Government and Politics of Ireland*, 2nd ed. (Stanford, Calif.: Stanford University Press, 1982), p. 18; and Chubb, *The Constitution and Constitutional Change in Ireland* (Dublin: Institute of Public Administration, 1978), pp. 40–80.

8. Commission on Emigration and Other Population Problems, *Commission on Emigration and Other Population Problems 1948–1954 Reports*, Pr. 2541 (Dublin: Stationery Office, 1956), p. 142, paragraph 324.

9. Ibid., p. 180, paragraph 458.

10. Memo from Minister Sean MacEntee to Prime Minister Eamon De Valera, on meeting of July 1958 with MacEntee and Monsignors Roche and Deskur. Robert Joseph Savage Jr., "Irish Television: The Political and Social Genesis," Ph.D. dissertation, Boston College, 1993, pp. 492–494.

11. Savage, pp. 492–494.

12. Ide O'Carroll, *Models for Movers: Irish Women's Emigration to America* (Dublin: Attic Press, 1990), p. 100. See also Kate Kelly and Trionna Nic Giolla Choille, *Emigration Matters for Women* (Dublin: Attic Press, 1990), p. 16: "The vast majority of women emigrate for employment-related reasons. . . . Having said that, women in particular have also emigrated because of what we may call 'social reasons,' e.g. to escape domestic violence by travelling to Women's Aid shelters in England, to have an abortion, to conceal a pregnancy, to escape a feeling of not "fitting in" because of beliefs or sexuality. For many the two referenda . . . added significantly to a social climate which they already felt was oppressive. For some women, these referenda were the final straw." Kelly and Nic Giolla Choille, at the time this book was published, were full-time education and information officers with Emigrant Advice in Dublin. Emigrant Advice succeeded the Catholic Social Welfare Bureau, which was established in 1942 by Archbishop McQuaid to assist emigrants of the 1950s, '60s, and '70s. The agency was updated in the '80s in response to renewed emigration, even after the Catholic Social Welfare Bureau was disbanded. It operates under the auspices of Centrecare, Dublin Diocesan Social Service Centre, and is funded by Church, government, and private grants.

In an interview in Dublin, October 21, 1994, Trionna Nic Giolla Choille said that the debates surrounding divorce and abortion in the mid-1980s split many families apart because of the emotion and passion engendered by the issues.

In a national referendum held November 24, 1995, the Irish electorate voted in favor of establishing divorce laws in Ireland. The bill passed by 9,000 votes, less than one percent of the votes cast. *Irish Voice*, November 29–December 5, 1995, p. 3.

13. See Linda Dowling Almeida, "'And They Still Haven't Found What They're Looking For': A Survey of the New Irish in New York City," in *The Irish World Wide: Patterns of Migration*, vol. 1, ed. Patrick O'Sullivan (Leicester, England: Leicester University Press, and

New York: St. Martin's Press, 1992), p. 211; and Almeida, "Women among the New Irish Immigrants," paper presented to New England Regional Conference of the American Conference for Irish Studies (ACIS), October 16, 1993, p. 12.

14. Persons under the age of 25 accounted for 46.4 percent of the total population in 1986 and 47.8 percent of the population in 1981. Central Statistics Office, *Ireland Census 86, Summary Population Report* (Dublin: Stationery Office, November 1987), p. vii.

15. Central Statistics Office, *Vital Statistics for Ireland: Fourth Quarter and Yearly Summary 1993* (Dublin: Stationery Office, September 1994), p. 77.

16. Pat O'Connor, "Defining Irish Women: Dominant Discourses and Sites of Resistance," *Eire-Ireland*, Fall 1995, p. 177.

17. For a discussion on the present power of the Church and the morality and conscience of Catholics in Ireland, see Lee, pp. 651–661. In an interview with the author on October 20, 1994, regarding the state of Catholicism in Ireland, Father Paul Byrne, director of the Irish Episcopal Commission in Ireland, said that he feared the Church had lost many of the young Irish and that they would not return. He and other Church leaders were working to bring them back into the fold.

18. Laurie Oaks, "Irishwomen, Eurocitizens, and Redefining Abortion."

19. See Oaks.

20. *Irish Voice*, October 13, 1992, p. 7.

21. The details about the Bronx Women's Group were gathered from an interview with R. H. on December 4, 1992. Notes in possession of the author.

22. William Shannon, *The American Irish: An American and Social Portrait* (New York: Macmillan, 1966), p. 136. Shannon notes than in 1886 thirty-five of the sixty-nine bishops in the country were Irish or Irish American; the Germans (including Swiss and Austrians) followed with fifteen. See also Jay P. Dolan, *The Immigrant Church: New York's Irish and German Catholics, 1815–1865* (Notre Dame, Ind.: University of Notre Dame Press, 1983), for a complete study of the struggle between the Irish and German clergy for control of the New York diocese in the nineteenth century. See in particular chapter 5, "Conflict in the Church," and chapter 9, "Transformation of the Church."

23. In 1966, the number of U.S. seminarians in theology or post-college studies numbered 8,325. By 1975, the number had dropped 38 percent to 5,137, and by 1994 the total was 3,328. Numbers published by the Center for Applied Research in the Apostolate (CARA) at Georgetown University and quoted in Jerry Filteau, "Numbers Drop: U.S. Seminary Enrollment Off by 3.4%," *Catholic New York*, February 2, 1995, p. 7.

"As a result of the dramatic decrease in the number of women becoming and remaining nuns, in 1974 lay teachers constituted 61 percent of the faculty of Catholic schools. In contrast, thirty years ago [in the mid-1940s], when these figures were first recorded, lay teachers were only 8 percent of the faculty of Catholic schools." Andrew M. Greeley, William C. McCready, and Kathleen McCourt, *Catholic Schools in a Declining Church* (Kansas City, Mo.: Sheed and Ward, 1976), p. 221.

24. Lawrence McCaffrey, *The Irish Diaspora in America* (Bloomington: Indiana University Press, 1976), p. 158, and Nathan Glazer and Daniel P. Moynihan, *Beyond the Melting Pot: The Negroes, Puerto Ricans, Jews, Italians, and Irish of New York City* (Cambridge: MIT Press and Harvard University Press, 1964), p. 276.

25. Most of the scholarship which exists on Irish America since the Great Famine centers on Irish Catholics, because the vast majority of migrants leaving the Republic were and are Catholic. See Kerby A. Miller, *Emigrants and Exiles: Ireland and the Irish Exodus to North America* (New York: Oxford University Press, 1985), p. 350, for statistics, and Lee, p. 661, who disputes one writer's attempt to defend a "polyglot" Ireland by arguing that the religions in Ireland are "Catholic and Protestant. Few Protestants are left in the Republic."

Kerby Miller is currently conducting research on the Irish Protestant community in the United States. According to the 1990 U.S. census, 5.6 million Americans identified themselves as Scotch-Irish, which would presumably mean they are Protestant. Kerby Miller discovered that 13.3 million or 34 percent of those Americans claiming to be Irish ethnics in the same census reside in the South. He assumes that most of these are descendants of Ulster Presbyterians, other Irish Protestant settlers, or converts from Catholicism since most famine and post-famine immigrants did not settle in the South. Of course this does not take into account Irish Catholics from around the country, particularly the Northeast, who relocated to the South in recent decades following job opportunities and a better quality of life. The numbers, however, do suggest a significant Irish Protestant population in the United States. Miller cites his reference: Bureau of the Census, *1990 Census of Population, Social and Economic Characteristics, United States,* vols. CP-2-1 through CP-2-52 (Washington, D.C., 1993).

26. McCaffrey, *Irish Diaspora;* see chapter 9, "From Ghetto to Suburb: From Someplace to No Place," especially pp. 167, 173, 176. McCaffrey also analyzes the writing of Monsignor John Tracy Ellis, who in the 1950s criticized the anti-intellectual thrust of American Catholicism and American Catholic educational institutions. "Ellis's censure of the low standard of American Catholic intellectualism was for all practical purposes a criticism of the Irish who have dominated the educational and administrative structure of the church in the United States. . . . And Ellis said that Catholic intellectualism was frustrated by the adoption of the anti-intellectual, materialistic values of American life and by the challenge of American nativism. American Catholics tried to achieve success in American terms, which meant amassing wealth, not knowledge" (p. 167). See also Glazer and Moynihan, especially pp. 251 and 262.

In 1972, Pete Hamill wrote that by the late 1960s "the Irish moment was over" in New York City. See "Notes on the New Irish: A Guide for the Goyim," *New York Magazine,* March 15, 1972, p. 33.

27. See Linda Dowling Almeida, "The Lost Generation: The Undocumented Irish in New York City in the 1980s," *New York Irish History Journal* (1989): 29, 48–52.

28. Marifeli Perez-Stable, "Father Andrew Greeley," *Culturefront* 4, no. 1 (1995): 25.

29. Ibid., pp. 25–27.

30. In the interview cited above, Father Greeley argued that there are similarities between urban and suburban parishes: "it depends a lot on the suburb and the part of the country. In many suburban parishes the sense of community is pretty much what it was in the old neighborhood. People are better educated and they have more money, but that does not make them any less enthusiastic about their parish community, especially perhaps the parochial schools where they continue to enroll their children." Perez-Stable, p. 27.

31. See Lee, pp. 659–687, for a thorough discussion of Irish identity vis-à-vis language, religion, and the country's entry into the world marketplace and culture, and how the Irish can maintain a national identity without parroting those of Ireland's larger, more successful neighbors, i.e., Great Britain and America.

32. James Joyce, *Dubliners* (New York: Viking Press, 1961).

33. In the opening scene of *Ulysses,* Joyce has Buck Mulligan lift his shaving bowl in a morning salute recited in Latin to his friend Stephen Dedalus, the main protagonist. Dressed in a loose fitting bathrobe, Mulligan's gesture is a rather comic reminder of the offertory, when the priest raises the chalice in sacrifice during the most sacred part of the Roman Catholic mass. James Joyce, *Ulysses* (New York: Vintage Books, 1961), p. 3.

34. Elizabeth Cullinan, *Yellow Roses* (New York: Viking Press, 1977). See "Estelle," pp. 5–6: "In its day, thirty or so years before I was born, the house [on the outskirts of New York] had been comfortable enough and the street picturesquely rural, but in my day the house, the street, and the neighborhood were a step removed from squalor. And majestically arrayed on that crucial step was St. John's. My grandmother [Norris] more than basked in the church's reflected glory, she traded on it. . . . She wanted to end her days there, which was understandable, and she wanted us to stay with her, which was unfair, but stay there we did, in the shadow of the church, which was supposed to compensate for the beauty and order that were missing from our lives."

Also, "Voices of the Dead," p. 103: ". . . at eighty-five she [Mary Nugent] was a woman accustomed to religious privilege. Her house [in Mount Vernon] was across the street from Holy Family Church, and as long as she was able she attended daily Mass, taking her place always at the end of the eighth pew from the front. Then, when her legs became so bad that she couldn't cross the street without worrying . . . she took to looking from her front porch at the services. In winter the images lasted only as long as the opening and closing of the door. . . . On clear nights, after Benediction, she always joined the voices, floating across the warm air. . . ."

35. For more background on Irish American fiction and writers in the postwar period see Charles Fanning, "The Heart's Speech No Longer Stifled: New York Irish Writing since the 1960s," in *The New York Irish*, ed. Ronald H. Bayor and Timothy Meagher (Baltimore: Johns Hopkins University Press, 1996), pp. 508–531; Daniel J. Casey, "Heresy in the Diocese of Brooklyn: An Unholy Trinity," in *Irish-American Fiction: Essays in Criticism*, ed. Daniel J. Casey and Robert F. Rhodes (New York: AMS, 1979), pp. 153–175; and Eileen Kennedy, "Bequeathing Tokens: Elizabeth's Cullinan's Irish-America," *Eire-Ireland*, Winter 1981, pp. 94–102.

36. Claire Grimes, "History of the *Irish Echo*," *New York Irish History Journal*, 1993–1994 (New York: New York Irish History Roundtable, 1994), p. 5. John Grimes's father, Paddy, bought the weekly in 1955 to promote the family's travel agency—Grimes Travel Agency. The *Echo* printing presses also produced most of the brochures and journals for the various county organizations in New York in the fifties and sixties.

37. John Grimes, *The Best of Times: Reminiscences,* Christmas 1989. Courtesy Claire Grimes.

38. *Irish Echo,* March 13, 1965, p. 35.

39. John Grimes, pp. 21–22.

40. Miller, p. 526.

41. Eric Foner, "Class, Ethnicity, and Radicalism in the Gilded Age: The Land League and Irish America," *Marxist Perspectives* (Summer 1978): 6–53.

42. Marion R. Casey, "Redefining 'Irish': Culture and Subculture in New York City, 1900–1940," paper presented to the Organization of American Historians, Atlanta meeting, April 14, 1994, p. 5. Courtesy Marion Casey.

43. Kerby Miller quotes a 1917 observation of British ambassador Thomas Spring Rice: ". . . all churchmen realized implicitly that for Irish-American Catholics hatred of Protestant England was 'necessary to true religion and the maintenance of due religious fervour.'" Miller, *Emigrants and Exiles,* p. 537.

44. Glazer and Moynihan, pp. 246–247.

45. "In the 1940s, parochial schools in American cities were dominated by Irish clerical and lay faculties teaching mostly Irish students." McCaffrey, *Irish Diaspora in America,* p. 158.

46. Diana Jean Schemo, "Hard-Fought Legacy of Catholic Power: Next Archbishop Will Inherit a History as Scrappy as New York," *The New York Times,* February 12, 2000, p. B1, is a good review of past Catholic leaders in New York, anticipating the resignation of John Cardinal O'Connor.

47. Robert I. Gannon, S. J., *The Cardinal Spellman Story* (New York: Doubleday and Company, 1962), pp. 66–90.

48. George C. Herring, *America's Longest War, The United States and Viet Nam 1950–1975* (New York: Alfred A. Knopf, 1986), pp. 48–49.

49. Gannon, p. 257.

50. Gannon, pp. 302–303.

51. *Survey of Nonpublic Schools, New York State, 1968–69,* University of the State of New York, State Education Department, Albany, July 1969, table 5.

52. See chapter 2. Except for the Mott Haven neighborhood, most of the communities discussed that had large concentrations of Irish had populations in which almost half—and

in the case of St. Simon Stock parish, almost two-thirds—of school-age children were in private schools in 1960.

53. Andrew M. Greeley, William C. McCready, and Kathleen McCourt, *Catholic Schools in a Declining Church* (Kansas City, Mo.: Sheed and Ward, 1976), pp. 221 and 223.

54. Ibid., p. 61.

55. Andrew Greeley, *From Backwater to Mainstream: A Profile of Catholic Higher Education* (New York: McGraw-Hill Book Company, 1969), p. 32, table 5.

56. Brother Charles B. Quinn, *Iona College: The First Fifty Years* (New Rochelle, N.Y.: Iona College, 1990), pp. 62 and 76.

57. Ibid., p. 20.

58. Ibid., p. 25.

59. See Greeley, McCready, and McCourt for discussion of the progress of ethnic Catholic groups in education, income, and social mobility, pp. 65–75.

60. Flynn was a member of the Irish American delegation that traveled to Northern Ireland in the late summer and early fall of 1994 to negotiate a peace settlement between the Unionists and the Republicans in the north.

61. "Business 100 1994," Special Supplement, November/December 1994, pp. S3–S43.

62. One Bronx second-generation Irish man remembered the nuns in his school telling the class that they were to grow up and take "a position," not just a job. J. D. interview, April 20, 1995.

63. Amber Coverdale Sumrall and Patrice Vecchione, eds., *Catholic Girls* (New York: Plume Books, 1992), pp. 2–3.

64. A Slavic American Catholic woman from Chicago remembers: "Sonya and I made black veils out of old pillowcases, which were really a deep navy blue, and we fastened them to our heads with white strips of gauze around our foreheads and faces. We tied several strands of black silver rosaries around our waists and hung plastic crucifixes around our necks with string . . . we installed our 'classrooms' in separate parts of my basement, with our various dolls as our students. We actually taught our dolls from our own school books, and hit them mercilessly when they misbehaved or didn't do their homework, just as the nuns beat us in real life." Irene Zabytko, "St. Sonya," in *Catholic Girls*, ed. Sumrall and Vecchione, p. 188.

A Hispanic woman from Los Angeles recalls being taught that a nun was the highest calling a young woman could have; marriage was second and singlehood was the last. Although she did not have a vocation, she shares a memory from her school days: "The afternoon sun coming through the window illuminated the entire space [in the chapel]. One of the sisters knelt in the first row of pews nearest the altar, praying. It was so holy and quiet and she seemed to be bathed in a golden light; in that moment I wished with all my heart that I could be one of them." Lin Florinda Colavin, "The Calling," *Catholic Girls*, ed. Sumrall and Vecchione, p. 266.

Novelist Mary Gordon, whose mother was of Irish and Italian parentage, remembers that "although I didn't want to be a martyr I did want to be a nun" and that her parents took her to the Convent of Mary Reparatrix on 29th Street in New York. Her memory of one nun at that cloister captures the mystery that pre-Vatican religious carried for the young: "I've never seen a color like that in a nun's habit, and I'm quite sure I didn't invent it . . . it was a color dreamed up for movie stars. It was the color of Sleeping Beauty's ball gown, and that was what I wanted for myself. I wanted be beautifully kneeling in light, my young, straight back clothed in the magic garment of the anointed." "Getting Here from There," *Catholic Girls*, ed. Sumrall and Vecchione, pp. 102–103.

65. Marilyn Murphy, "Girls at the Altar," *Catholic Girls*, ed. Sumrall and Vecchione, p. 183

66. Ibid., p. 186.

67. Hamill, *A Drinking Life*, p. 109.

68. Hamill, *New York*, p. 36.

69. McCaffrey notes, "In the 1940s, parochial schools in American cities were dominated by Irish clerical and lay faculties teaching mostly Irish students." *Irish Diaspora in America*, p. 158.

In "Twenty Years on Fordham Heights," a photocopied history of St. Nicholas of Tollantine Church in the Bronx, the names of successive parish priests from 1906 forward included Fathers Dohan, Driscoll, Murphy, Zeiser, Mauch, Stengel, and Hurley (1959). These priests were Augustinians, an order associated with Villanova University. In fact, several of the priests assigned to St. Nicholas were transferred from or went on to head the university. History courtesy of Father John Dello Russo, parish office.

A history of St. Simon Stock, also in the Bronx, shows that the parish was run by Irish Carmelites, whose names included O'Farrell, Gerhard, Russell, Daly, Flanagan, and McCarthy (a "St. Simon Stock boy," born and raised in the parish, according to Father Sean Reid, O. Carm., "Recollections of Some Sixty Years," ca. 1985, courtesy Father Reid). See Alfred Isacsson, O. Carm., "The Irish Carmelites Come to the Bronx," *Bronx County Historical Society Journal* 25, no. 1 (Spring 1988): 24–25.

Father Reid, also a Carmelite, worked in the parish Our Lady of the Scapular of Mt. Carmel on 28th Street in Manhattan for many years in the 1940s and 1950s, and taught at St. Simon Stock in the 1930s. He was so well known and regarded in the Irish community that he was elected in 1964 as grand marshal of the St. Patrick's Day Parade. By his own admission, he was the first grand marshal elect who began his acceptance speech in Gaelic and continued in English. See Reid, "Recollections of Some Sixty Years," p. 83.

70. Elizabeth Cullinan, "The Voices of the Dead," in *Yellow Roses*: "Before she reached the age of sixty, Mary Nugent had given six children to God—two nuns, one priest, the other three in early, tragic deaths," p. 102.

71. *Irish Echo*, September 7, 1957, p. 10.

72. *Irish Echo*, September 21, 1957, p. 15.

73. Interview with Jerry Brennan and his friend Eamon, October 11, 1994. Eamon went to mass at Tollantine.

74. Interview with Peggy Hegarty Tanner, June 28, 1995.

75. Reid, p. 90. Father O'Callaghan was grand marshal of the St. Patrick's Day Parade in 1951. See John Ridge, *The St. Patrick's Day Parade in New York* (New York: St. Patrick's Day Committee, AOH Publications, 1988), pp. 143–144.

76. Interview with Joseph P. McLaughlin and his mother, Rose, March 29, 1995. McLaughlin said that his father, whatever firehouse he was in, was the fireman in charge of selling tickets to the annual communion breakfast.

77. See *Irish Echo*, December 23, 1950, benefit dance and donations for Father Boran; the social guide, p. 3, on September 11, 1954, included four benefit dances for priests.

78. *Irish Echo*, September 25, 1965, p. 9, and July 31, 1965, p. 3.

See *Irish Echo*, September 7, 1957, p. 3, for story on Christian Brothers seminarians, and September 28, 1957, p. 13, "Queens News and Events," by James O'Neill, gossip column highlighting marriages, engagements, new emigrants, vacations, and daughters entering the convent.

See *Irish Echo*, December 23, 1950, p. 8; Nancy Burk enters Dominican convent at Mt. St. Mary's in Newburgh, party held at Inwood Civic Center.

79. See Reid.

80. See Reid.

81. J. D. interview.

82. Reid, p. 5.

83. Reid, "Recollections," and Ridge, *St. Patrick's Day Parade*, p. 176.

84. Reid, p. 8. The first annual feis sponsored by the United Irish Counties Association (UICA) was held in 1933 at Wingate Field in Brooklyn. Marion Casey, "Redefining 'Irish': Culture and Subculture in New York City, 1900–1940," p. 9.

85. Ridge, *St. Patrick's Day Parade*, p. 154.

86. Reid, pp. 48–50.

87. Glazer and Moynihan, p. 275.

88. In 1960, 37.6% of adults age 25 and older in the Inwood section of Manhattan, tracts 291, 293, 295, 303, and 307, had completed high school; the median number of years spent in school was 10.2.

89. Mary Ford, "To Monahan's!" *Culturefront* 4, no. 7 (Spring 1995): 24.

90. Mary Hennessy Trotta, "Memories of Rockaway Long Ago!" *The Wave*, 100th Anniversary Edition, July 24, 1993, p. 48.

91. Perez-Stable, p. 26.

92. Perez-Stable, pp. 25–27. Lawrence J. McCaffrey, *The Irish Catholic Diaspora in America* (Washington, D.C.: The Catholic University of America Press, 1997), pp. 195–196. Andrew Greeley, "Why Do Catholics Stay in the Church: Because of the Stories," *New York Times Magazine*, July 10, 1994, p. 38.

93. "From 1966 to 1969, an estimated 3,413 priests resigned. In 1964, 44,500 future priests were preparing for ordination. Twenty years later, the number had dropped to around 12,000 and 241 seminaries had closed. In the 1960s, the church also began to experience a decline in the number of women religious. From 1965, a peak year, to 1980, the number of numbers of nuns declined from 181,421 to 126,517. In 1965, 12,539 brothers taught high school or college or worked in hospitals. In 1980, their numbers had dropped to 8,563." Lawrence McCaffrey, *Textures of Irish America* (Syracuse, N.Y.: Syracuse University Press, 1992), p. 85.

94. Greeley, McCready, and McCourt, p. 10.

95. Sister M. M. interview in Dublin, October 20, 1994.

96. Figures courtesy Sister Francis Lowe, National Library of Ireland. Letter to Linda Dowling Almeida, November 20, 1995.

97. Interview with Father Paul Byrne, Dublin, October 20, 1994. A poll taken in Ireland by the *Sunday Independent* and a television program revealed that 57 percent of those interviewed felt the Church was "permanently damaged by recent scandals involving bishops and priests and cases of child sex abuse." *Irish Voice*, November 8–14, 1995, p. 4.

98. *Irish Voice*, March 16, 1991, p. 34. The *Voice* published the results of a survey the author conducted among 247 New Irish immigrants in the fall of 1990.

99. *Irish Voice*, November 8–14, 1995, p. 4.

100. This survey was conducted by the United Irish Counties Community Action Bureau in the Norwood section of the Bronx and in the the Bay Ridge/Fort Hamilton/Dyker Heights section of Brooklyn. However, the results for questions 63 and 64 regarding the religious behavior of the respondents in both communities are identical. This is either a great coincidence or the results to questions 63 and 64 were just mistakenly duplicated for the two communities. United Irish Counties Community Action Bureau, *The Needs of the American-Irish Community in the City of New York* (New York: United Irish Counties Community Action Bureau, n.d.), pp. 36, 53, 54.

101. Greeley, *From Backwater to Mainstream*, table 34, p. 94, and table 43, p. 104.

102. Suellen Hoy, "The Journey Out: The Recruitment and Emigration of Irish Religious Women to the United States, 1812–1914," *Journal of Women's History* 6/7, no. 1 (Winter/Spring 1995): 64–98. Ms. Hoy recounts the forces and personalities that drew hundreds of Irish Catholic religious women to minister to the immigrant population in America in hospitals and schools throughout the nineteenth century, responding to the hierarchy's fear that the immigrant population was losing its faith in America.

103. Commission on Emigration and Other Population Problems, *Commission on Emigration and Other Population Problems 1948–1954 Reports* (Pr. 2541) (Dublin: Stationery Office, 1956), p. 141, paragraph 319.

104. Sile Ni Chochlain, president, Concilium Legionis Mariae, letter to Linda Dowling Almeida, February 24, 2000. Anecdotally, I have heard stories of Legion of Mary volunteers who met emigrants on the docks in the 1950s as they boarded ships to America and England to encourage them to keep their faith.

105. See Kelly and Nic Giolla Choille, pp. 12–13.

106. According to the Legion of Mary in Dublin, it has no data on Irish emigration to the United States in the 1950s. The presumption was that most Irish traveling to the United States had relatives there, so the need for services was not great. Letter to Linda Dowling Almeida from Sile Ni Chochlain, president, Concilium Legionis Mariae, February 10, 2000.

107. Correspondence from the Legion of Mary confirms this assumption. There was concern that because of the youth of the emigrants leaving for England and the fact that they had no family to rely on away from home, they were more needy than their peers in America. According to the president of the legion, the Society of St. Vincent de Paul and social welfare offices associated with the bishops of Ireland and England were very active in the care of migrants in England. Letter to Linda Dowling Almeida from Sile Ni Chochlain, February 10, 2000.

108. C. B. interview, January 27, 1994. Notes in possession of author.

109. As reported in an earlier chapter, direct government aid for the migrants in the form of financial assistance and formal recognition of the community was slow in coming, at least too slow for the migrants themselves. One of the major complaints of the New Irish was that the Irish government funded migrant facilities and programs for the Irish in England and did not respond in kind to the Irish in America. See Almeida, "The Lost Generation: The Undocumented Irish in New York City in the 1980s," p. 50.

110. The following sequence of events between February and the end of 1987 are repeated as told by Monsignor Murray in an interview conducted on January 27, 1989.

111. Interviews with Patricia O'Callaghan, January 31, 1989, and November 2, 1988.

112. O'Callaghan, January 31, 1989.

113. Interviews with Father Joe Delaney, March 1989; Sister Lucia Brady, March 1989; Father Martin Keveny, October 19, 1988, and March 23, 1989; and Monsignor Murray, January 27, 1989.

114. Emigrant Advice, *Emigrant Advice Annual Report 1989* (Dublin: Emigrant Advice, 1989), p. 11.

115. Sister Veronica Dobson, CSB, Irish Pastoral Center, Archdiocese of Boston, remarks as quoted in *The New Irish Immigrant*, report on a conference sponsored by the National Conference of Catholic Bishops (NCCB) Committee on Migration and the United States Catholic Conference Office of Migration and Refugee Services, Boston College, February 25, 1989, p. 24.

116. Reverend Joseph Delaney, Project Irish Outreach, Archdiocese of New York, as quoted in *The New Irish Immigrant*, pp. 25 and 27.

117. The Most Reverend Theodore E. McCarrick, Archbishop Newark, chairman, NCCB Committee on Migration, quoted in *The New Irish Immigrant*, pp. 29, 30, 33.

118. Interviews with Paula O'Sullivan and Patricia O'Callaghan, December 2, 1992. Notes in possession of author.

119. *Irish Echo*, November 13–19, 1991.

120. Sister Bridgh interview, December 9, 1992. Notes in possession of author.

121. Sister Bridgh interview. December 2, 1992, interviews with O'Callaghan and O'Sullivan. *Irish Echo*, November 13–19, 1991.

122. *Irish Voice*, September 23, 1989.

123. Interviews with O'Callaghan and O'Sullivan, December 2, 1992.

124. *Irish Voice, St. Patrick's Day Supplement 1992*, March 17, 1992.

125. Murray, January 27, 1989.

126. *Irish Echo*, November 13–19, 1991.

127. Tir na n'Og was established with a grant from the Irish Government. *Irish Echo*, November 13–19, 1991.

6. WHO ARE THE IRISH?

1. Quoted in William D. Griffin, *The Book of Irish Americans* (New York: Times Books, 1990), p. 177.

2. Peter Quinn, *Banished Children of Eve* (New York: Viking Penguin, 1994); Eric Foner, "Class, Ethnicity, and Radicalism in the Gilded Age: The Land League and Irish-America," *Marxist Perspectives* (Summer 1978): 6–53; Marion R. Casey, "Redefining 'Irish': Culture and Subculture in New York City, 1900–1940," paper presented to the Organization of American Historians, Atlanta meeting, April 14, 1994.

3. Foner, pp. 8–53.

4. J. J. [Joseph] Lee, *Ireland 1912–1985: Politics and Society,* 6th ed. (Cambridge: Cambridge University Press, 1993), p. 658.

5. See Lawrence J. McCaffrey, *Textures of Irish America* (Syracuse, N.Y.: Syracuse University Press, 1992), and Lee, pp. 658–687.

6. United Irish Counties Community Action Bureau, *The Needs of the American-Irish Community in the City of New York* (New York: United Irish Counties Community Action Bureau, n.d.), p. 11. No publication date is provided, but the report is based on survey data financed by a grant awarded by the Office of Economic Opportunity in 1975.

The authors of the report do not define Irish ethnicity or identity directly, although they do describe "traditional Irish characteristics" as "clannishness, the desire to be left alone by government, along with the ancient attitude that help is for other groups" (pp. 10–11).

7. For a discussion of Eamon De Valera's failure to execute and sustain a language revival program, see Lee, p. 333.

8. Kevin O'Connor, *Irish Independent,* July 20, 1985, as found in Lee, p. 658.

9. Liam De Paor, *Irish Times,* July 18, 1985, as quoted in Lee, p. 658.

10. Vincent Buckley, *Memory Ireland,* pp. 48–50, as quoted in Lee, p. 658.

11. O'Connor, as quoted in Lee, p. 658.

12. Father Sean Reid wrote that the Kilkenny Association held monthly meetings on a Saturday night in the Peter Stuyvesant Hotel on Central Park West. He was the association's first chaplain, and remembered attending a St. Patrick's Day dance in a hall "somewhere near the Triboro Bridge" in the 1930s. Every year the association sponsored a mass for its deceased members on Memorial Day at the Carmelite Church on 28th Street. When Father Reid conducted the mass, he led the congregation to "Calvary Cemetery in Queens where the Association had a plot and had erected a Celtic Cross monument over the grave of John Locke the Kilkenny Fenian patriot and poet. I said a prayer, speeches were made and a recitation was given of Locke's poem 'Dawn on the Hills of Ireland'" (pp. 17–18).

Father Reid reported that the Westmeath Men's Association also used the Carmelite Church for its annual Thanksgiving Day mass (p. 19). After World War II, Father Reid formed a Kilkenny hurling club, because he and Dick Quinn "thought it time to bring the black and amber colors of Kilkenny back to Gaelic Park" (p. 46). See Father Sean Reid, O. Carm., "Recollections of Some Sixty Years," ca. 1985. Courtesy Father Reid.

13. The United Irish Counties Association (UICA) was formed in 1933 to coordinate the activities of the thirty-two county associations in the city. It also ran the feis, which began in 1933 and featured Irish traditional music, dance, and other cultural activities. See Casey, "Redefining 'Irish': Culture and Subculture in New York City, 1900–1940," p. 9.

14. Kevin Morrissey interview, February 9, 1995.

15. H. F., vice president, Donegal Association, interview, January 12, 1996.

16. UICA Community Action Bureau, prologue. A median age of almost 62 is quite old, and may refer to foreign-born Irish only. I have not verified the figure, and the UICA does not indicate from which census report it came.

17. Kevin Morrissey interview.

18. H. F. interview.

19. H. F. interview.

20. *Irish Echo,* September 7, 1957, p. 14.

21. *Irish Voice,* March 16, 1991, p. 35.

22. Phone interview with Shane Doyle, December 1, 1992. For more background on differences within the New Irish population, vis-à-vis lifestyle and communities, see Joe

Jackson, "Is That It?" *Irish Times,* undated (Fall 1992?), courtesy Marion R. Casey; and "The Jig's Up: To Be Young, Hip and Irish," *New York Live: Daily News Color Supplement,* March 15, 1992, p. 4.

23. *Irish Echo,* March 15, 1958, p. 13.

24. Interview with Officer V. D., officer of the Emerald Society, March 28, 1995. The officer said that the police department had a current total of 30,000 officers.

25. V. D. interview.

26. Emerald Society, Police Department, City of New York, *Newsletter,* vol. 3, no. 1 (Winter [n.d.]): 1–2. No year is listed, but the text refers to 1986 as the year that just passed. Courtesy V. D.

27. Emerald Society, Police Department, City of New York, *Newsletter,* vol. 3, no. 1 (Winter 1986); vol. 3, no. 1 (January–February 1980); vol. 3, no. 1 (Winter [n.d.; see note 26, above]); vol. 5, no. 1 (Summer 1987); vol. 6, no. 1 (Winter 1987); vol. 7, no. 1 (Winter 1988); vol. 7, no. 5 (Spring 1989). Courtesy V. D.

28. Emerald Society *Newsletter,* vol. 3, no. 1 (Winter [n.d.]).

29. In his memoirs, Sean Reid recalled that he was chaplain for the Kilkenny Association, divisions 1 and 11 of the AOH, and Father Donal O'Callaghan was chaplain of division 9 and state Hibernian chaplain for life (pp. 17, 88–89); Father Reid was unofficial chaplain for Union 32J of women office cleaners; Father O'Callaghan was the unofficial chaplain of 32B, the union of doormen, elevator operators, etc.; and the Dublin Society had a missionary priest as a chaplain. The Reverend Father Maher was identified in the *Irish Echo* for September 7, 1957, as the chaplain of the BMT Transit Authority Holy Name Society (p. 16).

30. Cathedral Club, *Ninety-Fifth Annual Dinner of the Cathedral Club,* dinner program (Brooklyn: Cathedral Club, January 26, 1995), inside front cover. In possession of the author.

31. Ibid.

32. Pete Hamill called the *Tablet* "a sick right-wing sheet that saw Communists oozing from every brick in Manhattan." In "Notes on the New Irish: A Guide for the Goyim," *New York Magazine,* March 15, 1972, p. 36. See Rodger Van Allen, *The Commonweal and American Catholicism* (Philadelphia: Fortress Press, 1974), p. 111. The author claimed that diocesan papers, especially the *Tablet,* were pro-McCarthy.

33. *Irish Echo,* September 11, 1954, p. 7.

34. Photocopy of 50th anniversary book of parish, pp. 17–18, circa 1956. The committee was featured in *Columbia* magazine in an article by John J. O'Connor, "So the Parish Rolled Up Its Sleeves," August 1939.

35. Van Allen, p. 111. Van Allen quoted one reader of the *Tablet,* who wrote to the paper on August 30, 1952: "McCarthyism to me is one hundred percent anti-Communism; I glory in my McCarthyism."

36. Thomas J. Rowland, "Irish-American Catholics and the Quest for Respectability in the Coming of the Great War, 1900–1917," *Journal of American Ethnic History* 15, no. 2 (1996): 3–31.

37. Van Allen, p. 132.

38. Kenneth Moynihan, "History as a Weapon for Social Advancement: Group History as Told by the American Irish Historical Society, 1896–1930," *New York Irish History Journal* (1993–94): 34. This article is excerpted from a Ph.D. dissertation, "History as a Weapon for Social Advancement: Group History as Told by Jewish, Irish, and Black Americans, 1892–1950," Clark University, 1973. In the journal article Moynihan argued, "Accepting also the proposition that equal rights as Americans had to be 'earned' by 'contributions,' the three groups demonstrated that their own forebears had done their share and more" (p. 34).

39. Casey, "Redefining 'Irish': Culture and Subculture in New York City, 1900–1940," pp. 10 and 11, courtesy Marion Casey. Inset quote taken from official program of the United Irish Counties Association annual feis, 1941; photocopies in possession of Ms. Casey.

40. A news feature broadcast on RTE on March 11, 1987, "Emigration USA," emphasized the problems faced by illegal aliens in America, including exploitation by employers

and unscrupulous immigration attorneys. Niall O'Dowd, publisher of the *Irish Voice* and *Irish America Magazine*, compared the "twilight world" of the undocumented to the famine emigrants of the last century. Archive account number: BN307/87L.

When testifying before Congress on behalf of the New Irish, Donald Martin recalled the heroism of Irish veterans who battled for the Union in the American Civil War, basing his plea on the heritage, contributions, and long tradition of Irish immigration to the United States. See written testimony on behalf of the IIRM before House Subcommittee on Immigration, Refugees and International Law Committee. September 16, 1988. Courtesy Donald Martin. In possession of author.

41. Kerby A. Miller, *Emigrants and Exiles: Ireland and the Irish Exodus to North America* (New York: Oxford University Press, 1985), p. 297.

42. Casey, "Redefining 'Irish': Culture and Subculture in New York City, 1900–1940," p. 5.

43. Sean Reid was an Irish speaker who used the language for special ceremonies, homilies, and presentations; see Reid memoirs. J. D. recalls Irish sermons at St. Simon Stock church in the Bronx, including those given by Father Reid; interview with J. D., April 20, 1995. Ads for the following groups' activities appeared in the *Irish Echo*: Bronx Gaelic League, September 21, 1957, p. 9; Cumann na Gaelige (Gaelic Society, New York), September 7, 1957; St. Brendan Gaelic Society, Brooklyn, September 7, 1957.

J. H. recalled in a memoir that his first introduction to the Gaelic League in New York was October 31, 1945, at a Halloween ceili at the Carmelite Church in Manhattan. He identified the active branches of the Gaelic League at the time to be the Bronx Gaelic League; the Philo-Celtic Society, which met at a settlement house on East 72nd Street, east of Second Avenue; and the Gaelic Society of New York, known as the Westside Gaelic Society, which met at St. Matthew's school hall on West 68th Street, west of Amsterdam Avenue. J. H., "Cuimhni Cinn [Remembrance]," *An Teanga Mharthanach* [Living Language], ca. Spring 1993, p. 22.

44. Casey, "Redefining 'Irish': Culture and Subculture in New York City, 1900–1940," p. 10.

45. Rebecca Miller, "Irish Traditional and Popular Music in New York City: Identity and Social Change, 1935–1975," in *The New York Irish*, ed. Ronald H. Bayor and Timothy Meagher (Baltimore: Johns Hopkins University Press, 1996), pp. 488–489.

46. J. H., pp. 22 and 24.

47. Interviews with Peggy Tanner, J. D., J. McLaughlin. See *Irish America Magazine* Business 100 surveys and questionnaires of returned emigrants to Ireland and Irish Americans.

48. Rebecca Miller, p. 11; Jerry Kerlin, "Dancing at Flannery's: The Transmission of Irish Set Dancing at a Manhattan Pub," *New York Irish History Journal* (1993–94): 41; J. D. interview.

49. "One of the reasons for Irish traditional music's demise during these years was its growing association with rural poverty." Rebecca Miller, pp. 486 and 494.

In his interview, Jerry Brennan said that his children are American and they identify with being American, and that is what he wants for them.

In an article in *Foreign Affairs*, John V. Kelleher commented that the general Irish population in the 1950s rejected the paternalism of Irish government and Church leaders, like De Valera, and were particularly opposed to compulsory Irish in the schools. "Today, three out of four Irish children still do not go beyond the sixth grade; and the education they receive is half-ruined by concentration on a language they will never speak again, anywhere." "Ireland . . . And Where Does She Stand?" *Foreign Affairs* 35, no. 3 (1957): 494–495. See also interviews with Peggy Hegarty Tanner and Joe and Rose McLaughlin.

50. See "Steppin' Out for Ireland," *Irish America Magazine*, January/February 1995, p. 20, about step dancing; Fall 1995 Calendar for Ireland House includes two evenings of "traditional song and conversation entirely in Irish" on November 9 and December 7.

51. See P. J. Curtis, *Notes from the Heart: A Celebration of Traditional Irish Music* (Dublin: Torc, 1994), pp. 14–45. In his interview, February 9, 1995, Kevin Morrissey also talked about the change in entertainment styles in the 1960s and 1970s away from big band dances.

52. Jerry Kerlin, p. 41. Differences in style may also emerge when comparing the dances learned for competition and the dancing performed at home for recreation.

53. *From Shore to Shore: Irish Traditional Music in New York City,* produced by Patrick Mullins and Rebecca Miller, Cherry Lane Productions, 1993.

54. Curtis, pp. 49–50.

55. *Irish America Magazine,* September/October 1994, pp. 19–21.

56. *Irish America Magazine,* September/October 1994, p. 20.

57. Mary Corcoran, "Emigrants, 'Eirepreneurs,' and Opportunists: A Social Profile of Recent Irish Immigration in New York City," in *The New York Irish,* ed. Ronald H. Bayor and Timothy Meagher (Baltimore: Johns Hopkins University Press, 1996), p. 477. See also Francis Morrone, "The New Irish," *City Journal,* Summer 1993, p. 103.

58. Morrone, p. 103.

59. U2, *The Joshua Tree,* Island Records Ltd., 1987; lyrics by Bono.

60. In personal interviews, in the surveys, and in an Irish radio program, New Irish repeatedly volunteered that if they could make the same amount of money in Ireland that they did in New York or anywhere else in America, they would go home. Similarly, other Irish were drawn in by the social freedom and diversity America offered, but felt compelled to return to Ireland because it was home.

See Morrone, p. 103; New Irish surveys #36 and #51, in possession of the author; and interview with C. M., October 21 and 22, 1994. Mrs. M. lived in New York from 1985 to 1990. She returned to County Clare to run a farm and raise a family with her husband and work on the administrative staff of the Department of Social Welfare. She found life much harder financially in Ireland, but has learned to live without.

Using phrases borrowed from the fifties, one New Irish emigrant described his experience as a returned Yank in "frugal" Ireland as difficult but necessary. He had always "meant to come back," but it was difficult, "the same begrudging bastards who bid good riddance to your back will sit in critical judgement on your return." Diarmuid O'Flynn, "Home and Away: To Go or Stay? United States: Never Again," *Irish Voice,* January 10–16, 1996, p. 17. The piece ran opposite an essay by Emer Mullins, who also returned to Ireland, but ultimately went back to New York because "there was no such thing as disposable income" in Ireland, she hated the "begrudgery" she found in Ireland, and she missed "the feeling that you really can be what you want to be and do what you want to do" in New York. "Home and Away: To Go or Stay? Ireland: Home Thoughts from Abroad," *Irish Voice,* January 10–16, 1996, p. 16.

61. *Irish Press,* February 9, 1994, p. 9.

62. Morrone, p. 103.

63. Curtis, p. 65.

64. Ibid.

65. Mary Corcoran quoted an Irish commentator who "argued that for many young Irish people today, America (rather than Ireland or the ethnic Irish community) is their cultural and spiritual homeland." "Emigrants, 'Eirepreneurs,' and Opportunists," p. 477. Her source was Fintan O'Toole, "Some of Our Emigrants Are Happy to Go," *Irish Times,* September 14, 1989.

66. Paul O'Dwyer, founder of the Irish Institute, held meetings at his home on Central Park West between 1948 and 1950 to discuss creating the institute. The history records that it was "founded" in 1953 and "established" in 1950, but it also lists past presidents from 1950 to 1984. *A Brief History of the Irish Institute,* Papers of the Irish Institute of New York, Inc., Archives of Irish America, Bobst Library, New York University.

67. In a 1996 brochure, "Next Door Neighbors: The Irish and Others in New York City," publicizing a seminar sponsored by the institute at New York University on March 2, 1996, the Irish Institute described itself as having "quietly pursued a policy of financial sup-

port for cultural projects in Ireland and America amounting to nearly one million dollars." Brochure in possession of author.

68. Rosaleen Fitzgibbon interview, December 1, 1993.

69. Background on Irish Arts Center taken from Donal Malone, "The Irish Arts Center: A Case Study in Ethnic Revival," *New York Irish History Journal* (1989): 39–41. Quote from Jim Dowd is found on p. 40 and is cited in "Irish Arts Center—A Proud Beginning," *New York Times*, December 7, 1972.

Malone notes that the center had a rocky existence, not least because it became associated with Irish nationalist causes, and although he suggested that attention to the problems in Northern Ireland during the seventies and eighties provided periodic boosts to membership from sympathetic Irish Americans, its political associations may have also cost it wider appeal. In examining the Irish American response to the plight of the New Irish, it seemed that the overwhelming support that Irish Americans who did not typically belong to ethnic institutions or organizations gave to the issue of immigration reform and the granting of visas to the undocumented was precisely because it was *not* related to the problems in the north or the IRA. Many Irish Americans were uncomfortable endorsing either of these because of the links to terrorism and violence.

70. American Irish Teachers Association newsletters, vol. 20, no. 7, September 1994; vol. 20, no. 8, October 1994; program for American Irish Teachers Association 19th Annual Irish American Conference, Saturday, November 12, 1994, Liederkranz Club, 6 East 87th Street, New York City—featured speakers included John McGoldrick, native of County Fermanagh, member of the Thomas Davis Players, poetry and readings; Dr. Terry Moran, professor of culture and communications at New York University, "Sons of Derry"; Edward O'Donnell, doctoral candidate, Columbia University, "The Irish and Henry George"; and John Ridge, author of *St. Patrick's Day Parade in New York, Erin's Sons in America,* and other works, "The Irish on the Titanic." Drama and readings were offered by Cill Cais players.

71. McCaffrey, *Textures of Irish America*, p. 177.

72. Hamill, "Notes on the New Irish," p. 31.

73. Alice Kessler-Harris, *Social History,* the New American History Series, ed. Eric Foner (Washington, D.C.: American Historical Association, 1990), p. 3.

74. Timothy Meagher argues in "Irish All the Time: Ethnic Consciousness among the Irish in Worcester, Massachusetts, 1880–1905" that it was actually second- and third-generation Irish who showed greater awareness of their ethnicity because they were more comfortable with their Americanness as well. *Journal of Social History* (Winter 1985): 273–290. See p. 289 in particular.

75. Linda Dowling Almeida, "The Lost Generation: The Undocumented Irish in New York City in the 1980s," *New York Irish History Journal* (1989): 49.

76. Reid, pp. 48–49. In the case of one hurler, he was promised a better job.

77. Mary Corcoran, "Ethnic Boundaries and Legal Barriers: The Labor Market Experience of Undocumented Irish Workers in New York City," unpublished paper for Columbia University, April 1998, pp. 14–15. Courtesy Marion R. Casey and Mary Corcoran.

78. Brendan Ward interview, October 24, 1994.

79. See Rebecca Miller, chapter section "All Roads Lead to City Center Ballroom," pp. 492–494.

80. Ibid., p. 493.

81. Ward interview; "Focus: Brendan Ward," *Irish Voice,* October 19–25, 1994, p. 18; Fitzgibbon interview; Rebecca Miller, p. 492.

82. Rebecca Miller, p. 492.

83. Mary Corcoran quotes a local Bronx priest, of St. Brendan's parish, Bainbridge Avenue, May 3, 1988: "Bars are [the New Irish] cultural center, and they tend to close in on themselves." Corcoran, "Emigrants, 'Eirepreneurs,' and Opportunists," p. 475; see pp. 475–478 for her impressions of New Irish cultural identity, which she sees as influenced by Irish American ethnicity, American culture, and contemporary Irish culture.

84. J. D. interview. Pete Hamill described a similar breakdown in bar culture in his own Brooklyn neighborhood in *A Drinking Life* (New York: Little, Brown and Company, 1994) and in his novel *The Gift* (New York: Random House, 1973).

85. "In personal interviews with the New Irish, as well as in the popular media, migrants complain about the lack of alternative social and recreational outlets for the population. They cite the absence of dance halls like those at home. Respondents to this survey offered similar observations, citing the need for a 'community centre' or a 'social club with . . . class' because the New Irish miss the 'discos.'" Linda Dowling Almeida, "'And They Still Haven't Found What They're Looking For,'" in *The Irish World Wide: Patterns of Migration*, vol. 1 (Leicester, England: Leicester University Press, 1992), p. 202. Good examples of migrant testimony include Connie Higgins's letter to the editor, *Irish Voice*, November 17, 1990, p. 9; and taped interviews with Ted and Tim on March 23, 1989; Ellen and Siobhan on September 27, 1987; and Avril, Ellen, and Ted on October 12, 1988. The names are aliases and tapes are in the possession of the author. New Irish survey questionnaires #210 and #37, in possession of author. Regarding the demand for discos, in Ireland socializing among young people continued in the discos after the pubs closed at 11 P.M.

86. New Irish survey #83, in possession of author.

87. Interview with Mary Corcoran, Dublin, November 11, 1988. Notes in possession of author. See also Mary Corcoran, "Ethnic Boundaries and Legal Barriers."

88. See comments of the Reverend Joseph Delaney, Project Irish Outreach, Archdiocese of New York, *The New Irish Immigrant*, report on a conference sponsored by the National Conference of Catholic Bishops Committee on Migration and the United States Catholic Conference Office of Migration and Refugee Services, Boston College, February 25, 1989, pp. 25 and 27, in which he speaks about the unhealthy environment created by the "circumstances" of the New Irish ghettoes: "They miss interplay that goes on in any natural or normal community that they have at home where you have a whole age range represented. Therefore, they miss maybe the constraints, maybe the advice, and the supports that come in any community from those who are older, those who are wiser, those who are younger and filled with enthusiasm. . . ."

89. Roy Rosenzweig made similar observations about working-class saloon life in nineteenth-century immigrant communities, including the networking and banking functions the saloons provided working men. *Eight Hours for What We Will* (Cambridge: Cambridge University Press, 1983), p. 53.

90. Mary Corcoran identified five types of immigrants: bread and butter immigrants or "economic refugees"; disaffected adventurers, who left in the absence of good career opportunities; holiday takers who make up the illegal population; the educated elite; and lottery winners. See Corcoran, "Emigrants, 'Eirepreneurs,' and Opportunists," p. 463.

91. Rosaleen Fitzgibbon said that the "big difference" between the migrants of the immediate postwar period and the New Irish was that in the forties and fifties "people didn't come to go back, they came to stay . . . they rooted as quickly as possible . . . there was a real sense of being Irish American. . . ." Interview, December 1, 1993.

92. Helena Sheehan, "Irish Identity Is Only Part of What We Are," *Irish Times*, November 29, 1991. Quote found in Corcoran, "Emigrants, 'Eirepreneurs,' and Opportunists," p. 475.

93. Fitzgibbon interview. Notes and tape in possession of author.

94. Letter from Berna Brennan to Linda Dowling Almeida, postmarked January 29, 1996, letter not dated. For reports on Irish reaction to Doyle's fiction and the TV drama *Family*, see Sean O'Riordan, "Author Faces His Fiercest Critics," *Cork Examiner*, September 15, 1994; Eoghan Corry, "Doyle Again Has Us Going Ha Ha Ha," *Irish Press*, August 6, 1994, p. 13; *Sunday Irish Press*, April 24, 1994, pp. 25f.; *Irish Independent*, September 15, 1994, p. 1; and *Irish Press*, February 5, 1994, p. 9.

95. Helena Mulkerns, "Not So Green in the Big Apple," *The Irish Times*, January 19, 1994, p. 10.

96. Ibid.

97. The Chieftains, *The Long Black Veil*, BMG Music, New York, 1995.

98. John Hill, "Images of Violence," in *Cinema and Ireland*, ed. Kevin Rockett, Luke Gibbons, and John Hill (Syracuse, N.Y.: Syracuse University Press, 1988), p. 147. The preface also offers a good overview of Irish film history. For a good discussion of tourism and Irish identity see Barbara O'Connor, "Myths and Mirrors: Tourist Images and National Identity," in *Tourism in Ireland: A Critical Analysis*, ed. Barbara O'Connor and Michael Cronin (Cork, Ireland: Cork University Press, 1993).

99. Interview with John Walley, Chemical Bank, and Jim Bourke, Forfas, the Policy and Advisory Board for Industrial Development in Ireland, October 17, 1994, in Dublin. In a full-page ad which appeared in a special advertising section devoted to Dublin in *Barron's-Market Week*, November 7, 1994, the IDA invited readers to "Profit by Us." It highlighted "The Place, The People, The Profits," with artwork that included a photo of an energetic young man in shirt and tie, sleeves rolled up, talking on the phone while he stared into a computer screen. Promising "an outstanding springboard to those big European markets" and "a maximum tax rate of only 10%," it also boasts of "an intelligent, youthful, enthusiastic workforce"; p. MW9.

An IDA brochure dated September 1993, entitled *Ireland: Put Yourself in Our Hands in the 90s*, opens with photos and copy about the young educated workforce and closes with a full page devoted to lifestyle—"Ireland: a unique blend of traditional and contemporary living . . . Dublin . . . its ethos is cosmopolitan but welcoming"; pp. 1 and 13. Brochure courtesy IDA.

100. Brian Rohan, "'Brothers': Released, at Last," *Irish Voice*, July 26–August 8, 1995, pp. 26–27.

101. Burns said in an interview with Brian Rohan of the *Irish Voice* (July 26–August 8, 1995, p. 27), that the subject of the film is "something I don't think has really been done before. We've had tons of movies about the Jewish-American experience, and the African-American experience, but what have we got from the Irish-American experience? *State of Grace*? *Far and Away*? Please. . . ."

102. The boys attended Catholic school and their rooms are decorated with Notre Dame pennants, but it is not clear that any of them attended that university, although they did attend college.

103. Helena Mulkerns, "Making Movies: Maturity and Money Make Ed Burns a Better Movie Maker," *Irish Echo*, August 21–27, 1996, p. 28.

104. Joe McLaughlin in his March 29, 1995, interview complained that the list never included any representatives from labor unions.

105. Chris McNickle, *To Be Mayor of New York: Ethnic Politics in the City* (New York: Columbia University Press, 1993), p. 64.

106. Ibid., p. 63.

107. Ibid., p. 167.

108. Ibid., pp. 152, 167, 175–179.

109. These two politicians are listed among the six council members on the *EIIC Newsletter*, October/November 1995, acknowledging major funding from the City of New York.

110. See Reid memoirs, pp. 79–80.

111. See Tim Pat Coogan, *The IRA: A History* (Niwat, Colo.: Roberts Rinehart Publishers, 1994), pp. 3–29, for a good background on the IRA.

112. Coogan, *The IRA*, pp. 507, 209–212.

113. Ibid., p. 209.

114. The January 6, 1951, edition of the *Irish Echo*, vol. 16, no. 1168, p. 2, announced a Clan na Gael and IRA Veterans Ball at the Yorkville Casino at 210 East 86th Street on January 6, 1951. The December 23, 1950, *Echo*, vol. 16, no. 1166, p. 6, announced a Clan na Gael/IRA Veterans 25th Annual Ball at the Palm Gardens, 306 W. 52nd Street, on December 30, 1950. The events in subsequent years suggest an active membership and successful turnout for the dances.

115. Coogan, *The IRA*, p. 210. The Irish Freedom Committee, 326 W. 48th Street, held

its "1st Annual Dance and Entertainment to Aid the Irish Republican Movement at City Center Ballroom." See ad in July 14, 1957, *Irish Echo*, p. 10.

116. Jack Deacy, "The IRA, New York Brigade," *New York*, March 15, 1972, p. 42. Paul O'Dwyer, founder of the Irish Institute, successfully defended Harry Barrett by calling his client a patriot and comparing his actions to those of the Hungarian freedom fighters. "If the Freedom Fighters in the streets of Budapest had had the kind of support that Harry Barrett is giving his brothers in Northern Ireland, perhaps they would be free men today, your honor." Deacy, p. 43.

117. Coogan, *The IRA*, p. 229.

118. Ibid., p. 248.

119. See Coogan, *The IRA*, pp. 249–268, 277–292.

120. Andrew J. Wilson, "The American Congress for Irish Freedom, 1967–70," *Eire-Ireland*, Spring 1994, pp. 61–75.

121. Coogan, *The IRA*, p. 273.

122. Jack Deacy, "The IRA, New York Brigade," pp. 40–43; Hamill, "Notes on the New Irish," p. 39, and Coogan, *The IRA*, pp. 273–274.

123. Wilson, pp. 72–73.

124. John T. Ridge, *The St. Patrick's Day Parade in New York* (New York: St. Patrick's Day Parade Committee, AOH Publications, 1988), p. 160. Courtesy John T. Ridge.

Pete Hamill wrote in response to Northern Ireland demonstrations at the 1972 parade, "For the first time in years, it will be possible this year to march in the St. Patrick's Day Parade without being embarrassed." "Notes on the New Irish," p. 39.

125. See Ridge, *St. Patrick's Day Parade*, pp. 162–163, on the 1973 and 1974 parades.

126. *New York Times*, March 18, 1978, found in Ridge, *St. Patrick's Day Parade*, p. 166.

127. Ridge, *St. Patrick's Day Parade*, p. 170; Morrone, p. 102.

128. Ridge, *St. Patrick's Day Parade*, p. 170.

129. Ibid., p. 171.

130. In its premier editorial the *Irish Voice* vowed to be "forthright in its attempts to win for the estimated 135,000 Irish illegals, their proper places as full members of this society." December 5, 1985, p. 4.

131. In 1994, after five years of immigration reform and the legalization of many in the New Irish community, *Irish Voice* publisher Niall O'Dowd led a contingent of Irish American business and political leaders to Ireland to negotiate a peace treaty with Northern Ireland, refocusing attention on the prospect of union between north and south for the entire immigrant and Irish American community, as well as the general public in America.

132. Father Martin Keveny interview, March 23, 1989.

133. Paul Stone, Floral Park, N.Y., letter to the *Irish Voice*, February 18, 1989, p. 9.

134. Rose Fitzgibbon, Brooklyn, N.Y., letter to *Irish Voice*, March 11, 1989, p. 11.

135. Coogan, *The IRA*, p. 449.

136. Morrone, p. 103.

137. Coogan, p. 452.

138. President Clinton has been the most proactive American president working for a peaceful solution to the Northern Ireland political crisis. He was the first president to grant Gerry Adams, Sinn Fein leader, a visitor's visa to come to America and raise money and awareness about the north. He also appointed George Mitchell to monitor the peace accord negotiations in 1998. His selection of Jean Kennedy Smith as ambassador to Ireland in his first term of office also ensured that peace in Northern Ireland would remain a high priority.

139. For a good review of the peace process to date, the Ireland.com website (http://www.ireland.com) includes a "Path to Peace" site on the *Irish Times* page that includes current and past news about the Northern Ireland situation. See in particular Gerry Moriarty, "'Sad but Inevitable Outcome,' Says Trimble," February 12, 2000, and "Northern Ireland Government Suspended after Only 8 Weeks," February 11, 2000.

140. Almeida, "'And They Still Haven't Found What They're Looking For,'" p. 217.

141. John McCarthy, *Dissent from Irish America* (New York: University Press of America, 1993), pp. 225–226.

142. Peggy Hegarty Tanner wrote that on a 1985 visit to her home village of Kilgarvan, County Killarney, she noticed that the town had "advanced and changed somewhat" from the village she remembered with no "television, no electricity, no sewage and no paved roads . . . [and where] every house had a rain barrel for the run off from the roof, the rain always being plentiful. Drinking water was obtained from Camblin Well every day." Mrs. Tanner emigrated to England and worked there as a nurse in the late 1940s. She left for New York in 1953 and worked as a nurse until she married. The above quote was taken from an article she submitted to a local Kilgarvan publication. The photocopy of the article is undated and includes no publication title. In the possession of the author, courtesy Peggy Tanner.

143. J. D. interview; Kerby A. Miller collection of immigrant letters, courtesy Kerby A. Miller.

144. *Irish America Magazine,* November/December 1994, pp. S11, S13, S34.

CONCLUSION

1. Mary Robinson, "Cherishing the Irish Diaspora," address to the Houses of the Oireachtas, February 2, 1995. On the website for the *Irish Emigrant*: http://www.emigrant.ie/emigrant/historic/diaspora.htm.

EPILOGUE

1. Brian Harvey, *Emigration and Services for Irish Emigrants: Towards a New Strategic Plan* (Dublin: Irish Episcopal Commission for Emigrants and Irish Commission for Prisoners Overseas, 1999), p. 14, for the years 1988 and 1992–1998. The 1999 figures for emigration are taken from the Central Statistics Office of the Republic of Ireland for the year ended April 1999, courtesy Patrick O'Sullivan, Irish-diaspora@Bradford.ac.uk, October 19, 1999.

2. Harvey, pp. 14 and 19.

3. Figures taken from Central Statistics Office for Republic of Ireland as reported in "The Celtic Tiger Draws Many of City's Irish Home," *New York Times,* December 5, 1999. Courtesy Marion R. Casey, Irish-diaspora@Bradford.ac.uk, December 13, 1999.

4. Harvey, pp. 14 and 19.

5. Employment and inflation figures found at http://www.ireland.com: Arthur Beesley and Padraig Yeates, "Live Register Figures Fall to 18-Year Low," *Irish Times,* February 5, 2000; and Jane O'Sullivan, "EU Inflation Data Puts Republic's Rise at 4.4%," *Irish Times,* February 23, 2000.

6. The question to ask here is, how many of those who returned to Ireland left with their green card? The green card allows aliens to work in the United States and travel outside its boundaries. In order to travel, an alien must have a valid green card and a valid passport. Green card holders are permitted to leave the United States for up to eleven months and twenty-nine days at a time. But advocates warn the immigrants that staying out of the country for longer than six months without solid proof of residency may, when they attempt to re-enter the country, cause the INS to suspect that they have abandoned their U.S. residency. If immigrants wish to remain outside the country for a longer continuous period they must file for a re-entry permit which is good for up to two years and can be extended in case of emergency. But if they stay out for more than two years without appropriate permission, they lose their green card. According to the INS, almost 88,000 Irish citizens legally immigrated to the United States between 1981 and 1996. Presumably some of these are among the return migrants. Will they move back and forth between the United States and Ireland to maintain a valid visa and work toward naturalization? Or will they stay in Ireland for the long term? How many of the Irish who received visas in the 1980s and 1990s remain, where they settle down in the United States, and how many become U.S. citizens cannot be determined with certainty until the 2000 census is completed. Visa regulations taken from phone interview with INS counselor, February 23, 2000, and Patricia O'Callaghan, March 2, 2000.

7. Harry Keaney and Patrick Markey, "The New Generation: Celtic Tiger Roars, but, for Many, Uncle Sam Still Beckons," *Irish Echo,* November 24–30, 1999. The authors cite an Immigration and Naturalization report that about 25 percent of Irish immigrants heading to the United States between 1981 and 1996 settled in the New York area.

8. Harvey, p. 23.

9. Harvey, p. 33, and *Summary of the New Grounds of Inadmissibility under the Illegal Immigration Reform and Immigrant Responsibility Act of 1996,* white paper highlighting regulations of the IIRIRA. Courtesy Patricia O'Callaghan, Project Irish Outreach, New York Archdiocese Catholic Charities.

10. *Summary of the New Grounds of Inadmissibility under the IIRIRA.* The possibility of amnesty was raised in discussions with Sister Edna MacNicholl at the Aisling Center in the Bronx, November 10, 1999, and February 22, 2000, and with Father Tim O'Sullivan, national director of the Irish Chaplaincy Program, February 22, 2000.

11. Harvey, p. 34, and "Diversity Visa 2001 also known as Green Card Lottery," http://immigrationvisa.com/lottery.

12. *EIIC News,* vol. 2, issue 1, January 2000, p. 2; *EIIC News,* vol. 2, issue 2, April 2000, p. 3. The new program experienced a certain amount of growing pains. Some attrition occurred among the first groups of recipients as the program evolved. Ray O'Hanlon, "No Show New Arrivals, Make Quick Return," *Irish Echo,* April 12–18, 2000. http://www.irishecho.com. Interview with Carolyn Ryan, EIIC, May 22, 2000.

13. Interviews with Sister Edna MacNicholl, November 10, 1999, and Carolyn Ryan, Emerald Isle Immigration Center, November 8, 1999.

14. Interview with Patricia O'Callaghan, Project Irish Outreach, New York Catholic Charities, October 21, 1999.

15. Interview with Father Tim O'Sullivan, February 22, 2000.

16. The mother and child programs evolved into the Irish American Family Association in 1996 with chapters in Boston, New York and San Francisco. The objective of the association is to create a family and social network for young parents and children who have no extended family of their own in the United States. Interview with Father Tim O'Sullivan, February 22, 2000. Focus of ministry was explained by Sister Edna MacNicholl in November 10, 1999, interview.

17. Interview with Sister Edna MacNicholl and visit to Aisling Center, November 10, 1999. Ads taken from St. Barnabas Church bulletin, November 7, 1999.

Bibliography

INTERVIEWS

Avril, Ellen, and Ted (aliases). October 12, 1988.
Bourke, Jim. October 17, 1994.
Brady, Sister Lucia. March 1989.
Brennan, Jerry. October 11, 1994.
Bridgh, Sister. December 9, 1992.
Byrne, Father Paul. October 20, 1994.
C. B. January 27, 1994.
C. M. October 21 and 22, 1994.
Corcoran, Mary. November 11, 1988.
Curley, Margaret. October 19, 1994.
Delaney, Father Joe. March 1989.
Derham, Robert H. "An Oral History of Irish Immigrants." University of California, Berkeley. December 4, 1976.
Doyle, Shane. December 1, 1992.
Ellen and Siobhan (aliases). September 27, 1987.
Farrell, James. September 28, 1988.
Fitzgibbon, Rosaleen. December 1, 1993.
G. Q. February 8, 1989.
H. F. January 12, 1996.
Hurley, Pat. October 15, 1988.
J. B. October 17, 1994.
J. D. April 20, 1995.
J. M. March 1995.
Jamison, Joe. February 1, 1989.
Keveny, Father Martin. October 19, 1988, and March 23, 1989.
M. M., Sister. October 20, 1994.
MacNicholl, Sister Edna. November 10, 1999.
Maeve and Margaret (aliases). December 1, 1988.
Maura (alias). October 26, 1988.
McIntyre, James. April 6, 1995.
McLaughlin, Joe and Rose. March 29, 1995.
McNicholas, Sister Edna. December 1992, November 10, 1999.
Minihane, Sean. October 20, 1994, and December 27, 1988.
Morrissey, Kevin. February 9, 1995.
Mulvey, Kathleen. April 26, 1995.
Murphy, Nick. January 29, 1989.
Murray, Monsignor James. January 27, 1989.
Nic Giolla Choille, Trionna. October 21, 1994.

O'Callaghan, Patricia. November 2, 1988; January 31, 1989; December 2, 1992; October 21, 1999; and March 2, 2000.
O'Sullivan, Father Tim. February 22, 2000.
O'Sullivan, Paula. December 2, 1992.
R. H. December 4, 1992.
Reid, Father Sean, O. Carm. January 27, 1994.
Ryan, Carolyn. November 8, 1999; May 22, 2000.
St. Mel's Discussion Group. October 3, 1994.
Sheila. February 1, 1989.
Tanner, Peggy Hegarty. June 28, 1995.
Ted and Tim (aliases). March 23, 1989.
Teresa. November 1988.
V. D. March 28, 1995.
W. Family. October 19, 1994.
Walley, John. October 17, 1994.
Ward, Brendan. October 24, 1994.

SURVEYS

Irish America Business 100 Surveys, 1995.
Irish American Surveys (IA94), 1994–1995.
New Irish Surveys, #1 through #247, Fall 1990.
Returned Emigrant Surveys (RE94), 1994.

LETTERS/MEMOIRS

Boyd, Colleen S., and Helen Hughes. "Catskills: A Paradise Lost." Letters. *Irish Voice*, August 16, 1995, p. 11.
Brennan, Berna. Letter to Linda Dowling Almeida, postmarked January 29, 1996.
Casey, Marion. E-mail to Irish-diaspora@Bradfor.ac.uk, subject: Return migration, December 13, 1999.
D. O. Letter to Linda Dowling Almeida. October 25, 1994.
———. Letter to Linda Dowling Almeida. November 1, 1994.
———. Letter to Linda Dowling Almeida. November 29, 1994.
De Valera, Eamon. Letter to T. Q., September 2, 1961 (photocopy). Courtesy T. Q.
F. D. Letter to Linda Dowling Almeida, July 21, 1995.
Fitzgibbon, Rose. Letter. *Irish Voice*, March 11, 1989. p. 11.
Grimes, John. *The Best of Times: Reminiscences.* Christmas 1989. Courtesy Claire Grimes.
H. L. G. Letter and memoir to Linda Dowling Almeida, December 12, 1994.
Hannon, Michael. "'Filthy, Lazy, Drunken,' Etc." Letter, *Irish Voice*, January 17–23, 1996, p. 11.
Hegarty, Peggy. Letter to Mom [D. Hegarty] and Den [brother], Co. Kerry, Ireland, March 14, 1957. Courtesy Peggy Hegarty Tanner.
———. Letter to Mom and Den. Tuesday, November 24, 1953. Courtesy Peggy Hegarty Tanner.
Immigrant X. Letter to F. and R. M. January 21, 1957. Kerby A. Miller collection. Courtesy Kerby A. Miller.
J. D. Letter to Linda Dowling, August 1, 1995.
J. H. Letter to Linda Dowling Almeida, August 16, 1994.
J. J. S. Letter to Linda Dowling Almeida, February 6, 1995.
Lingg, Barbara A. Letter to Linda Dowling Almeida, June 1, 1995.
Lowe, Sister Francis. Letter to Linda Dowling Almeida, November 20, 1995.
M. M. Letter to Linda Dowling Almeida and clippings, December 2, 1994.
———. Letter to Linda Dowling Almeida, March 22, 1995.
Mary, a documented alien, Bronx, N.Y. Letter. *Irish America Magazine*, September 1987, p. 7.

McLaughlin, Joseph. "Track of the Macs," family memoir, undated. Courtesy Joseph P. McLaughlin, son of Joseph McLaughlin.

Miller, Kerby A. Collection of immigrant letters.

Ni Chochlain, Sile. President, Concilium Legionis Mariae. Letters to Linda Dowling Almeida, February 10 and 24, 2000.

Nolan, Freda, private secretary, Office of the Minister for Labour, Ireland. Letter and appendix to Linda Dowling Almeida, July 30, 1991.

O'Gainm, Sean. Letter. *Irish Voice*, November 29–December 5, 1995, p. 11.

O'Sullivan, Dermot. Letter to Linda Dowling Almeida, November 1, 1994.

———. Letter to Linda Dowling Almeida, November 29, 1994.

O'Sullivan, Patrick. E-mail to Irish-diaspora@Bradford.ac.uk, subject: Ir-D Ireland—Immigrants and Emigrants, October 19, 1999.

P. M. Letter to M. M. May 14, 1952. Kerby A. Miller Collection. Courtesy Kerby A. Miller.

———. Letter to M. M. August 8, 1953 (?). Kerby A. Miller collection. Courtesy Kerby A. Miller.

Price, Mary L. Letter. *Irish America Magazine*, November 1987, p. 9.

Reid, Father Sean S., O. Carm. "Recollections of Some Sixty Years." ca. 1985. Courtesy Father Sean Reid.

———. Letter to Linda Dowling Almeida, March 1, 1995.

Ryan, Father Gerald. Letter to Linda Dowling Almeida, March 24, 1995.

Stone, Paul. Letter. *Irish Voice*, February 18, 1989, p. 9.

T. Q. Letter to Linda Dowling Almeida and clippings, June 30, 1994.

W. F. Letter to Linda Dowling Almeida, December 5, 1994.

GOVERNMENT DOCUMENTS: UNITED STATES

Congressional Research Office "U.S. Immigration Law and Policy, 1952–1986." December 1987.

Department of Commerce. *1990 Census of Population and Housing, Population and Housing Characteristics for Census Tracts and Block Numbering Areas, New York, Northern New Jersey, Long Island NY-NJ-CT CMSA (Part) New York, NY PMSA.* 1990 CPH-3-245H. Washington, D.C.: Government Printing Office, July 1993.

———. *1990 Census of Population and Housing.* Summary Tape File 3A on CD for New York State. Courtesy New York University Computer Center.

———. *1980 Census of Population, Ancestry of Persons, New York by Census Tracts, NY-NJ SMSA.* PHC80-2260. Washington, D.C.: Government Printing Office, August 1983.

———. *1980 Census of Population: Vol. 1, Sec. 2, Characteristics of Population: Chapter C, General Social and Economic Characteristics.* pt. 34, New York. PC80-1-C34. Washington, D.C.: Government Printing Office, July 1983.

———. *1980 Census, by Census Tracts, New York Selected Areas.* pt. 34. PHC80-2-34. Washington, D.C.: Government Printing Office, August 1983.

———. *1980 Census, Population Characteristics, New York State.* pt. 34. PC80-1-D34. Washington, D.C.: Government Printing Office, November 1983.

———. *1980 Census: Supplementary Report.* PC80-S110. Washington, D.C.: Government Printing Office, April 1983.

———. *1970 Census of Population and Housing: Census Tracts, New York, NY, Standard Metropolitan Statistical Area.* PHC(1)-145, pt. 1. Washington, D.C.: Government Printing Office, 1972.

———. *1970 Census of Population and Housing: Census Tracts, New York, NY, Standard Metropolitan Statistical Area.* PHC(1)-145, pt. 2. Washington, D.C.: Government Printing Office, 1972.

———. *1960 Census of Population: Characteristics of the Population, U.S. Summary.* Vol. 1, pt. 1. Washington, D.C.: Government Printing Office, 1961.

————. *1960 Census of Population: Characteristics of the Population, New York*. Vol. 1, pt. 34. Washington, D.C.: Government Printing Office, 1963.

————. *1960 Census of Population: Final Report, New York, NY, Standard Metropolitan Statistical Area, Part 1, New York City*. PHC (1)-104, pt. 1. Washington, D.C.: Government Printing Office, 1961.

————. *1960 Census of Population: Final Report, Subject Reports, Nativity and Parentage, Social and Economic Characteristics of the Foreign Stock by Country of Origin*. PC(2)-1A. Washington, D.C.: Government Printing Office, 1964.

————. *1960 Census of Population: Characteristics of Population*. Vol. 1, pt. 34. New York. Washington, D.C.: Government Printing Office, 1963.

————. *1960 Census of Population and Housing: Final Reports. Series PHC. By Census Tracts*. PHC(1). Washington, D.C.: Government Printing Office, 1961–1962.

————. *1960 Census of Population and Housing: Final Reports. Series PHC. By Census Tracts. New York, NY*. Pt. 1, New York City. PHC(1)-104. Washington, D.C.: Government Printing Office, 1962.

————. *1950 Census of Population: Census Tract Statistics New York, NY. Selected Population and Housing Characteristics*. P-D37. Vol. 3, chap. 37. Washington, D.C.: Government Printing Office, 1952.

————. *1950 Census of Population: Characteristics of Population. U.S. Summary*. Vol. 2, pt. 1. Washington, D.C.: Government Printing Office, 1953.

————. *1950 Census of Population: Characteristics of Population. New York*. Vol. 2, pt. 32. Washington, D.C.: Government Printing Office, 1952.

————. *1950 Census: Special Reports, Nativity and Parentage*. P-E 3A. Washington, D.C.: Government Printing Office, 1954.

Human Resources Administration, Medicaid Eligibility Administration. "Changes in Medicaid Eligibility of Aliens: July 1988," *Medicaid Alert*. New York: Human Resources Administration, September 1988.

Immigration and Naturalization Service (INS). *The I&N Reporter*. vol. 11, no. 4, Washington, D.C.: Department of Justice, April 1954.

————. *1997 Statistical Yearbook of the Immigration and Naturalization Service*. Washington, D.C.: Government Printing Office, October 1999.

————. *1992 Statistical Yearbook of the Immigration and Naturalization Service*. Washington, D.C.: Government Printing Office, October 1993.

————. *1987 Statistical Yearbook of the Immigration and Naturalization Service*. Washington, D.C.: Government Printing Office, October 1988.

————. *1982 Statistical Yearbook of the Immigration and Naturalization Service*. Washington, D.C.: Government Printing Office, October 1983.

————. *Annual Report of the Immigration and Naturalization Service, 1967*. Washington, D.C.: Department of Justice, 1967.

————. *Annual Report of the Immigration and Naturalization Service, 1961*. Washington, D.C.: Department of Justice, 1961.

————. *Annual Report of the Immigration and Naturalization Service, 1960*. Washington, D.C.: Department of Justice, 1960.

————. *Annual Report of the Immigration and Naturalization Service, 1959*. Washington, D.C.: Department of Justice, 1959.

————. *Annual Report of the Immigration and Naturalization Service, 1958*. Washington, D.C.: Department of Justice, 1958.

————. *Annual Report of the Immigration and Naturalization Service, 1957*. Washington, D.C.: Department of Justice, 1957.

————. *Annual Report of the Immigration and Naturalization Service, 1956*. Washington, D.C.: Department of Justice, 1956.

————. *Annual Report of the Immigration and Naturalization Service, 1955*. Washington, D.C.: Department of Justice, 1955.

————. *Annual Report of the U.S. Immigration and Naturalization Service, 1954.* Washington, D.C.: Department of Justice 1954.

Information Center on Education, University of the State of New York. *Nonpublic School Enrollment and Staff, New York State 1973–1974.* Albany, N.Y.: The State Department of Education, April 1975.

"Irish Immigration Adversely Affected by Immigration and Nationality Act of 1965." *Congressional Record,* House 113, pt. 10, pp. 13166–8.

Koch, Edward I. "City Policy on Undocumented Aliens." October 15, 1985.

New York City Department of City Planning. *The Newest New Yorkers 1990–1994: An Analysis of Immigration to NYC in the Early 1990s.* DCP96-19, December 1996.

New York State Department of Social Services. *Medicaid: How New York State Helps with Medical Expenses.* New York: Department of Social Services, March 1987.

Office of the Health and Hospital Corporation and Legal Services Staff, Community Action for Legal Services, Inc. *If You Can't Pay Your Hospital Bill—Medicaid or HHC's Fee Settlement Program May Be Able to Help You Out.* New York: n.p., December 1987.

Schick, Joe, ed. *New York City Health and Hospitals Corporation Annual Report 1988.* New York: Office of Public Affairs and Special Projects, November 1989.

Social Security Administration. *Annual Statistical Supplement to the Social Security Bulletin, 1995.* Washington, D.C.: Government Printing Office, August 1995.

————. *Annual Statistical Supplement to the Social Security Bulletin,* excerpts from 1955, 1956, 1957, 1958, 1959, 1960, 1961, 1962, 1964, 1965, 1966, 1967, 1968, 1969, 1970, 1971, 1972, 1973, 1974, 1976, 1977, 1979, 1980, 1982, 1983, 1984, 1985, 1986, 1987, 1988, 1989, 1990, 1991, 1992, 1993, 1994. Washington, D.C.: Government Printing Office. Courtesy Barbara A. Lingg, acting leader, Division of RSDI Research Statistics, Office of Research and Statistics, Social Security Administration.

————. *Social Security Bulletin,* vol. 57, no. 1. Washington, D.C.: Government Printing Office, Spring 1994.

Survey of Nonpublic Schools, New York State, 1968–69. University of the State of New York. Albany, N.Y.: State Education Department, July 1969.

Works Progress Administration (WPA). Historical Records Survey, Federal Writers Project. Box 3579, "Irish in New York"; folder 5, "Occupations and Location"; A. Fitzpatrick, "The Irish Race in Various Industries, Professions, Etc." 1938.

GOVERNMENT DOCUMENTS: IRELAND

Barrington, Anne. "Emigration from Ireland: Why and How Many?" New York: Consul General, Ireland, May 1991.

Central Statistics Office. *Ireland Census 91, Vol. 1, Population Classified by Area.* Dublin: Stationery Office, June 1993.

————. *Ireland Census 86, Summary Population Report.* Dublin: Stationery Office, November 1987.

————. *Labour Force Survey 1987.* Dublin: Stationery Office, August 1988.

————. *Population and Labour Force Projections, 1991–2021.* Dublin: Stationery Office, April 1988.

————. *The Trend of Employment and Unemployment 1979–1985.* Dublin: Stationery Office, August 1988.

————. *Vital Statistics for Ireland: Fourth Quarter and Yearly Summary 1993.* Dublin: Stationery Office, September 1994.

Commission on Emigration and Other Population Problems. *Commission on Emigration and Other Population Problems 1948–1954 Reports.* (Pr. 2541) Dublin: Stationery Office, 1956.

Industrial Development Authority [Ireland]. *Ireland: Put Yourself in Our Hands in the 90s.* September 1993.

————. *Ireland: The Skills Center of Europe for the Electronics Industry.* Dublin: IDA, September 1993.

National Economic and Social Council (NESC). *The Economic and Social Implications of Emigration.* Dublin: National Economic and Social Council, March 1991.

Office of the Minister for Labour. "Appendix A: Briefing Notes on Emigration for Officials; Dion—The Advisory Committee on Emigrant Welfare Services." Dublin, n.d.

Robinson, Mary. "Cherishing the Irish Diaspora," Address to the Houses of the Oireachtas, February 2, 1995. On the website of the *Irish Emigrant*: http://www.emigrant.ie/emigrant/historic/diaspora.htm.

FRATERNAL ORGANIZATION AND
INSTITUTIONAL STUDIES/DOCUMENTS

American Irish Teachers Association. Newsletters. Vol. 20, no. 7, September 1994; vol. 20, no. 8, October 1994.

———. Program for 19th Annual Irish American Conference, Saturday, November 12, 1994.

Cathedral Club. *Ninety-Fifth Annual Dinner of the Cathedral Club.* Dinner program. Brooklyn: Cathedral Club, January 26, 1995.

Emigrant Advice. *Emigrant Advice Annual Report 1990.* Dublin: Emigrant Advice, 1990.

———. *Emigrant Advice Annual Report 1989.* Dublin: Emigrant Advice, 1989.

———. *Emigrant Sunday: October 2nd, 1988: The Rising Tide of Emigration.* Dublin: Emigrant Advice, 1988.

Emerald Isle Immigration Center. *Education: Your Passport to Success 1991.* New York: Emerald Isle Immigration Center, 1991.

———. Newsletters 1990–1996, 1999, 2000.

———. Website: http://www.eiic.org.

Harvey, Brian. *Emigration and Services for Irish Emigrants: Towards a New Strategic Plan.* Dublin: Irish Episcopal Commission for Emigrants and Irish Commission for Prisoners Overseas, 1999.

Irish Immigration Reform Movement. Newsletters 1987–1990.

Irish Institute. *A Brief History of the Irish Institute.* Courtesy Kevin Morrissey.

———. *Next Door Neighbors: The Irish and Others in New York City.* Brochure for seminar held at New York University March 2, 1996.

———. Papers of the Irish Institute of New York, Inc. Archives of Irish America, Bobst Library, New York University.

Kerry Emigrant Support Group. *Emigration Awareness,* ed. Sister Anne McNamara, PBVM. Tralee: Kerry Emigrant Support Group, n.d. (includes 1993 data).

Martin, Donald. Written testimony on behalf of the IIRM before House Subcommittee on Immigration, Refugees, and International Law Committee. September 16, 1988.

Migration and Refugee Services Staff, U.S. Catholic Conference. "Undocumented Irish in the U.S." March 1988.

The New Irish Immigrant. Printed remarks of conference sponsored by the National Conference of Catholic Bishops Committee on Migration and United States Catholic Conference Office of Migration and Refugee Services. Boston College, February 25, 1989.

New York Archdiocese Catholic Charities. *Summary of the New Grounds of Inadmissibility under the Illegal Immigration Reform and Immigrant Responsibility Act of 1996.* White paper for use by staff. Courtesy Patricia O'Callaghan.

O'Callaghan, Patricia. *Immigrating USA: A Guide for Irish Immigrants.* New York: Project Irish Outreach, Catholic Charities, Archdiocese of New York, 1989.

Quinn, Gerard, ed. *The Irish Banking Review Autumn 1987.* Dublin: Irish Bankers' Federation, 1987.

St. Nicholas of Tollantine Roman Catholic Church. Baptismal Records 1953–1959, 1977–1985. Courtesy Father John Dello Russo, OSA, associate, and Father Brian Frawley, OSA, pastor.

———. *50th Anniversary Book* (photocopy). Bronx, N.Y.: St. Nicholas of Tollantine Parish, ca. 1956. Courtesy Father John Dello Russo, OSA, associate, and Father Brian Frawley, OSA, pastor.

————. *75th Anniversary Book: Diamond Jubilee*. Bronx, N.Y.: St. Nicholas of Tollantine Parish, October 10, 1981. Courtesy Father John Dello Russo, OSA, associate, and Father Brian Frawley, OSA, pastor.

————. *Twenty Years on Fordham Heights* (photocopy). Bronx, N.Y.: St. Nicholas of Tollantine Parish, n.d. Courtesy Father John Dello Russo, OSA, associate, and Father Brian Frawley, OSA, pastor.

NEWSPAPERS/PERIODICALS

Irish America Magazine, 1994–2000.

Irish Echo, 1950–2000.

Irish Voice, 1987–2000.

RTV Guide [Ireland], vol. 1, no. 4, January 1977; vol. 6, no. 6, February 1982; vol. 6, no. 10, March 1982.

BOOKS

Alba, Richard. *Ethnic Identity: The Transformation of White America*. New Haven: Yale University Press, 1990.

Allitt, Patrick. *Catholic Intellectuals and Conservative Politics in America, 1950–1985*. Ithaca, N.Y.: Cornell University Press, 1993.

Barkan, Elliott Robert. *And Still They Come: Immigrants and American Society 1920 to the 1990s*. Wheeling, Ill.: Harlan Davidson, 1996.

Bayor, Ronald H. *Neighbors in Conflict: The Irish, Germans, Jews, and Italians of New York City, 1929–1941*. 2nd ed. Urbana: University of Illinois Press, 1987.

Bayor, Ronald H., and Timothy Meagher, eds. *The New York Irish*. Baltimore: Johns Hopkins University Press, 1996.

Bodnar, John. *The Transplanted: A History of Immigrants in Urban America*. Bloomington: Indiana University Press, 1985.

Caro, Robert. *The Power Broker: Robert Moses and the Fall of New York*. New York: Knopf, 1974.

Carroll, Jim. *The Basketball Diaries*. New York: Penguin Books, 1995.

Casey, Daniel J., and Robert E. Rhodes, eds. *Irish-American Fiction: Essays in Criticism*. New York: AMS, 1979.

Chafe, William H. *The Unfinished Journey: America since World War II*. New York: Oxford University Press, 1986.

Chubb, Basil. *The Constitution and Constitutional Change in Ireland*. Dublin: Institute of Public Administration, 1978.

————. *The Government and Politics of Ireland*. 2nd ed. Stanford, Calif.: Stanford University Press, 1982.

Cogley, John. *Catholic America*. New York: Doubleday, 1974.

Coogan, Tim Pat. *The IRA: A History*. Niwat, Colo.: Roberts Rinehart Publishers, 1994.

————. *Eamon De Valera: The Man Who Was Ireland*. New York: HarperCollins Publishers, 1993. Orig. pub. *De Valera: Long Fellow, Long Shadow*. London: Hutchinson, 1993.

Cooney, John. *The American Pope: The Life and Times of Francis Cardinal Spellman*. New York: Times Books, 1984.

Corcoran, Mary P. *Irish Illegals: Transients between Two Societies*. Westport, Conn.: Greenwood Press, 1993.

Cullinan, Elizabeth. *Yellow Roses*. New York: Viking Press, 1977.

Curtis, P. J. *Notes from the Heart: A Celebration of Traditional Irish Music*. Dublin: Torc, 1994.

Diner, Hasia. *Erin's Daughters in America*. Baltimore: Johns Hopkins University Press, 1983.

Dinnerstein, Leonard. *Natives and Strangers*. New York: Oxford University Press, 1996.

Dinnerstein, Leonard, and David Reimers. *Ethnic Americans: A History of Immigration*. 3rd ed. New York: Harper and Row, 1988.

Dolan, Jay P. *The Immigrant Church: New York's Irish and German Catholics, 1815–1865*. 2nd ed. Notre Dame, Ind.: University of Notre Dame Press, 1983.

Erie, Steven P. *Rainbow's End: Irish Americans and the Dilemmas of Urban Machine Politics, 1840–1985*. Berkeley: University of California Press, 1988.

Fogarty, Michael, Joseph Lee, and Liam Ryan. *Irish Values and Attitudes: The Irish Report of the European Value Systems Study*. Dominican Publications, 1984.

Foster, R. F. *Modern Ireland 1600–1972*. London: Allen Lane, the Penguin Press, 1988.

Gannon, Robert I., S.J. *The Cardinal Spellman Story*. New York: Doubleday, 1962.

Glazer, Nathan, and Daniel Patrick Moynihan. *Beyond the Melting Pot: The Negroes, Puerto Ricans, Irish, Jews, and Italians of New York City*. Cambridge: MIT Press and Harvard University Press, 1963.

Goren, Arthur. *New York Jews and the Quest for Community: The Kehillah Experiment, 1908–1930*. New York, 1970.

Greeley, Andrew. *The American Catholic: A Social Portrait*. New York: Basic Books, 1977.

———. *Catholic Myth: The Behavior and Beliefs of American Catholics*. New York: Charles Scribner's Sons, 1990.

———. *From Backwater to Mainstream: A Profile of Catholic Higher Education*. First of a series of profiles sponsored by the Carnegie Commission on Higher Education. New York: McGraw-Hill Book Company, 1969.

———. *That Most Distressful Nation: The Taming of the American Irish*. Chicago: Quadrangle Books, 1972.

Greeley, Andrew, and Peter Rossi. *The Education of Catholic Americans*. Chicago: Aldine, 1966.

Greeley, Andrew, William C. McCready, and Kathleen McCourt. *Catholic Schools in a Declining Church*. Kansas City, Mo.: Sheed and Ward, 1976.

Griffin, William D. *The Book of Irish Americans*. New York: Times Books, 1990.

Gutierrez, Ramon. *When Jesus Came, the Corn Mothers Went Away: Marriage, Sexuality, and Power in New Mexico, 1500–1846*. Stanford, Calif.: Stanford University Press, 1991.

Halberstam, David. *The Fifties*. New York: Villard Books, 1993.

Hamill, Pete. *A Drinking Life*. New York: Little, Brown and Company, 1994.

———. *The Gift*. New York: Random House, 1973.

Hechter, Michael. *Internal Colonialism: The Celtic Fringe in British National Development, 1536–1966*. Berkeley: University of California Press, 1975.

Hennesy, James, S.J. *American Catholics: A History of the Roman Catholic Community in the United States*. New York: Oxford University Press, 1981.

Herring, George C. *American's Longest War: The United States and Viet Nam 1950–1975*. New York: Alfred A. Knopf, 1986.

Jackson, Kenneth T. *Crabgrass Frontier*. New York: Oxford University Press, 1985.

Joyce, James. *Dubliners*. New York: Viking Press, 1961.

———. *Ulysses*. New York: Vintage Books, 1961.

Katznelson, Ira. *City Trenches: Urban Politics and the Patterning of Class in the United States*. Philadelphia: Temple University Press, 1981.

Kelly, Kate, and Trionna Nic Giolla Choille. *Emigration Matters for Women*. Dublin: Attic Press, 1990.

Kenny, Kevin. *Making Sense of the Molly Maguires*. New York: Oxford University Press, 1998.

Kessler-Harris, Alice. *Social History*. The New American History Series, ed. Eric Foner. Washington, D.C.: American Historical Association, 1990.

Lee, Joseph. *Ireland 1912–1985: Politics and Society*. 6th ed. Cambridge: Cambridge University Press, 1993.

———. *The Modernisation of Irish Society, 1848–1918*. Dublin: Gill and Macmillan, 1973.

MacLaughlin, Jim, ed. *Location and Dislocation in Contemporary Irish Society: Emigration and Irish Identities*. Notre Dame, Ind.: University of Notre Dame Press, 1997.

Mannion, Lawrence J., and Richard C. Murphy. *The History of the Society of the Friendly Sons of St. Patrick in the City of New York: 1784 to 1955*. New York: Society of the Friendly Sons of St. Patrick, 1962.

Marcuson, Lewis R. *The Stage Immigrant: The Irish, the Italians, and Jews in American Drama, 1920–1960*. New York: Garland Press, 1990.

May, Elaine Tyler. *Homeward Bound: American Families in the Cold War*. New York: Basic Books, 1988.

McCabe, Patrick. *The Butcher Boy*. New York: Delta, 1994.

McCaffrey, Lawrence J. *The Irish Catholic Diaspora in America*. Washington, D.C.: The Catholic University of America Press, 1997. Rev. ed. of *The Irish Diaspora in America*. Bloomington: Indiana University Press, 1976.

———. *Textures of Irish America*. Syracuse, N.Y.: Syracuse University Press, 1992.

McCarthy, John P. *Dissent from Irish America*. New York: University Press of America, 1993.

McIlroy, Brian. *Irish Cinema: An Illustrated History*. Dublin: Anna Livia Press, 1988. Orig. pub. *World Cinema 4: Ireland*. Trowbridge, England: Flicks Books, 1988.

McNickle, Chris. *To Be Mayor of New York*. New York: Columbia University Press, 1993.

Miller, Kerby A. *Emigrants and Exiles: Ireland and the Irish Exodus to North America*. New York: Oxford University Press, 1985.

Miller, Kerby A., and Paul Wagner. *Out of Ireland: The Story of Irish Emigration to America*. Washington, D.C.: Elliott and Clark Publishing, 1994.

Moore, Deborah Dash. *At Home in America: Second Generation New York Jews*. New York: Columbia University Press, 1981.

Murphy, John A. *Ireland in the Twentieth Century*. 2nd ed. The Gill History of Ireland, ed. James Lydon and Margaret MacCurtain. Dublin: Gill and Macmillan, 1977.

Murphy, Thomas. *A Crucial Week in the Life of a Grocer's Assistant*. Dublin: Gallery Press, 1978.

New York and the Irish Famine: A Symbolic Meal and Keynote Address on the Occasion of the Tenth Anniversary of the New York Irish History Roundtable. St. Paul the Apostle Undercroft, New York City, October 28, 1994. New York: Irish History Roundtable, 1994.

Nolan, Janet. *Ourselves Alone*. Lexington: University Press of Kentucky, 1989.

O'Carroll, Ide. *Models for Movers: Irish Women's Emigration to America*. Dublin: Attic Press, 1990.

O'Connor, Barbara, and Michael Cronin. *Tourism in Ireland: A Critical Analysis*. Cork: Cork University Press, 1993.

O'Connor, Richard. *Hell's Kitchen: The Roaring Days of New York's Wild West Side*. Philadelphia and New York: J. B. Lippincott Co., 1958.

The Official Catholic Directory AD 1995. New Providence, N.J.: P. J. Kennedy and Sons, in association with R R. Bowker, 1995.

O'Hanlon, Ray. *The New Irish Americans*. Niwot, Colo.: Roberts Rinehart Publishers.

O'Sullivan, Patrick, ed. *Patterns of Migration*. Vol. 1 of *The Irish World Wide*. Leicester, England: University of Leicester Press, and New York: St. Martin's Press, 1992.

———. *The Irish in New Communities*. Vol. 2 of *The Irish World Wide*. Leicester, England: University of Leicester Press, and New York: St. Martin's Press, 1992.

O'Toole, Fintan. *The Lie of the Land: Irish Identities*. New York: Verso, 1997.

O'Tuathaigh, Gearoid. *Ireland before the Famine 1798–1848*. The Gill History of Ireland. Dublin: Gill and MacMillan, 1972.

Quill, Shirley. *Mike Quill, Himself*. Greenwich, Conn.: Devin-Adair, 1985.

Quinn, Brother Charles B. *Iona College: The First Fifty Years*. New Rochelle, N.Y.: Iona College, 1990.

Quinn, Peter. *Banished Children of Eve*. New York: Viking Penguin, 1994.

Reimers, David. *Still the Golden Door: The Third World Comes to America*. New York: Columbia University Press, 1985.

Ridge, John T. *Erin's Sons in America: The Ancient Order of Hibernians*. New York: Ancient Order of Hibernians, 150th Anniversary Committee, 1986.

———. *The History of the Ancient Order of Hibernians and Ladies' Auxiliary of Brooklyn*. Brooklyn: Ancient Order of Hibernians, 1973. Reprint, 1985.

———. *The St. Patrick's Day Parade in New York.* New York: St. Patrick's Day Committee, AOH Publications, 1988.

Rockett, Kevin, Luke Gibbons, and John Hill. *Cinema and Ireland.* Syracuse, N.Y.: Syracuse University Press, 1988.

Rosenwaike, Ira. *Population History of New York City.* Syracuse, N.Y.: Syracuse University Press, 1972.

Rosenzweig, Roy. *Eight Hours for What We Will.* Cambridge: Cambridge University Press, 1983.

Scally, Robert James. *The End of Hidden Ireland: Rebellion, Famine, and Emigration.* New York: Oxford University Press, 1995.

Shannon, William. *The American Irish: A Political and Social Portrait.* New York: Macmillan, 1966.

Sharp, Monsignor John K. *The History of the Diocese of Brooklyn, 1853–1953.* 2 vols. New York: Fordham University Press, 1954.

Silinonte, Joseph M. *Tombstones of the Irish Born: Cemetery of the Holy Cross, Flatbush, Brooklyn.* Brooklyn, N.Y.: privately published, 1992.

Solomon, Barbara Miller. *In the Company of Educated Women: A History of Women in Higher Education in America.* New Haven, Conn.: Yale University Press, 1985.

Sumrall, Amber Coverdale, and Patrice Vecchione, eds. *Catholic Girls.* New York: Plume, 1992.

Teitelbaum, Michael S., and Myron Weiner, eds. *Threatened Peoples, Threatened Borders: World Migration & U.S. Policy.* New York: W. W. Norton and Company, 1995.

Tobin, Fergal. *The Best of Decades: Ireland in the Nineteen Sixties.* Dublin: Gill and Macmillan, 1984.

United Irish Counties Community Action Bureau. *The Needs of the American-Irish Community in the City of New York.* New York: United Irish Counties Community Action Bureau, n.d. Courtesy Marion R. Casey.

Van Allen, Rodger. *The Commonweal and American Catholicism.* Philadelphia: Fortress Press, 1974.

Wakefield, Dan. *New York in the Fifties.* Boston: Houghton Mifflin/Seymour Lawrence, 1992.

Whyte, J. H. *Church and State in Modern Ireland: 1923–1979.* 2nd ed. Dublin: Gill and Macmillan, 1980.

Williams, Niall, and Christine Breen. *The Luck of the Irish: Our Life in County Clare.* New York: Soho Press, 1995.

Wilson, Andrew J. *Irish America and the Ulster Conflict, 1968–1995.* Washington, D.C.: The Catholic University of America Press, 1995.

MAGAZINES/PERIODICALS/SCHOLARLY ARTICLES AND PRESENTATIONS

Adelman, M. "The Irish Observed: E. O'Connor's Novels." *Furrow 2* (December 1961): 718–724.

Almeida, Linda Dowling. "'And They Still Haven't Found What They're Looking For': A Survey of the New Irish in New York City." In *The Irish World Wide: Patterns of Migration,* vol. 1., ed. Patrick O'Sullivan, pp. 196–221. Leicester, England: Leicester University Press, and New York: St. Martin's Press, 1992.

———. "The Lost Generation: The Undocumented Irish in New York City in the 1980s." *New York Irish History Journal* (1989): 25ff.

———. "Women among the New Irish Immigrants." Paper presented to New England Regional Conference of American Conference for Irish Studies. October 16, 1993.

Banning, N. C. "There Is Still Hope for the Irish." *Jubilee 1* (January 1954): 7–11.

Beesley, Arthur, and Padraig Yeates, "Live Register Figures Fall to 18-Year Low." *Irish Times,* February 5, 2000: http://www.ireland.com/newspaper/archive.

Berkow, Ira. "Just Another Down-to-Earth Guy." *New York Times,* February 8, 1995, pp. B11f.

Birmingham, Stephen. "From the Banks of the Shannon to the Banks of Wall Street." *U.S. Catholic* 39: 30–35.

Borrill, Rachel. "Invisible Pain of the Emigrant." *Irish Times,* March 6, 1995, p. 11.

Broderick, Patricia. "Emigration from Ireland: Vice or Virtue?" http://www.maths.tcd.ie/pub/econrev/ser/html/emigration.html

Brooks, Thomas R. "Lindsay, Quill, and the Transit Strike." *Commentary,* March 1966.

Bushe, Andrew. "Diaspora Light Turns Off Browne." *The Sunday Times,* January 14, 1996.

"Business 100 1994." Special Supplement. *Irish America Magazine,* November/December 1994.

"Cardinal Spellman Overreaches: Barden Bill for Aid to Public Schools." *Christian Century,* August 3, 1949.

Casey, Daniel J. "Heresy in the Diocese of Brooklyn: An Unholy Trinity." In *Irish-American Fiction: Essays in Criticism,* ed. Daniel J. Casey and Robert F. Rhodes, pp. 153–175. New York: AMS, 1979.

Casey, Marion R. " 'From the East Side to the Seaside': Irish Americans on the Move in New York City." In *The New York Irish,* ed. Ronald H. Bayor and Timothy Meagher, pp. 395–418. Baltimore: Johns Hopkins University Press, 1996.

———. "Intraurban Migrations of the Irish in America: Boston, Chicago, Philadelphia, and New York, 1850–1950." *Retrospect* (1987): 28–40. *Retrospect* is the publication of the Irish History Students' Association.

———. Minutes of November 30, 1990, meeting, Columbia University Seminar on Irish Studies. Speaker Dennis Clark: "The Exile's Embrace: The Social Extension of Irish-American Networks," January 31, 1991.

———. "Redefining 'Irish': Culture and Subculture in New York City, 1900–1940." Paper presented to Organization of American Historians, Atlanta meeting, April 14, 1994.

———. "Redefining 'Irish': The Impact of New Immigration on the New York Irish Community 1900–1950." Ph.D. dissertation proposal. February 10, 1992.

———. "Twentieth Century Irish Immigration to New York City: The Historical Perspective." *New York Irish History Journal* 3 (1988): 25–29.

"The Celtic Tiger Draws Many of City's Irish Home." *New York Times,* December 5, 1999.

Clines, Francis X. "Ireland's Woes Again Forcing Out the Young." *New York Times,* April 24, 1987, pp. A1f.

Conzen, Kathleen Neils, David A. Gerber, Ewa Morawska, George E. Pozzetta, and Rudolph J. Vecoli. "The Invention of Ethnicity: A Perspective from the USA." *Journal of American Ethnic History* 12, no. 1 (1992).

Corcoran, Mary. "Emigrants, 'Eirepreneurs,' and Opportunists: A Social Profile of Recent Irish Immigration in New York City." In *The New York Irish,* ed. Ronald H. Bayor and Timothy Meagher, pp. 461–480. Baltimore: Johns Hopkins University Press, 1996.

———. "Ethnic Boundaries and Legal Barriers: The Labor Market Experience of Undocumented Irish Workers in New York City." Unpublished paper presented at Columbia University, New York, April 1988.

Corry, Eoghan. "Doyle Again Has Us Going Ha Ha Ha." *Irish Press,* August 6, 1994, p. 13.

Corry, J. "Cardinal Spellman and New York Politics." *Harper's,* March 1968.

Courtney, Damien A. "Summary of Recent Trends in Emigration from Ireland." Development Studies Association Annual Conference. Queens University of Belfast. September 1989.

Daly, Mary. "The Economic Ideals of Irish Nationalism: Frugal Comfort or Lavish Austerity?" *Eire-Ireland,* Winter 1994, pp. 77–100.

Deacy, Jack. "The City Politic: The Greening of James Buckley." *New York,* March 15, 1972, pp. 8f.

———. "The IRA, New York Brigade." *New York,* March 15, 1972, pp. 40–43.

Doherty, Michael, Hugh Garavan, and Aidan Moran. "The Irish Mind Abroad: The Experiences and Attitudes of the Irish Diaspora." *Irish Journal of Psychology* (1994): 300–315.

Donnelly, Fiona. "Ireland Down Under." *Irish Times,* March 7, 1995, p. 11.

Donovan, Katie. "How Many Irish Out There Now?" *Irish Times,* March 8, 1995, p. 11.

Doyle, Joseph. "The Chelsea Irish and the Old Westside." *Ais Eiri* (Magazine of the Irish Arts Center), Spring 1982, pp. 8–11.

———. "The Controversial History of the TWU." *New York Irish History Journal* (1986): 8–10.

"Dublin: Special Advertising Section." *Barron's Market Week,* November 7, 1994.

Duffy, Martha. "Not Your Father's Jig." *Time,* March 18, 1996, p. 92.

Duggan, Dennis. "Judge Comerford and the Politics of the Parade." *New York,* March 13, 1972, p. 38.

Dunphy, Liam. "County Cork in New York: A History of the County Cork Association." *New York Irish History Journal* (1988): 21–23.

Dwyer, Jim. "Why Old Dublin Is My Brand New Love." *New York Daily News,* December 3, 1995, p. 2.

Dwyer, Michael. "Paper 3: Roddy Doyle. Discuss." *Irish Times,* April 30, 1994.

Emerald Society, Police Department, City of New York. *Newsletter.* Vol. 3, no. 1 (Winter [n.d.]); vol. 3, no. 1 (January–February 1980); vol. 3, no. 1 (Winter 1986); vol. 5, no. 1 (Summer 1987); vol. 6, no. 1 (Winter 1987); vol. 7, no. 1 (Winter 1988); vol. 7, no. 5 (Spring 1989).

"European Demographic Information." *Migration 1966–1971,* Bulletin 7, no. 4 (1976): 125–144.

Fanning, Charles. "The Heart's Speech No Longer Stifled: New York Irish Writing since the 1960s." In *The New York Irish,* ed. Ronald H. Bayor and Timothy Meagher, pp. 508–532. Baltimore: Johns Hopkins University Press, 1996.

Filteau, Jerry. "Numbers Drop: U.S. Seminary Enrollment Off by 3.4%." *Catholic New York,* February 2, 1995, p. 7.

Fitzgerald, Garret. "Mass Emigrant Movement Shows Strength of Family." *Irish Times,* December 23, 1995.

Flaherty, Joe. "The Men of Local 1268, God Bless Them All, the Last of a Bad Breed." *New York,* March 13, 1972. pp. 56–58.

"Focus: Brendan Ward." *Irish Voice,* October 19–25, 1994, p. 18.

Foner, Eric. "Class, Ethnicity, and Radicalism in the Gilded Age: The Land League and Irish America." *Marxist Perspectives* (Summer 1978): 6–53.

Ford, Mary. "To Monahan's!" *Culturefront* 4, no. 7 (Spring 1995): 23–24.

Freeman, Joshua B. "Catholics, Communists, and Republicans: Irish Workers and the Organization of Transport Workers Union." In *Working-Class America: Essays on Labor, Community, and American Society,* ed. Michael H. Frisch and Daniel J. Walkowitz (Chicago: University of Illinois Press, 1983).

Fuchs, Lawrence H. "Comment: 'The Invention of Ethnicity': The Amen Corner." *Journal of American Ethnic History* 12, no. 1 (1992): 53–58.

Gaffney, Maureen. "In Two Places at One Time." *Irish Times* "Weekend," March 4, 1995, pp. 1–2.

Gallagher, Thomas, "Paddy's Lament: Through the Golden Door." *New York Irish History Journal* (1989): 31–33.

Gans, Herbert J. "Comment: Ethnic Invention and Acculturation—A Bumpy-Line Approach." *Journal of American Ethnic History* 12, no. 1 (1992): 42–52.

Gerber, David A., Ewa Morawska, and George E. Possetta. "Response." Forum on "The Invention of Ethnicity." *Journal of American Ethnic History* 12, no. 1 (1992): 59.

Granovetter, Mark. "The Strength of Weak Ties: A Network Theory Revisited." In *Sociological Theory,* ed. Randall Collins. Washington, D.C.: Jossey Bass Publishers, 1983.

Gray, Kate Martin. "The Attic LIPs: Feminist Pamphleteering for the New Ireland." *Eire-Ireland,* Spring 1994, pp. 105–122.

Greeley, Andrew. "Why Do Catholics Stay in the Church: Because of the Stories." *New York Times Magazine,* July 10, 1994, pp. 38–41.

Greeley, Andrew, and William McCready. "The Transmission of Cultural Heritages: The Case of the Irish and Italians." In *Ethnicity: Theory and Experience,* ed. Nathan Glazer and Daniel P. Moynihan. Cambridge: Harvard University Press, 1975.

Hamill, Pete. "Notes on the New Irish: A Guide for the Goyim." *New York,* March 15, 1972, pp. 33–39.

Healy, Orla. "No More Blarney: The New Irish March to a Different Drummer." *New York Live: Daily News Color Supplement,* March 15, 1992, pp. 4–7.

Hill, John. "Images of Violence." In *Cinema and Ireland,* ed. Kevin Rockett, Luke Gibbons, and John Hill, pp. 147–193 (Syracuse: Syracuse University Press, 1988).

Hogan, Capt. Robert J. "A History of the Pipes and Drums of the Emerald Society New York City Police Department." *New York Irish History Journal,* 1990–1991, pp. 21–27.

Hone, Kathryn. "Charmed by the Craic." *Irish Times,* March 6, 1995, p. 11.

Hoy, Suellen. "The Journey Out: The Recruitment and Emigration of Irish Religious Women to the United States, 1812–1914." *Journal of Women's History* 6/7 no. 1 (Winter/Spring 1995): 64–98.

Infusino, Divian. "Get Your Enyas Out." *American Way,* March 1, 1996, pp. 76f.

Irish America Magazine. December 1988, pp. 20ff.

"The Irish Arts Center—A Proud Beginning." *New York Times,* December 7, 1972.

Irish Independent, September 15, 1994, p. 1.

Irish Press, February 5, 1994, p. 9

Irish Times, November 8, 1988, p. 8.

Irish Voice, December 5, 1987, p. 4.

Irish Voice, St. Patrick's Day Supplement 1992, March 17, 1992.

Isacsson, Alfred, O. Carm. "The Irish Carmelites Come to the Bronx." *The Bronx County Historical Society Journal* 25, no. 1 (1988).

J. H. "Cuimhni Cinn [Remembrance]." *An Teanga Mharthanach* [Living Language], ca. Spring 1993, pp. 22–26.

Jackson, Joe. "Is That It?" *Irish Times,* Fall 1992?

Jackson, Pauline. "Women in 19th Century Irish Migration." *International Migration Review* 18, no. 4 (Winter 1984): 1004–20.

"The Jig's Up: To Be Young, Hip, and Irish," *New York Live: Daily News Color Supplement,* March 15, 1992, p. 4.

Juri, Carmen. "(Irish) Talk of the Airwaves Celebrates 25th Anniversary with Music and Chat." *The Star-Ledger,* November 17, 1995, p. 76.

Keaney, Harry, and Patrick Markey, "The New Generation: Celtic Tiger Roars, but, for Many, Uncle Sam Still Beckons." *Irish Echo,* November 24–30, 1999.

Keely, Charles B. "The Effects of International Migration on U.S. Foreign Policy." In *Threatened Peoples, Threatened Borders: World Migration and U.S. Policy,* ed. Michael S. Teitelbaum and Myron Weiner. New York: W. W. Norton and Company, 1995.

Kelleher, John V. "Ireland . . . And Where Does She Stand?" *Foreign Affairs* 35, no. 3 (1957).

Kelton, Jane Gladden. "New York City St. Patrick's Day Parade: Invention of Contention and Consensus." *Drama Review* 29, no. 3 (1985): 93–105.

Kennedy, Eileen. "Bequeathing Tokens: Elizabeth Cullinan's Irish-America." *Eire-Ireland,* Winter 1981, pp. 94–102.

Kennedy, Eugene. "Day with Jimmy Breslin." *Critic* 33 (October/November 1974): 18–29.

Kennedy, Kieran A., Thomas Giblin, and Deirdre McHugh. "Outward Re-orientation, 1947–1972." In *The Economic Development of Ireland in the Twentieth Century* (New York: Routledge, 1988).

Kerlin, Jerry. "Dancing at Flannery's: The Transmission of Irish Set Dancing at a Manhattan Pub." *New York Irish History Journal,* 1993–1994, pp. 41–45.

Lacey, Colin. "Focus: Michael McNicholas." *Irish Voice,* July 26–August 8, 1995, p. 18.

Larkin, Emmett. "The Devotional Revolution in Ireland, 1850–1875." *American Historical Review* 77, no. 3 (1972): 625–652.

Lord, Miriam. "But He Does Not Need Defense of Boys in Blue." *Irish Independent*, September 15, 1994.

MacEinri, Piaras. "Some Recent Demographic Developments in Ireland": http://migration.ucc.ie/activities (retrieved from Internet October 19, 1999). Site for Irish Centre for Migration Studies at the National University of Ireland at Cork.

———. "States of Becoming: Is There a 'Here' Here and 'There' There? Some Reflections on Home, Away, Displacement, and Identity": http://migration.ucc.ie/activities (retrieved from Internet October 19, 1999).

Malone, Donal. "The Irish Arts Center: A Case Study in Ethnic Revival." *New York Irish History Journal*, 1989, p. 39.

"Mass Attendance Down by 27%." *Irish Voice*, November 8–14, 1995, p. 4.

"Master Builder." *Time*, December 8, 1967.

McCaffrey, Lawrence J. "Irish America." *The Wilson Quarterly* (Spring 1985): 78–93.

McCarthy, Joe. "The Gra-a-nd Parade." *American Heritage* 20, no. 2 (1969).

McCauley, Bernadette. "Taking Care of Their Own: Irish Catholics, Health Care, and Saint Vincent's Hospital, 1850–1900." *New York Irish History Journal* (1993–1994): 51–54.

McEvoy, Dermot Kavanagh. "PW Interviews: Pete Hamill." *Publishers Weekly*, January 10, 1994, pp. 38–39.

McGill, William J. "New York Irish." *The Recorder* (Journal of the American Irish Historical Society) 39 (1978): 96–102.

McGreevy, Ronan. "Roddy Roasted." *Irish Press*, September 15, 1994.

McNamara, John. "Irish in the Bronx." *The Bronx Historian* (Newsletter of the Bronx County Historical Society) 5, no. 4 (March/April 1983). A lecture given by John McNamara to the Celtic Medical Society on the same topic on January 17, 1985, is on file with the society as well.

McShane, Kieran. "A Study of Two New York Irish-American Newspapers in the Early Nineteenth Century." *New York Irish History Journal* 8 (1993–94): 13ff.

Meagher, Timothy. "Irish All the Time: Ethnic Consciousness among the Irish in Worcester, Massachusetts, 1880–1905." *Journal of Social History* (Winter 1985): 273–303.

Meener, J. "Some Features of Irish Emigration." *International Labour Review* 69 (1954): 126–139.

"Meeting the Murphia." *Irish Times*, March 6, 1995, p. 11.

Milkovits, Joseph. "The New York GAA: Origins to Golden Jubilee." *New York Irish History Journal*, 1988, pp. 4–7.

Miller, Kerby A., with David Doyle and Patricia Kelleher. "For Love and for Liberty: Irishwomen, Emigration, and Domesticity in Ireland and America, 1815–1920." University of Missouri, April 22, 1992. Paper presented at New York University. Later published in *Irish Women and Irish Migration*, pp. 41–65, vol. 4 of *The Irish World Wide*, ed. Patrick O'Sullivan. London: University of Leicester Press, 1995.

Miller, Rebecca S. "Irish Traditional and Popular Music in New York City: Identity and Social Change, 1935–1975." In *The New York Irish*, ed. Ronald H. Bayor and Timothy Meagher, pp. 481–507. Baltimore: Johns Hopkins University Press, 1996.

Moriarty, Gerry. "'Sad but Inevitable Outcome,' Says Trimble." *Irish Times*, February 12, 2000: http://www.ireland.com/newspaper/archive.

Morrone, Francis. "The New Irish." *City Journal*, Summer 1993, pp. 100–103.

Moynihan, Daniel Patrick. "When the Irish Ran New York." *The Reporter*, June 6, 1961, pp. 32–34.

———. "The Irish of New York." *Commentary* 36, no. 2 (1963): 32–34.

———, and Nathan Glazer. "The Irish." In *Beyond the Melting Pot: The Negroes, Puerto Ricans, Irish, Jews, and Italians of New York City*. Cambridge: MIT Press and Harvard University Press, 1963.

———. "The Irish of New York." In *American Ethnic Politics*, ed. Lawrence H. Fuchs (New York: Harper and Row, 1968).

Moynihan, Kenneth. "History as a Weapon for Social Advancement: Group History as Told by the American Irish Historical Society, 1896–1930." *New York Irish History Journal*, 1993–1994, pp. 34ff.

Mulkerns, Helena. "The Brothers McMullen." *Irish Edition*, August 1995, p. 21.

——. "Making Movies: Maturity and Money Make Ed Burns a Better Movie Maker." *Irish Echo*, August 21–27, 1996, p. 28.

——. "Not So Green in the Big Apple." *Irish Times*, January 19, 1994, p. 10.

Mullins, Emer. "Home and Away: To Go or Stay? Ireland: Home Thoughts from Abroad." *Irish Voice*, January 10–January 16, 1996, p. 16.

Newsweek. October 5, 1987, p. 35.

New York Times Magazine. November 20, 1988, pp. 28f.

"1994 Business 100." *Irish America Magazine*, November/December 1994, pp. S3–S43.

"Northern Ireland Government Suspended after Only 8 Weeks." *Irish Times*, February 11, 2000: http://www.ireland.com/newspaper/archive.

Oaks, Laurie. "Irishwomen, Eurocitizens, and Redefining Abortion." Paper presented at New England Regional Conference for American Conference for Irish Studies. October 16, 1993.

O'Brien, David. "Toward an American Catholic Church." *Cross Currents* 31, no. 4 (Winter 1981–1982).

O'Clery, Conor. "Irish Nation—Overseas." *Irish Times*, March 7, 1995, p. 11.

O'Connor, Barbara. "Myths and Mirrors: Tourist Images and National Identity." In *Tourism in Ireland: A Critical Analysis*, ed. Barbara O'Connor and Michael Cronin, pp. 68–85. Cork, Ireland: Cork University Press, 1993.

O'Connor, John J. "So the Parish Rolled Up Its Sleeves." *Columbia Magazine* (August 1939).

O'Connor, Pat. "Defining Irish Women: Dominant Discourses and Sites of Resistance." *Eire-Ireland*, Fall 1995, pp. 177–187.

O'Dowd, Niall. "Periscope: ILGO Insights." *Irish Voice*, January 17–23, 1996, p. 10.

O'Faolain, Nuala. "Little Women Learn the Joy of Sex." *Irish Times*, March 6, 1995, p. 12.

O'Flynn, Diarmuid. "Home and Away: To Go or Stay? United States: Never Again." *Irish Voice*, January 10–16, 1996, p. 17.

O'Gara, J. "Catholic Super Patriots." *Commonweal*, May 12, 1967.

O'Riada, Lorcan. "Illegal Immigrants: Show Us the Facts." *Boston Irish News*, April 1989, pp. 1f.

O'Riordan, Sean. "Author Faces His Fiercest Critics." *Cork Examiner*, September 15, 1994.

O'Rourke, Hugh E. "The Arrival of the Fenian Exiles to New York." *New York Irish History Journal*, 1993–1994, pp. 46–51.

O'Sullivan, Jane. "EU Inflation Data Puts Republic's Rise at 4.4%." *Irish Times*, February 23, 2000: http://www.ireland.com/newspaper/archive.

O'Toole, Fintan. "Some of Our Emigrants Are Happy to Go." *Irish Times*, September 14, 1989.

Parnes, Brenda. "Collecting Oral Histories of the TWU." *New York Irish History Journal*, 1987, pp. 25–27.

Perez-Stable, Marifeli. "Father Andrew Greeley." *Culturefront* 4, no. 1 (1995): 25–27.

Reimers, David H. "History of Recent Immigration Regulation." *Proceedings of The American Philosophical Society* 136, no. 2 (1992). Presented as part of the Symposium on Immigration at the autumn general meeting of the society, November 7–8, 1991.

——. "Overview: An End and a Beginning." In *The New York Irish*, ed. Ronald H. Bayor and Timothy Meagher, pp. 419–438. Baltimore: Johns Hopkins University Press, 1996.

Rohan, Brian. "'Brothers': Released, at Last." *Irish Voice*, July 26–August 8, 1995, pp. 26–27.

Rowland, Thomas J. "Irish-American Catholics and the Quest for Respectability in the Coming of the Great War, 1900–1917." *Journal of American Ethnic History* 15, no. 2 (1996): 3–31.

Sachs, Susan. "From a Babel of Tongues, a Neighborhood." *New York Times*, December 26, 1999, pp. 1, 25.

Schemo, Diana Jean. "Hard-Fought Legacy of Catholic Power: Next Archbishop Will Inherit a History as Scrappy as New York." *New York Times*, February 12, 2000, p. B1.

Sheehan, Helena. "Irish Identity Is Only Part of What We Are." *Irish Times,* November 29, 1991.

Sheehy, Gail. "The Fighting Women of Ireland." *New York,* March 15, 1972, pp. 45f.

Sheridan, John D. "A Dublin Family at Work and Play." *The Sign,* March 1957, pp. 18–22.

———. "Irish Are Not Vanishing," *The Sign,* March 1957.

Silinonte, Joseph M. "Brooklyn's Cemetery of the Holy Cross." *New York Irish History Journal,* 1991–1992, pp. 31–34.

Snyder, Robert W. "The Neighborhood Changed: The Irish of Washington Heights and Inwood since 1945." In *The New York Irish,* ed. Ronald H. Bayor and Timothy Meagher, pp. 439–460. Baltimore: Johns Hopkins University Press, 1996.

Staunton, Denis. "Ireland's New Foreign Legion." *Irish Times,* March 7, 1995, p. 11.

"Steppin' Out for Ireland." *Irish America Magazine,* January/February 1995, pp. 20f.

"Strike in the Graveyard." *Time,* March 14, 1949, p. 63.

Sunday Irish Press, April 24, 1994, pp. 25f.

Tanner, Peggy Hegarty. "Kilgarvan Have You Changed." Photocopy taken from Kilgarvan, Ireland, publication. Undated. Courtesy Peggy Tanner.

Tansey, John Paul. "Rabbitte Family Out of the Stew." *Irish Independent,* February 5, 1994, p. 9.

Teevan, Richard F. "A West Side Story of a Sort: The Teevan and Byrnes Families." *New York Irish History Journal,* 1990–1991, pp. 49–50.

Trauth, Eileen M. "Women in Ireland's Information Industry: Voices from Inside." *Eire-Ireland,* Fall 1995.

Trotta, Mary Hennessy. "Memories of Rockaway Long Ago!" *The Wave.* 100th Anniversary Edition, July 24, 1993, p. 48.

"Under Catholic Church Fire: Kennedy's School Plan. Statement January 17." *U.S. News and World Report,* January 30, 1961, pp. 54–55.

U.S. News and World Report, March 2, 1987, p. 15.

Warren, Robert. "Annual Estimates of Nonimmigrant Overstays in the United States: 1985 to 1988." Urban Institute Conference on Illegal Immigration before and after IRCA. July 21, 1989. Washington, D.C..

Wiemers, Amy J. "Rural Irishwomen: Their Changing Role, Status, and Condition." *Eire-Ireland,* Spring 1994, pp. 76–92.

Wilson, Andrew J. "The American Congress for Irish Freedom, 1967–70." *Eire-Ireland,* Spring 1994, pp. 61–75.

MASTER'S THESES

Blanch, Frank K. "Relocation in Two Contrasting Urban Renewal Sites in New York City: Seaside and Hammels." Brooklyn College of City University of New York (CUNY), 1965.

Comerford, James J. "Adjustment of Labor Unions to Civil Service Status: The TWU and the New York City Government." Columbia University, 1941.

Giordano, Richard. "A History of a Neighborhood in the South Bronx: Morrisania in Three Periods: 1875; 1925; 1975." Columbia University, 1981.

Weiser, Bruce L. "Hammels, Rockaway (1900–1976): A Case Study of Ethnic Change and Urban Renewal." Queens College, 1976.

PH.D. DISSERTATIONS

Appel, John J. "Immigrant Historical Societies in the United States, 1880–1950." University of Pennsylvania, 1960.

Gordon, Michael A. "Studies in Irish and Irish-American Political Thought and Behavior in Gilded Age New York City." University of Rochester, 1977.

Lyman, Kenneth C. "Critical Reaction to Irish Drama on the New York Stage: 1900–1958." University of Wisconsin, 1960.

Malone, Donal J. "The Irish Arts Center: A Case Study in Ethnic Revival." CUNY, 1988.

Moynihan, Kenneth J. "History as a Weapon for Social Advancement: Group History as Told by Jewish, Irish, and Black Americans, 1892–1950." Clark University, 1973.

Nelson, Dale D. "Ethnicity and Political Participation in New York City: A Theoretical and Empirical Analysis." Columbia University, 1977.

Savage, Robert Joseph Jr. "Irish Television: The Political and Social Genesis." Boston College, 1993.

Truslow, Marion A. "Peasants into Patriots: The New York Irish Brigade Recruits and Their Families in the Civil War Era, 1850–1890." New York University, 1994.

VIDEOS/FILM/TELEVISION/MUSIC

The Boxer. Directed by Jim Sheridan; written by Terry George; produced by Jim Sheridan. Hell's Kitchen/Universal, 1997.

The Brothers McMullen. Directed by Ed Burns; written by Ed Burns; produced by Ed Burns and Dick Fisher. 1995.

The Chieftains. *The Long Black Veil.* BMG Music, 1995.

Circle of Friends. Directed by Pat O'Connor; written by Andrew Davies; produced by Arlene Sellers, Alex Winitsky, and Frank Price. Savoy Pictures, 1994.

The Commitments. Directed by Alan Parker; written by Dick Clement, Ian La Frenais, and Roddy Doyle; produced by Roger Randall-Cutler and Lynda Myles. 20th Century Fox, 1991.

Did Your Mother Come from Ireland? Produced by Mick Moloney. Available from Ethnic Arts Center, New York.

Emigration USA. Produced by RTE [Irish television]. March 11, 1987. Archive account number: BN307/87L.

From Shore to Shore: Irish Traditional Music in New York City. Produced by Patrick Mullins and Rebecca Miller. Cherry Lane Productions, 1993.

In the Name of the Father. Directed by Jim Sheridan; written by Jim Sheridan and Terry George, exec.; produced by Gabriel Byrne. Universal, 1993.

Into the West. Directed by Mike Newell; written by Jim Sheridan. Touchstone Home Video and Miramax Films, 1993.

Irish Music and America: A Musical Migration. 1992 documentary.

Kennedy's Ireland. Executive produced by Peter Owens; produced by Charles Davis and Doug Wilson. Dublin Productions, 1963.

U2. *The Joshua Tree.* Island Records, 1987.

My Left Foot. Directed by Jim Sheridan; written by Shane Connaughton and Jim Sheridan; produced by Noel Pearson. Miramax, 1990.

Odd Man Out. Directed by Carol Reed; written by F. L. Green and R. C. Sheriff; produced by Carol Reed. General Film Distributors, 1947.

The Playboys. Directed by Gillies MacKinnon; written by Shane Connaughton and Kerry Crabbe; produced by William P. Cartlidge and Simon Perry. Samuel Goldwyn Company, 1992.

The Quiet Man. Directed by John Ford; written by Frank Nugent; produced by Herbert Yates. Republic, 1952.

Ryan's Daughter. Directed by David Lean; written by Robert Bolt; produced by Anthony Havelock-Allan. Faraway/Goldwyn/Mayer/Metro/MGM, 1970.

The Snapper. Directed by Stephen Frears; written by Roddy Doyle; produced by Lynda Myles. Miramax, 1993.

Some Mother's Son. Directed by Terry George; written by Terry George; produced by Jim Sheridan, Arthur Lappin, and Ed Burke. Castle Rock/Columbia TriStar/Sony, 1996.

Water Wisdom. Produced and directed by Colm O'Laoghaire for the Department of Local Government, Ireland. 1962.

Index

LINDA DOWLING ALMEIDA is Adjunct Professor of History at New York University. She received her B.A. and M.A. degrees from Boston College and her Ph.D. from NYU. A long-time member of the New York Irish History Roundtable, she has published articles on the New Irish in America and edited volume 8 of the journal *New York Irish History*.